HUMAN ECOLOGY AND COGNITIVE STYLE

HUMAN ECOLOGY AND COGNITIVE STYLE

Comparative Studies in Cultural and Psychological Adaptation

JOHN W. BERRY

SAGE PUBLICATIONS

Halsted Press Division
JOHN WILEY & SONS
New York – London – Sydney – Toronto

Distributed by Halsted Press, a Division of
John Wiley & Sons, Inc., New York

Printed in the United States of America

Library of Congress Cataloging in Publication Data

Berry, John W., 1939-
  Human ecology and cognitive style.

  (Cross-cultural research and methodology series)
  Bibliography, p. 229
  1. Personality and culture. 2. Environmental psychology.
3. Cognition. 4. Acculturation. I. Title.
GN504.B47   301.2'1   76-9803
ISBN 0-470-15103-X

FIRST PRINTING

CONTENTS

ACKNOWLEDGEMENTS

Cross-cultural studies such as those reported in this volume necessarily involve the support of many individuals—some willingly and knowingly, and some not. To these many individuals, I offer my thanks for their inspiration and help: to J. W. Bridges for originally showing me that psychology and anthropology could be fruitfully combined; to James Drever for first allowing me to try it; to John Dawson for introducing me to the theory of "psychological differentiation"; and to Herman Witkin for his continuing criticism and support in its cross-cultural use.

In the field many individuals have made life considerably easier, and I thank: Mr. W. Muir and Mr. U. R. Koroma of the Sierra Leone Development Company; Mr. C. E. McKee, Mr. A. Okpik, and Mr. W. J. Berry of the Department of Northern Affairs (Baffin Island Region); Mr. D. Ramsay of Inverkeilor; Father J. Clancy of Santa Teresa; Ruth and Barry Craig of Sydney and Telefomin; and Hugo Georgekish and John Murdock of Wemindji.

In most field areas the work was only made possible with the day-to-day help of interpreters, translators, and field assistants. For this help I am grateful to: Ibrihim Kabia, Bill Allen, Danielie, Muktah, Stanislaus Palmer, George Gorey, Kamipsep, Reg Mark, Margery Mark, Ted Wilson, Shirley Reece, Laurie Price, Rose Pierre, Alec Pierre, Brenda Prince, Fred Sam, Nora Atlooken, Florence Towedo, Laurence Longpeter, Irvine Layarde, Irene Papassay, and Robert Cosco. And to Bob Annis, Tom Mawhinney, and John Kane, I am extremely grateful for their work as field supervisors during the Amerindian studies.

For financial support I have been considered with generosity by the Canada Council (Doctoral Fellowships in 1964 and 1965, and Research Awards: S 70-0103, S 71-0330 and S 72-0184), the Province of Quebec

(Travel Award, 1963-1964), the University of Sydney (Research Grant, 1967), the Australian Research Grants Committee (Research Awards 1968, 1969), Queen's University (Research Grant, 1969), and Communications Canada (Research Contracts in 1972 to 1974 to the QUIST group, John Beal coordinator). And for a Fellowship during the year 1974-1975, I am extremely grateful to the Netherlands Institute for Advanced Study; this award enabled me to complete the research, and (with the secretarial skills of Marina Voorman) to prepare the manuscript.

Finally, at various times during the writing of this report, I have received supportive and critical comments from numerous colleagues. I thank for help but absolve from blame: Herman Witkin, Pierre Dasen, Ype Poortinga, Jos Jaspars, Rich Brislin, and Walt Lonner.

J.W.B.
Kingston

November 1975

FOREWORD

The conceptual sweep and methodological scope of the work reported in this book place it among cross-cultural psychology's most ambitious research undertakings. Its exemplary use of theory and the richness of its findings rank it among cross-cultural psychology's best achievements.

What we have here is an integrated account of the conceptual and empirical content of an evolving research program, in progress for over a decade now. Typical of programmatic research, theory-building has been at the heart of the enterprise from its inception; and the empirical part of the enterprise has been in the service of its theoretical purposes throughout. Again typical of programmatic research, its long history has seen continual interplay between theory and evidence. At each stage of its development, the theory served as a guide to the next research step. In turn, the evidence produced by that research step contributed to further elaboration of the theory and to more specific and more testable formulations. By the very nature of the course Berry's work has been following, this latest statement of the theory and its supporting evidence is hardly a final one. The book in fact ends with an account of the steps that need to be taken next to check some of the theory's newer and still untested propositions. Indeed, Berry is in the midst of a study in the Central African Republic in which these checks are now being made.

Unique even among programmatic undertakings is the large conceptual canvas on which Berry paints. He has chosen to engage himself all at once with a constellation of behaviors and with a number of the salient forces that shape them. His theory aims at general principles of behavior and of person-environment relationships, and seeks to accommodate individual differences as well; in addition, it places the phenomena of interest in a developmental perspective.

Berry's theoretical model seeks to integrate three classes of dimensions: ecological, cultural, and behavioral. The behaviors of interest are those subsumed under psychological differentiation, particularly as manifested in a field-dependent or field-independent cognitive style. These behaviors, in turn, implicate specific ecological and cultural variables conceived as relevant to them. In the collective, these variables constitute an ecocultural dimension, characterized at one end by a nomadic hunting existence, loose social organization, and socialization for autonomy, and, at the other end, by a sedentary agricultural existence, tight social organization, and socialization for conformity. The constellation at the nomadic loose end is conceived to be associated with more differentiated behavior, the constellation at the sedentary tight end with less differentiated behavior. A more recently introduced segment of the theory relates differentiation to acculturation, in regard to both shifts toward the contact culture and response to acculturative stress.

As may be inferred from the amount of ground the theory covers, testing of the many hypotheses derived from it has required an elaborate empirical effort. Basically, the testing has taken the form of a series of experiments in nature: the independent background variables have been systematically varied by selecting for study cultures varying along the ecocultural dimension, and, within cultures, samples varying along an acculturation dimension. To achieve the variation needed, Berry has studied twenty samples, from many different parts of the globe, using both ethnographic and psychological methods. Results of the examination made of the behavioral variables, as a function of ecocultural and acculturation variables, are, on the whole, in good agreement with expectations.

The conceptual path Berry has chosen to travel engages him with a very large and rocky terrain. It commits him as well to a vastly complex empirical enterprise. A narrower effort, limited to some particular component of the conceptual scheme, would avoid the risks that so large an enterprise inevitably carries with it, would be less demanding of empirical effort, and would very likely bring quicker rewards as well. It is a tribute to Berry's courage that, despite the risks involved, he has preferred to deal with "things as they are," in their full complexity. It is as much to Berry's credit that he is extremely sensitive to the pitfalls so huge an enterprise entails. As has been said of the turtle, he is very willing to stick his neck out, but while doing so he keeps all four feet on the ground. And it is to be remembered that only when the turtle sticks his neck out does he make real progress.

While risks are inherent in any large-scale theoretical undertaking, they are likely to be compounded in the cross-cultural domain. It is worth identifying these risks, about which Berry himself is quite explicit, and some of the guards against them inherent in the conceptualization itself and in the methodology used.

A first potential risk of any large theoretical effort is that, particularly in its early stages, its constructs may be vague and global. One remedy here is continual feedback into the theoretical framework of evidence gathered under its guidance, moving the theory toward greater specificity. This has

indeed been the history of Berry's project. A second way in which the risk of globality was diminished in Berry's case is that in developing his conceptual framework he was able to draw at the outset upon the theory of psychological differentiation. While that theory has itself been evolving in much the same way as Berry's own framework, it provided Berry with a network of constructs relevant to his conceptual goals, as well as a large body of supporting evidence from western sources. Minimally, that network, and the evidence bearing upon it, had the heuristic value of suggesting "where to look," both in forming the theory and in identifying ways of checking it. For dealing with a third difficulty of large-scale conceptual enterprises—meeting the very demanding task of developing a wide array of methodological approaches and specific test procedures needed to check the theory in its various parts—the work connected with differentiation theory also provided Berry with an armamentarium of methods and tests. Minimally, these provided suggestions as to "how to look" for evidence to assess the theory.

While drawing on differentiation theory for his own conceptual goals served these positive purposes for Berry, the very fact that differentiation theory, and its surrounding evidence and methodology, had their origin in western settings itself carries the risks attending exportation of any conceptual system of primarily western origin to other cultures. One guard against the dangers of exportation is provided by the central role of ecology in Berry's theory. To consider ecology means for Berry giving constant attention, both conceptually and in data gathering, to the concrete conditions prevailing in each local situation. Such an emphasis helps insure that what is unique to each cultural setting will not be overlooked, thus protecting against assignment of universal status to western concepts and observations. This emphasis is institutionalized in Berry's research strategy of following both an emic approach, which focuses on local behavioral and cultural characteristics, and an etic approach, which focuses on the generality of phenomena. From the very beginning then, Berry's thinking has been rooted in both the intra- and intercultural worlds.

Also mitigating, though hardly eliminating the risks of exportation in the present instance is the nature of the differentiation concept itself. Differentiation refers to structural rather than to content properties of an individual's psychological makeup. Compared to content properties, the variety possible in structural properties is quite limited. Beyond that, structural properties are more likely to follow a characteristic sequence in human ontogeny and to show stability over time. For these reasons, transfer of a concept such as differentiation across cultures is more supportable than transfer of concepts of a content nature.

A third guard against the common negative consequences of exportation lies in Berry's cultural relativism. Such a perspective makes it less likely that whatever is western will be valued; and it again focuses attention on the nature of each local situation. On a cultural level, Berry explicitly rejects the idea that cultural adaptation leads to "higher forms." Adaptiveness must be judged with reference to the requirements of each particular setting, so that adaptation may show itself in a variety of ways. As Berry puts it, the fact of cultural adaptation carries no judgment on progress or regress, advance or retreat. On a behavioral level, Berry again takes a relativist stand, and the impressive evidence in this book that members of nomadic, loose cultural groups tend to be field independent in their cognitive style and members of sedentary, tight cultural groups to be field dependent seems to justify this stand. When we consider that the cluster of characteristics at the field-independent end of the field-dependence-independence dimension includes skills in cognitive analysis and structuring and limited social sensitivity, and the cluster at the field-dependent end includes social skills and limited analytical and structuring skills, we can see that each mode is adaptive to the ecocultural setting in which it is predominant.

On the issue of relativism, it may be noted that the field-dependence-independence cognitive style, so central in Berry's work, is inherently value-neutral in the sense that each pole has qualities adaptive in particular circumstances. Though the sequence during growth is from a field-dependent to a field-independent mode, an individual's or group's standing in this developmental ordering is not to be used as a basis for making absolute value judgments. Such judgments, as Berry argues, must be based rather on the usefulness of each mode in specified contexts. In this connection, the non-western groups Berry studied present considerable variety among themselves with regard to cognitive style, ranging from very field dependent to very field independent. That variety is meaningfully related to standing on the eco-cultural dimension. Altogether, then, the relativist value perspective we find in Berry's work is another clear antidote to the danger of importing western-ethnocentric biases along with western-originated theory.

Particularly in its present state of development, cross-cultural psychology needs to maintain its distinctiveness as a discipline, in both substance and method. At the same time, cross-cultural psychology is part of general psychology, and it will come closer to realizing its full potential as its commerce with general psychology increases. For what it has done to bring together concepts, findings, and methods of general psychology with indigenous cultural phenomena, this work signals an important forward step toward the maturity of cross-cultural psychology.

Herman A. Witkin

*To Joan, Heather, Susan
and Michael*

Chapter 1

INTRODUCTION

To study the ecology of a phenomenon is to examine its distribution in relation to its environmental setting. In this book we consider one particular behavioural phenomenon—cognitive style—as an adaptation to both the natural and cultural environments in which it develops. The comparative study of such adaptive behaviour requires that a highly diverse set of peoples be included, and, as we shall see, these range widely from agriculturalists in West Africa and highland New Guinea to hunters and gatherers in Central Australia and Arctic Canada.

Lest the scope of the study begin to appear overly grandiose, it must be noted at the outset that there are several limitations which have helped to focus the study and to anchor it to established theoretical positions in behavioural science. First, the peoples included are those who operate at or near the *subsistence level;* it is among these cultures where adaptation to ecological press is most likely to be worth investigating (Vayda, 1969). Second, not all features of the natural and cultural environment are taken into consideration; rather there is a focus upon those features subsumed within the term *nomadic style* by Lee and Devore (1968: 11). And third, the examination of cognitive style has been guided by the systematic approach of Witkin and his colleagues (Witkin, Dyk, Faterson, Goodenough, and Karp, 1962); in this study cognitive style is examined largely in relation to their concept of *psychological differentiation.*

A fourth limitation is that the study has placed a relatively greater emphasis upon the hunting and gathering ecological adaptation, and a lesser emphasis upon the agricultural subsistence mode. As Lee and Devore have argued, "To date the hunting way of life has been the most successful and persistent adaptation man has ever achieved" (1968: 3); he has been a hunter and gatherer for over ninety-nine percent of his existence. This success and

[1]

time span constitute a significant element of mankind's natural history, one which psychologists (and other social scientists) have some obligation to attend to. Moreover, this life style is under great ecological and cultural pressure, not so much now from subsistence-level agriculturalists, but from the expansion of the technological and industrial societies of the world; this scientific obligation now carries great urgency and no small degree of social responsibility.

And last, the comparative method itself constitutes a limitation, as well as providing a tremendous opportunity. By its very nature, the comparative study of human behaviour runs a gamut of risks from social and political repercussions through to measurement error. However, such problems must be risked, for most behavioural science is culture-bound and culture-blind; it ignores the great panorama of human variation which could not only enrich its content, but which could also test and evaluate its theory. Naturally occurring human variation constitutes a tremendous resource, one which enables the social and behavioural scientist to gain comparative perspective on his study. For psychologists to ignore such a resource, despite the conceptual and practical difficulties involved in such a study, is to leave the job half done.

THE BROADENING PERSPECTIVE

During the past decade there has been a renewed awareness among psychologists and others that a complete understanding of the behaviour of human beings cannot emerge from laboratory studies alone (e.g., Willems and Rausch, 1969; Brandt, 1972). One result of this awareness has been a growth in field studies which observe and gauge behaviour in settings more natural than those which have characterized the traditional laboratory emphasis. Paralleling this shift from lab to field has been a more novel movement to a wide variety of cultural settings; this movement out of the lab has continued farther afield so that many researchers are now working with cultural-variable ranges which had been unattended since the classic studies of Rivers (1901).

Within the discipline of psychology this movement has been known by various names, the most common of which is *cross-cultural psychology*. In other disciplines, this search for some generality in the study of human behaviour has been differently titled: in anthropology, this movement is referred to as *psychological anthropology* (or *culture and personality*), in psychiatry it is known *as transcultural psychiatry*, and in sociology as *comparative sociology*. Whatever the terms employed and whatever the nature of the observations, these parallel trends have all been concerned with the wider description of behavioural variation, and with the broader exploration of functional relationships between behaviour and its antecedent variables.

WHAT DOES CROSS-CULTURAL MEAN?

No adequate definition of this term exists in the psychological literature, although many have been proposed (e.g., Whiting, 1968; Jahoda, 1970a; Triandis et al., 1971). To direct attention toward those aspects of the term which are considered to be important for this volume, yet another definition will be attempted. One way to begin is to examine the term *cultural psychology* in relation to the more familiar term *social psychology*. Brown (1965: xix) has argued that the latter is not a special system of psychology; it is an approach to the study of behaviour that takes into account new kinds of variables, employing novel methodologies, in an attempt to deal with a set of topics which has "exceeded the grasp" of a general psychology. Cultural psychology might be viewed in a similar light and might be defined as another set of topics which now exceeds the grasp of both a general and a social psychology. Briefly, cultural psychology may be viewed as a specialized attempt to deal with the behaviour of the individual as a function of background cultural (recurrent forms of learned and shared behaviour) variables, leaving to social psychology those behaviours of the individual which may be viewed as a function of background *social* variables (forms of interaction among two or more persons).

At this level the distinction is not very great; they have a degree of overlap (for example in a concern with language, socialization, and ideologies), but since they do emphasize differing kinds of antecedent variables, the distinction is a useful one. However in two other (mutually related) ways the separation of the fields may be demonstrated. First, a major distinction arises in the essentially *comparative strategy* employed in most cultural psychology; the field thus becomes one of cross-cultural psychology. This strategy is based upon the recognition that one cannot increase the variation in background cultural variables without crossing cultural boundaries; in so doing comparisons become inevitable and a methodology to deal with them becomes necessary. The field is thus largely defined by its *methodology* rather than by its *content* (cf. Lijphart, 1971). Second, there seems to be no limit to the set of topics which is studied cross-culturally; virtually all psychological variables studied by general and social psychology have now been included in cross-cultural behavioural research (e.g., perception, learning, memory, emotional expression, psycholopathology, and a variety of social behaviours). In summary, the emerging field of cross-cultural psychology cannot claim to be a system or even a well-defined set of topics, but it is characterized by an established scientific methodology and by an interest in independent variables which are broadly cultural. Furthermore, it is now generally recognized that, as one crosses cultural boundaries, one also crosses *ecological* ones as well, and the field comes to require the observation of physical-environmental as well as of cultural variation. A crude definition of cross-cultural psychology might now be attempted: the study of aspects of individual human behaviour as it develops and is displayed in a wide variety of ecological and cultural settings.

AIMS OF CROSS-CULTURAL PSYCHOLOGY

Quite simply, the overriding goal of cross-cultural psychology is to reduce the "culture-bound and culture-blind" nature of general psychology. And in pursuit of this goal at least three sequential steps may be discerned (Berry, 1969a: 124; Triandis et al., 1971: 1; Berry and Dasen, 1974: 14). The first is to *transport* our available psychological knowledge (observations, theories, and laws) to test its applicability and generality in other cultural systems; this is an essential step toward reducing culture-boundedness. The second is to *explore* behaviour in other cultural systems in order to discover variations and differences which have not appeared in our own cultural system; this step should reduce culture-blindness. And third, cross-cultural psychology seeks to *generate* universal psychological knowledge by comparing and integrating the original and the newly discovered materials. If this proves possible, then a truly *general* psychology may emerge, and the need for a specialized cross-cultural psychology will be reduced and eventually eliminated.

With respect to how to pursue such a goal, much has been written about the special methodology now employed in cross-cultural psychology (Whiting, 1968; Strodtbeck, 1964; Frijda and Jahoda, 1966; Berry, 1969a; Brislin, Lonner, and Thorndike, 1973; Price-Williams, 1974; Edgerton, 1974). In addition, many reviews of the field have appeared in recent years (French, 1963; Triandis, 1964; Honigmann, 1969; Jahoda, 1970a; Dawson, 1971; Triandis, Malpass and Davidson, 1971, 1973). There is thus no need to draw together these detailed methodological and empirical summaries in this research monograph. However the studies reported in this volume are firmly set in this emergent tradition, and the reader may wish to obtain a more comprehensive view of the field by referring to them.

AIM OF THE BOOK

Over the past ten years data have been collected in a number of field settings, and on a number of related topics. Some of this material has appeared as journal articles (in particular Berry, 1966, 1967, 1969b, 1971a, 1975), but much of the material has not been in a form suitable to the brief journal style of publication. The aim of this volume is to present, in a comprehensive and integrated form, the thoughts and field observations (both cultural and behavioural), which have accumulated over this period. However it is not merely an assemblage of unrelated clips; rather the overall cultural sampling has been guided by a dimension rooted in the school of cultural ecology (Cohen, 1968, 1971; Vayda and Rappoport, 1968), and the behavioural sampling has been guided by the theory of psychological differentiation (Witkin et al., 1962) and its cross-cultural elaboration (Witkin and Berry, 1975).

Over and above the reporting of this work, our aim is also to illustrate a strategy for cross-cultural research. All too often such research has been haphazard, both in the selection of the cultural variables and the behavioural variables sampled. One-shot studies (which have been very often carried out while on a sabbatical leave or in correspondence with a colleague in another country), have added much to our information about the variety of behaviour exhibited by human beings, but they have contributed little to our systematic understanding of the functional relations among cultural and behavioural variables. By pursuing samples which display differential characteristics on ecological and cultural dimensions, and by examining differential behavioural characteristics in these samples, it is hoped that valid and systematic inferences might be made about the nature of cultural-behavioural interactions.

OUTLINE OF THE BOOK

An ecological perspective upon cultural and behavioural variation is presented in Chapter 2. It is argued that an examination of the physical environmental setting of the group, of the culture which is adapted to that setting, and of the individual behaviour appearing in that cultural group are all necessary, since they may all be functionally interrelated. It is thus no longer possible to simply treat cultural variables as antecedent and behavioural variables as consequent; they can be viewed as group-shared and individual behavioural patterns responsive not only to each other, but to the surrounding ecology. However, no return to environmental determinism is advocated in this volume, merely a serious look at a possible source of cultural and behavioural variation in subsistence-level settings where ecological press may be operative.

In Chapter 3 the concept of differentiation, and in particular a theory of psychological differentiation, are outlined, based largely upon the work of Witkin and his colleagues (1954, 1962, 1971, 1975). Many behaviours can be and have been examined in the history of cross-cultural research; however the comparability and the meaning of these varied observations may be open to serious question when they are not theoretically integrated. The work reported here is not intended simply as a cross-cultural check of the theory of differentiation; this would constitute only the first of many possible aims of cross-cultural research. It is primarily an exploration of the compatibility of this theoretical system in psychology and the cultural characteristics exhibited by subsistence-level peoples. This use of the theory is consistent with the second and third goals of cross-cultural research, the consideration of specific cultural variations and their integration into the original theoretical system.

A model which attempts to structure the interrelationships among the three classes of variables (ecological, cultural, and behavioural) is presented in Chapter 4. This model is the most recent elaboration of earlier versions (Berry, 1966, 1969b, 1971a, 1975) which considered ways in which these variables might be structured. In the present case a new level dealing with acculturation as an alternative source of cultural and behavioural development and change has been incorporated.

In Chapter 5, we introduce the ten subsistence-level cultures and two western groups which are included in the study. In addition, specific details of the samples are provided. Much of this material is descriptive, and its style may be unfamiliar to some psychologists. However this detail increasingly forms an integral part of the literature of cross-cultural psychology, and is most necessary if the behaviour is to be comprehended.

Experimental design is considered in Chapter 6, along with a discussion of some methodological issues which arise in the study of behaviour and the use of tests cross-culturally. Also in this chapter, the independent ecological and cultural variables are quantified; this operationalization of the model leads to a statement of hypotheses about the level and kinds of behaviours to be found, and their relationships to each other and to the independent variables in the model.

Two chapters (7 and 8) then present the bulk of the behavioural data on differentiation, and on the relationships between acculturation, differentiation, and the stress being experienced by individuals in the samples.

In Chapter 9, the patterning of the behavioural findings in relation to the hypotheses and the model is discussed. In addition to evaluating the model (a hypothesis-testing approach), the whole set of ecological, cultural, and behavioural data is returned for examination; a multiple regression analysis is employed to indicate not whether our model and the hypotheses derived from it are supported or correct, but how to better structure the relationships among our ecological, cultural, and behavioural variables for maximum prediction.

Finally, in Chapter 10, we return to some basic questions about the meaning and use of studies in cross-cultural psychology: why bother; do they mean anything, make any difference; of what possible value can they be to the peoples who were involved in the study? In attempting to answer, attention is paid to the process, goals, and results of social change, in particular to the issues of education, mental health, and development.

As the reader may have surmised, this study falls somewhere between natural history and experiment as traditions in the social and behavioural sciences. No apologies are offered for being in this state of transition: questions of who does what, where, and in apparent relation to which variables constitute the historical basis for every social science; questions of causation and operations constitute their optimistic futures.

Chapter 2

AN ECOLOGICAL AND CULTURAL PERSPECTIVE

There is no shortage of definitions for the concept of *culture* in the discipline of anthropology; indeed Kroeber and Kluckhohn (1952) have outlined more than 150 which have been employed in the literature. In their summary statement, they emphasize a number of characteristics of the concept as it is currently used:

> A set of attributes and products of human societies, and therewith of mankind, which are extra-somatic and transmissible by mechanisms other than biological heredity, and are as essentially lacking in sub-human species as they are characteristic of the human species as it is aggregated in its societies [1952: 284].

In substance, and in colloquial terms, we may define culture quite simply as "the way of life of a group of people." Such a common usage is consistent with the definition employed in the present research: Culture is a learned and shared pattern of behaviour which is characteristic of a group living within fairly definite boundaries and which is interacting socially among themselves.

Two levels of culture are usually discerned (Krech, Crutchfield, and Ballachey, 1963). One is an overt form (often called *explicit* culture) which is the readily observable regularity in the behaviour of the group; and the other is a covert from (often called *implicit* culture) which is the set of patterns, rules, or the structure inferred to account for this observed regularity.

This dual approach is not acceptable to all, however; many anthropologists prefer to limit the concept to the implicit level, and to leave the directly observable behaviour, especially individual behaviour, to other disciplines (notably psychology). Kroeber and Kluckhohn (1952: 305) are clearly of this view:

[9]

Whether behaviour is to be included in culture remains a matter of dispute. The behaviour in question is of course the concrete behaviour of individual human beings, not any collective abstraction. The two present authors incline strongly to exclude behaviour as such from culture. This is on two grounds. First, there also is human behaviour not determined by culture, so that behaviour as such cannot be used as a differentiating criterion of culture. Second, culture being basically a form or pattern or design or way, it is an abstraction from concrete human behaviour, but is not itself behaviour. Behaviour is of course a pre-condition of culture; just as the locus or residence of culture can only be in the human individuals from whose behaviour it is inferred or formulated. It seems to us that the inclusion of behaviour in culture is due to confusion between what is a pre-condition of culture and what constitutes culture.

This conceptual distinction between culture and behaviour is an important one. In part it helps to define two distinctive and legitimate approaches to the study of human affairs—anthropology and psychology; without such a distinction between the two focal concepts the scientific pursuits of each would become hopelessly confused. Lest this argument for the maintenance of disciplinary boundaries sound like a justification for the maintenance of disciplinary isolation, a second argument may be advanced: Maintaining conceptual distance between "culture" and "behaviour" permits the development of an interdisciplinary study of their relationships. Without such conceptual independence, the cross-cultural study of behaviour-culture interactions would remain at a purely descriptive level.

CULTURAL ECOLOGY

Among the many views of culture (see, for example, Feldman, 1975), one relates the concept to the physical—environmental setting in which a particular group of people develops its distinctive life style; this kind of definition is the hallmark of the branch of anthropology known as cultural ecology. Such an approach to the study of culture emphasizes the role of the physical-environmental factors in shaping, limiting, or determining various forms of group-shared behaviour and the regularities which lie behind them.

Although earlier ethnographers and geographers had considered the role of ecological factors in the development of cultural variations, it was Daryll Forde (1934) in his classic *Habitat, Economy and Society*, who established the point of view in anthropology. This work was a systematic and integrative account of sixteen cultural groups, classified as food gatherers, cultivators, and pastoral nomads. In his summary chapters on habitat and economy, he was very much aware of the diversity of cultural forms within these broad categories, but he was also concerned to demonstrate that there were "complex relations between the human habitat and the manifold technical and social devices developed for its exploitation" (1934: 460) among traditional peoples. This classic statement remains one of the more balanced presentations of the view of cultural ecology, and has withstood arguments from less-restrained investigators on both sides of the question.

Many anthropologists do not admit any role for ecological factors, while those who do, claim a number of differing points of interaction and influence. Essentially, there are two extremes between which cultural ecologists vary. As Vayda (1969: xi) has put it:

Two main ways of relating cultural behaviour to environmental phenomena may be distinguished: either showing that items of cultural behaviour function as part of systems that also include environmental phenomena, or else showing that the environmental phenomena are responsible in some manner for the origin or development of the cultural behaviour under investigation.

The former (the "weak" version) is a correlative approach which emphsizes the functional interdependencies between physical-environmental and cultural variables, while the latter, (the "strong" version) is a causal approach which attempts to account for cultural origins.

Within the "weak" version, opinions range from apologetic to assertive. Consider, for example, the two following quotations:

The present work in no sense represents a relapse toward the old environmentalism which believed it could find the causes of culture in the environment. While it is true that cultures are rooted in nature, and can therefore never be completely understood except with reference to that piece of nature in which they occur, they are no more produced by that nature than a plant is produced or caused by the soil in which it is rooted [Kroeber, 1939: 1].

Culture is man's most important instrument of adaptation. A culture is made up of the energy systems, the objective and specific artifacts, the organization of social relations the modes of thought, the ideologies, and the total range of customary behaviour that are transmitted from one generation to another by a social group and that enable it to maintain life in a particular habitat [Cohen, 1968: 1].

Spokesmen for the deterministic or "strong" version have also ranged over a similar dimension. For example Wissler (1926: 214) asserted that

the environment is in some way a determiner, and a principle or law may be formulated as: when two sections of a continent differ in climate, florae and faunae, or in their ecological complexes, the culture of the tribal groups in one section will differ from that in the other.

A somewhat stronger position has been taken by Boas (1911: 159) when he asserted:

> It is not difficult to illustrate the important influence of geographical environment upon forms of inventions. The variety of habitations used by tribes of different areas offer an example of its influence. The snow house of the Eskimo, the bark wigwam of the Indian, the cave dwelling of the tribes of the desert, may serve as illustrations of the way in which protection against exposure is attained, in accordance with the available materials. Other examples may be found in the forms of more special inventions: as in the complex bows of the Eskimo, which seem to be due to the lack of long elastic material for bow-staves; and in the devices for securing elasticity of the bow where elastic wood is difficult to obtain, or where greater strength of the bow is required; and in the skin receptacles and baskets which often serve as substitutes for pottery among tribes without permanent habitation. We may also mention the dependence of the location of villages upon the food-supply, and of communication upon available trails or upon the facility of communication by water. Environmental influences appear in the territorial limits of certain tribes of peoples, as well as in the distribution and density of population. Even in the more complex forms of the mental life, the influence of environment may be found; as in nature myths explaining the activity of volcanoes or the presence of curious land forms, or in beliefs and customs relating to the local characterization of the seasons.

However as Thomas (1925: 279) has pointed out, Boas was well aware of the limits of such influences and of alternatives which may account for differing cultural forms:

> We must remember, that, no matter how great an influence we may ascribe to environment, that influence can become active only be being exerted upon the mind; so that the characteristics of the mind enter into the resultant forms of social activity. It is just as little conceivable that mental life can be explained satisfactorily by environment alone, as that environment can be explained by the influence of the people upon nature, which, as we all know, has brought about changes of water-courses, the destruction of forests, and changes of fauna. In other words, it seems entirely arbitrary to disregard the part that physical elements play in determining the forms of activities and beliefs which occur with great frequency all over the world.

The most assured statements about the determining role of ecological factors have often been attributed to geographers, such as Ellsworth Huntington. However it is difficult to find clear, unattenuated assertions about such determinants in his writings. A close reading of Huntington's works (e.g., 1915, 1945) fails to turn up the strong positions often attributed to him. Indeed as Sprout and Sprout (1965: ch. 3) and Vayda and Rappoport (1968:

480) have all correctly observed, Huntington and his colleagues did not take an extreme deterministic position. It is thus difficult to find a scholar who has taken an extremely strong view on the question of environmental determinism.

Current emphasis in studies of cultural ecology may be gauged from an examination of two recent volumes devoted to cultural adaptation (Damas, 1969; Vayda, 1969). Both volumes illustrate that broad generalizations about relations between cultural forms and environmental factors cannot easily be made. However, as a tool for examining local cultural adaptations, or as a conceptual tool for understanding some cross-cultural regularities, the method has proved to be extremely valuable. Most recently it has been used to great advantage, in the Culture and Ecology Project, directed by Walter Goldschmidt. In particular, one of the volumes deriving from the project (Edgerton, 1971) has provided a wealth of information on the differential cultural and individual adaptations of groups of pastoralists and farmers in East Africa. These three sets of studies, taken as a whole, have served to demonstrate that careful and sensitive analyses of environmental-cultural interactions may lead to the conclusion that there are indeed systematic relationship to be discovered, and that the more simplistic determinist position (and its equally simplistic rejection) need no longer worry the serious student of cultural ecology.

CULTURAL EVOLUTION

One potential difficulty, which should be made explicit at this point, is the often-found confusion between the cultural-ecology and the cultural-evolution points of view. In the latter approach, it is argued that new cultural forms emerge in adaptation to environmental elements, and that, over time, one may discern a progressive movement in these forms toward some higher or more advanced state of affairs. The former, however, is concerned simply with exploring the nature of cultural adaptations without taking any position on the question of progress or advance. The most detailed treatment of this issue is contained in a set of essays by Sahlins and Service (1960). They make a clear initial statement that, in their view,

> evolution moves simultaneously in two directions. On one side, it creates diversity through modification: new forms differentiate from old. On the other side, evolution generates progress: higher forms arise from, and surpass lower. The first of these is Specific Evolution and the second, General Evolution [1960: 12-13].

Thus it should be clear that a cultural ecologist may adopt the former ("diversity through adaptive modification") while being free to reject the latter ("progress" and "higher forms" resulting from adaptation). This is the point of view adopted in the present research; no judgments of progress or regress, advance or retreat, will be made. On the contrary, a relativist position is maintained (Berry, 1972), in which no general criteria of cultural or behavioural excellence are possible. And in the view of Sahlins and Service (1960: 15) this argument is internally consistent:

> Adaptive improvement is relative to the adaptive problem; it is so to be judged and explained. In the specific context each adapted population is adequate, indeed superior, in its own incomparable way.

Such a position has most recently been illustrated by Lomax and Berkowitz (1972) in their development of an evolutionary scale of culture. Although the scale exhibits an *order* of cultural developments, it is clearly based upon geographical and chronological criteria, rather than upon judgements of value.

In summary, then, cultural ecology and cultural evolution share a concern for the process of cultural adaptation to the environmental setting or habitat, and both may be either value-free or value-laden. In the present research an explicit value-free approach is taken; adaptation is a value unto itself.

VARIETIES OF ADAPTATION

The term *adaptation* is an ambiguous one. In our present usage it refers to the changes in culture or behaviour which are associated with changes in an environmental setting. However if we accept the proposition that culture or behaviour will change as a function of environmental change, we cannot accurately predict either the kind or the degree of change which will occur.

These varieties of change may be termed as *adjustment, reaction,* and *withdrawal,* and maybe defined in the following way. In the case of adjustment, behavioural changes are in a direction which reduces the conflict (that is, increases the congruence) between the environment and the behaviour by bringing the behaviour into harmony with the environment. In general, this variety is the one most often intended by the term adaptation and may indeed be the most common form of adaptation. In the case of reaction, behavioural changes are in a direction which retaliates against the environment; these may lead to environmental changes which, in effect, increases the congruence between the two, but not by way of cultural or behavioural adjustment. In the case of withdrawal, behaviour is in a direction which reduces the pressures from the environment; in a sense, it is a removal from the adaptive arena.

These three varieties of adaptation are similar to the distinctions in the psychological literature (Horney, 1955; Lewin, 1936; Harvey, 1966) made between *moving with or toward, moving against,* and *moving away from* a stimulus.

It is important to note that the third mode (withdrawal) is often not a real possibility, either from physical-environmental pressures for those living at subsistence level, or from acculturation pressure for those being influenced by larger and more powerful cultural systems. And for the second mode (reaction), in the absence of an advanced technology to change the physical environment, and in the absence of political power to divert acculturative pressures, many traditional societies cannot successfully engage in retaliatory responses. Thus, for most peoples, the adjustment mode of adaptation is the only realistic response, and this assumption will guide our basic predictions in Chapter 6. However evidence for the other two modes of adaptation will be sought in the data presented in the later chapters.

In conclusion the studies to be reported in this volume will be set firmly in the context of cultural ecology. Behaviour will be viewed both as a function of a set of cultural factors which are in adaptation to an environmental setting, and (as is more usual in behavioural studies) as a function of direct (culturally unmediated) stimulation impinging from that same environment. A model, linking these sets of variables (ecological, cultural, and behavioural) will be outlined in Chapter 4.

ECOLOGICAL PSYCHOLOGY

The re-emergence of an ecological perspective has not been limited to the field of anthropology; in psychology, Egon Brunswik and Roger Barker, among others, have been at the forefront of a similar movement. The term *ecological psychology* is used here to refer to only a portion of those concerns now popularly subsumed under the label of environmental psychology (Proshansky, Ittelson, and Rivlin, 1970; Wohlwill and Carson, 1972). It is limited to those areas concerned with the study of behaviour as a function of the molar physical environment. Excluded are studies devoted to the molecular physical environment (the *stimulus* in conventional terms), and those studies concerned with the application of psychology to the solution of environmental (ecological) problems such as pollution and conservation management.

A major review and evaluation of the work of Egon Brunswik has been edited by Hammond (1966) and includes expositions and critiques by many psychologists who have been influenced by him; there is thus no need to cover the entire ground here. Rather our focus here will be on a few key points which relate to the previous discussion of cultural ecology, and which lead to a consideration of the model guiding the present research.

For Brunswik, the task of psychology is "the analysis of the inter-relation between two systems, the *environment* and *the behaving subject*" (Hammond, 1966: 23). These interrelations are viewed largely as adaptive events, and this places his theoretical approach in a functionalist school along with those working in cultural ecology. Brunswik considered individual behaviour as a "coming to terms" with the environment (Brunswik, 1957: 5), just as Cohen (1968: 1) viewed culture as man's most important instrument of adaptation to a particular habitat.

The use of the term *ecology* by Brunswik has been less than precise or consistent, as Leeper (1966: 432) has pointed out. However there is a constant theme in his employment of the term, a theme which is related to the core meaning of the term for cultural ecologists: "natural-cultural habitat" (Leeper, 1966: 412). Note, however, that Brunswik includes culture as a part of the overall habitat to which the individual adapts, while cultural ecologists consider culture as the entity which adapts to the natural habitat.

At other times, Brunswik (1957) has employed a more limited psychological definition of the term:

> It will have been noted that by environment we mean the measurable characteristics of the objective surroundings of the organism rather than the psychological environment or life space, in the sense which Lewin has used the term. We may specify the sum total of these objective surroundings as the "ecology" of an individual or species.

It is apparent that Brunswik wishes to distinguish his use of the term from the environment as perceived by the organism (Koffka's and Lewin's "psychological environment") and from the immediate environment at the surface of the organism (the "stimulus" in experimental psychology). Indeed, he devoted considerable thought and effort to the problem of distinguishing the "distal" (or "molar") environment from the "proximal" environment which is so highly controlled and attended to so much in conventional psychological experimentation. The relationship between the two is one of "ecological validity," its measure being a correlation co-efficient, which (since it is necessarily less than unity) leads him to emphasize the "probabilistic" or "equivocal" nature of environment-organism relations.

Brunswik thus considered the ecology to be that complex of physical and cultural elements surrounding the behaving organism. Behaviour was viewed as adaptive to this ecology, but because of equivocal transactions between the two, he came to view his system as one of "probabilistic functionalism" thereby avoiding the charge of determinism which hounded the earlier cultural ecologists.

More recently work by Barker (1963, 1965, 1969) has emphasized both the "pre-perceptual," "non-psychological," or objective environment of Brunswik, and the "life space" or psychological environment of Lewin as substantial factors in understanding the variability of human behaviour. In Barker's view behaviour takes place within ecological units termed "behaviour settings" (1963: 26), and there is impressive evidence that there are real "differences in the behaviour of the same persons in different behaviour settings" (1963: 28). That is, behaviour settings "regulate the behaviour episodes within them as molecules regulate atoms" (1963: 29). However, the environment and behaviour are "mutually causally related systems" (1965: 9), so that the direction of the relationship and the regulation are not simply one way; in a sense, returning to our earlier argument, behaviour is adaptive to environment both by adjustment and reaction, the latter tending to regulate the impinging features of the environment.

Finally and most importantly for our purposes, in contrast to Brunswik, Barker recognizes the distinction between physical and sociocultural components of the environment and proposes a rather novel hypothesis: that "in relatively stable environments, people are the source of behaviour variance," while in "varied and changing environments, the contribution of environmental input to the variance of behaviour is enhanced" (1965: 13). From one point of view such a proposition is a truism; if there are only two sources of variance in behaviour, when one is held constant, the other will be operative. However, as an empirical question, it will be useful to examine the relative contributions of ecological and cultural factors to the observed behavioural variance.

ECOLOGY IN CROSS-CULTURAL PSYCHOLOGY

It is quite apparent that we must include, and distinguish between, both natural and cultural elements in our set of external antecedents to behaviour. Immediately we are faced with the problem that when we sample behavioural variation cross-culturally, we must inevitably also sample it across natural habitats. Thus, research which has been limited to only cultural-behavioural relations is necessarily incomplete; alternative explanation based upon uncontrolled variation in the natural ecology cannot be ruled out. Alternatively, research which has attended only to ecological variation is also incomplete; alternative cultural explanations may be equally plausible. However, to the extent that ecological and cultural factors covary (as indeed they are considered to do within the framework of cultural ecology), this problem of alternative explanations will disappear. But to the extent that they do covary, a major difficulty will be encountered when attempting to comprehend the relative contributions of ecological and cultural factors. In practice, though, cultural adaptation, as we have seen, is not entirely determined; it is probabilistically related to ecological setting. This being the case, our assertion that both ecological and cultural variables should be monitored received further support. And, recalling our earlier argument that culture and behaviour should remain conceptually distinct, we arrive at a set of at least three variables which must be taken into account in any satisfactory cross-cultural research: ecology, culture, and behaviour.

These three factors, in various combinations, have received considerable attention in the short history of cross-cultural psychology. Initially some aspect of either the environmental (e.g., Porteus 1937) or the sociocultural (e.g., Kardiner, 1945) background was argued to be related to some aspect of behaviour (e.g., intelligence or personality). A turning point was reached by Whiting and Child (1953), when they considered the role of economic "maintenance systems" as a contributor to cultural and behavioural variation. In its present form, the Whiting (1973) model gives full recognition to all three levels: Ecological elements include the physical environment and the learning environment, as well as some economic and demographic features of the maintenance system; among cultural variables are the indigenous social structure and diffusions from other cultures; and behavioural elements include both learned and innate behaviours, as well as the "projective-expressive" systems characteristic of a group of people. This latter element may be argued to be a matter of culture, returning as it does to group-shared forms of behaviour.

Another tradition of ecocultural research was pioneered by Segall, Campbell, and Herskovits (1963, 1966). In these studies both natural and cultural environmental stimulus factors were examined in relation to susceptibility to various forms of visual illusions. However, in those studies, the input from "culture" was merely to alter the frequencies of various geometric shapes in the visual ecologies of their samples; in a sense these cultural products then became part of the physical-enivronmental setting in which the organism carried out its day-to-day behaviour. Absent from their study was concern for the more usual "cultural" variables of socialization, social structure, language, and social relations which are often at the core of a definition of culture.

The general distinction, between behaviour which is a function of the physical environment (natural ecolgoy and culturally introduced physical elements) and behaviour which is mediated by cultural factors, has been outlined by Berry (1969b). It was argued that cross-cultural/cross-ecology studies should consider independently two kinds of functional relationships between ecology and behaviour. One (termed a "direct relationship") is represented in intracultural studies by topics such as perceptual response in relation to frequency of prior-exposure to aspects of visual ecology (reviewed by Johnson, Thompson, and Frincke, 1960); it is this aspect which is represented cross-culturally by the Segall, Campbell, and Herskovits, (1966) illusion studies. The other relationship (termed an "indirect relationship") has cultural mediation between the ecology and the behaviour. Intraculturally, this relationship can be illustrated only partially (because ecological variation is not normally available) by such studies as language, socialization, or social class relations with a variety of behaviours; cross-culturally this relationship has been illustrated for example by Berry (1968) who was able to demonstrate "within ecology" variation in illusion response which was associated with such cultural variables as education and socialization. More recent work with these illusions has tended to confirm the link originally established by Segall between ecology and behaviour (e.g., Berry, 1971c; Stewart, 1973); but the point of this discussion is not to evaluate this relationship alone, but to point out that other (in this case, cultural) explanations might have been more powerful if all three variables had been included in the original investigations.

Within a "bio-social" framework, Dawson (1967, 1969) has also been considering cultural and behavioural relationships. In the more recent elaborations of his framework (1973) he has made explicit reference to the ecology as a setting for the biosocial system. He has paid particular attention to such factors as physique, malnutrition, disease, and hormonal changes on the one hand, and laterality and responses to Western influence on the other.

And, as we have already noted, Edgerton (1971) had employed all three variables in his study of individual and group adaptations among East African pastoralists and agriculturalists. At the ecological level, in addition to the basic contrast between maintenance systems, Edgerton was interested in land shortage, population and crowding, and food production, while at the cultural and behavioural levels (which are not always clearly distinguishable) his concern was for a variety of attitudes, social behaviours, and internalized states such as guilt and fear. As in the case of the other other research programs briefly reviewed in this chapter, Edgerton was able to discern some systematic relationship among his ecological, cultural, and behavioural variables, once again supporting the value of the ecological approach.

Left out of this overview has been the development of the three-variable model which is employed in the present research (Berry, 1966, 1969b, 1971a) and a critical overview of the use of such analyses by Frijda and Jahoda (1966); these will be considered within the context of Chapter 4, in which a detailed statement of the model is presented. However, they are considered to be an integral part of this general growth of ecological analyses within anthropology and psychology in general, and in cross-cultural psychology in particular. Before turning to an exposition of this model, however, it is necessary to examine the behavioural phenomena which will be included and the theoretical system which led to the selection of these behaviours; this system is the developmental notion of differentiation, particularly as elaborated by Witkin et al. (1962).

Chapter 3

COGNITIVE STYLE AND DIFFERENTIATION

Although there are many meanings of the term *cognitive style* in the psychological literature, the meaning attributed to the notion in this study derives primarily from its relationship to the broader notion of *psychological differentiation* (Witkin et al. 1962). The notion of differentiation also has a number of meanings, particularly in biological and cultural sciences, in addition to those in psychological science. Since a basic goal of this study is to examine potential interrelationships among ecological, cultural, and behavioural variables, it is useful to consider the range of meanings attributed to the term in both cultural and behavioural domains.

In this chapter we consider differentiation in both sociocultural and psychological systems and attempt to draw out sufficient communal meaning to enable later discussions of relationships between sociocultural and psychological variables. At the outset we should note that the etymology of the term "differentiation" implies the process of becoming more different; systems become more heterogeneous. And heterogeneity implies not only more parts, but also more complex organization among the parts of the system.

DIFFERENTIATION IN SOCIOCULTURAL SYSTEMS

The concept of differentiation has appeared often in the history of sociological and anthropological thought. Perhaps its most noteworthy use has been in Spencer's famous definition of evolution (1864: 216): "Evolution is a change from a state of relatively indefinite, incoherent homogeneity to a state of relatively definite, coherent heterogeneity, through continuous differentiations and integrations." In this definition, differentiation is accompanied by a parallel term (integration), and this conjoint usage matches the general meaning which we noted above.

First considering differentiation itself, the study of sociocultural groups may be approached from the point of view of the number and nature of positions in a particular social group. A position is simply a socially recognized location in relation to others in the group such as brother, slave, carpenter, or competitor. Any individual may hold numerous positions and, as in the foregoing case, all of these positions may be held simultaneously by any one person. The development and elaboration of positions (and behaviour which is considered appropriate to them) is referred to as the process of *role differentiation*. A social group which has a large number of positions may be said to be a highly differentiated group.

When these many positions are assigned ranks on the basis of their prestige or value to the group, then the notion of status emerges. If a group which is highly differentiated in terms of positions and roles adopts a hierarchical or status dimension for them, then the group is said to be vertically organized or *stratified*. Thus, in observations of social groups (often made across cultures), sociologists and anthropologists have come to describe a range of groups which differ in their number of roles and degree of stratification; these may be said to differ in their levels of sociocultural differentiation.

In addition to the basic structural features of role differentiation and social stratification, there is a large set of sociocultural variables which has been extensively discussed in the recent literature of cultural complexity and evolution. This set includes "the relative complexity of societies in terms of increasing specialization of function or the degree of elaboration and cumulation of cultural elements" (Tatje and Naroll, 1970: 766). Both Naroll (1956) and Freeman and Winch (1957) have been concerned with these variables, scaled on an undimensional scale, while more recently Bowden (1969, 1972) has argued for a curvilinear arrangement for the variables. Carneiro (1970) and McNett (1970), as well, have performed scale analyses on many of these variables, with a view to deriving a scale of sociocultural evolution and complexity. For example, Naroll (1956: 687) has asserted that "that society is the most evolved which has the highest degree of functional differentiation." To pursue this assertion Naroll rated nineteen societies on three variables: craft specialization, organizational complexity, and the degree of urbanization. Similarly Freeman and Winch (1957) rated fifty-eight societies on eleven variables such as the presence or absence of trade with other societies, social stratification or slavery, and full-time craft or magical-religious specialists. Correlational analyses between these two sets of ratings reveal a high degree of similarity (+.89) in the rankings of the two approaches. The conclusions which are generally drawn (for example by Tatje and Naroll, 1970: 782; by Carneiro, 1970: 854; and by Murdock and Provost 1973: 931) are that the mutual support provided by these studies strongly indicates that sociocultural changes have taken place over time, and that the direction of this movement has been toward greater differentiation and complexity.

However there is emerging evidence that a single, linear dimension is not an accurate description for these multiple changes. This evidence tends to support a fairly linear change for differentiation (heterogeneity) of elements over time, but suggests that integration (coherence and organization) of elements may not be linear (Lomax and Berkowitz, 1972; Blumberg and Winch, 1973; Murdock and Provost, 1973). In the study by Lomax and Berkowitz (1972) two factors emerged from their analyses of cultures, which they labelled "differentiation" and "integration" (1972: Figure 5, p. 237). Differentiation tended to increase in a linear way along their scale of cultural evolution (from African and Australian gatherers through Amerindian hunters and villagers to African agriculturalists and early classical cultures).

However the integration factor increased (in parallel with differentiation) only in the central range of this scale (from Amerindian hunters to African agriculturalists); prior to this range, integration of sociocultural elements was relatively high (for example, among African and Australian gatherers), and subsequent to this central range, the integration of elements was relatively low (for example, among classical cultures). This curvilinear trend for some other sociocultural elements has been reinforced by Blumberg and Winch (1973) with respect to family complexity and by Murdock and Provost (1973) for rules of descent. The implications of these two trends are not entirely clear. One point which is clear is that it is no longer possible to refer to a single trend in sociocultural change: The increased diversity of elements is not always accompanied by an increase in their organization or coherence. In any systematic study of relationships between sociocultural variables and ecological or behavioural ones, this nonlinearity must now be taken into account.

Another point which is clear is that, in sociocultural systems, differentiation is both conceptually and empirically distinct from integration. At the conceptual level, differentiation tends to refer to the separation or multiplicity of parts, while integration refers to the organization among them. And empirically it has been demonstrated that these two processes do not always move in parallel. In contrast, the term differentiation as it is employed in the study of psychological systems tends to encompass both processes; it is to this second use that we now turn.

DIFFERENTIATION IN PSYCHOLOGICAL SYSTEMS

The major theoretical and empirical advances in the use of the notion of differentiation in psychology have been made by H. A. Witkin and his colleagues. Earlier, both Lewin (1935) and Werner (1948) made extensive use of the notion, and more recently others have made valuable contributions, especially in the area of cognition (e.g., Bieri, 1961, 1966; Kelly, 1955; Harvey, Hunt and Schroder, 1961; Scott, 1963); however it is Witkin who has consistently tackled the wider problems, and it is his formulation of the issues which has guided the present research. The following outline of the concept adheres closely to the exposition made by Witkin et al. (1962: ch. 2), and the discussion of measures and findings also derive from the work of him and his colleagues. A later section will consider the contributions of others in both the general and in the cross-cultural literature.

For Witkin, the concept of differentiation pertains to the structure of a system, "whether psychological, biological or social" (1962: 9). The general and specific features of systems, with respect to differentiation, are succinctly phrased by Witkin himself:

> In broadest terms differentiation refers to the complexity of a system's structure. A less differentiated system is in a relatively homogeneous structural state; a more differentiated system is in a relatively heterogeneous state. The emphasis on "relative" is important for even the most rudimentary system is to some degree differentiated. This is implicit in the very definition of "system."

> The description of a system as more differentiated or less differentiated carries definite implications about how it functions. In fact it is mainly through particular functional manifestations that extent of differentiation of a system may be judged. Before the differentiation concept can be applied to the description of individual behaviour or the study of psychological problems its implications for function must be delineated.

> Among the major characteristics of the functioning of a highly differentiated system is specialization. The subsystems which are present within the general system are capable of mediating specific functions which, in a relatively undifferentiated state, are not possible or are performed in a more rudimentary way by the system as a whole.

> When used to describe an individual's psychological system, specialization means a degree of separation of psychological areas, as feeling from perceiving, thinking from acting. It means as well specificity in manner of functioning within an area. Specific reactions are apt to occur in response to specific stimuli as opposed to diffuse reaction to any of a variety of stimuli. Parts of a perceptual field are experienced as discrete, rather than fused with their background. Impulses are channelized, contrasting with the easy "spilling over" characteristic of the relatively undifferentiated state. More or less discrete feelings and needs are likely to be present.

> Psychological systems, like biological ones, are open in the sense that they are in continuous commerce with the environment. With respect to relation with the surrounding field, a high level of differentiation

implies clear separation of what is identified as belonging to the self and what is identified as external to the self. The self is experienced as having definite limits or boundaries. Segregation of the self helps make possible greater determination of functioning from within, as opposed to a more or less enforced reliance on external nurturance and support for maintenance, typical of the relatively undifferentiated state.

Degree of differentiation also has implications for the way in which a system is integrated. Integration is an essential property of any system, again by definition. It refers particularly to the form of the functional relationships among system components and so speaks first of all on the patterning of the total system. When we are dealing with open systems, as in psychology, integration also refers to the form of the relationships between the system and its surroundings [Witkin et al., 1962: 9-10].

Witkin goes on to argue (1962: 10-11) that *complexity* of integration and *effectiveness* of integration must be carefully distinguished. Complexity refers to the number and elaboration of parts within the system. Effectiveness on the other hand refers to *adjustive adaptation* (as previously discussed in Chapter 2). These two aspects are independent: A system may be complex but discordant with its environment, or conversely, it may be relatively simple, but well-adapted to its milieu. Complexity of integration is probably related to the level of differentiation, while effectiveness (adjustment) is related to the local adaptive problem. In essence, the thrust of this separation of complexity from effectiveness is to leave open for later discussion the difficult question (especially in a cross-cultural context) of the value of differentiation.

Although the concept of *psychological differentiation* has not been employed phylogenetically in (animal) comparative psychology, its most frequent employment has been ontogenetically in (human) developmental psychology. For Witkin the major comparative dimension of differentiation is between infancy and adulthood: "The difference between the psychological pictures found in infancy and at later stages of development provides maximal contrast between a low and a high level of differentiation; the difference is obviously greater than that which exists between adults most widely separated with regard to extent of differentiation" (1962: 11). This last passage introduces a second dimension on which comparisons may be made— that of differences among individuals at similar age levels. An assumption here is that these individual differences may be accounted for by differential movement along the developmental dimension, from a system state of low differentiation to one of high differentiation.

Since differentiation of the organism must be inferred from overt behaviours, Witkin has explored a number of "indicator areas" of behaviour. His "differentiation hypothesis" (1962: 15-16) is that these various behaviours will tend to be consistent among themselves in the level of differentiation exhibited, as judged in comparison with the usual characteristics of early and later behaviour: "Differentiation thus serves as a construct for conceptualizing communality in behaviour in several areas of psychological functioning" (1962: 16). Thus the concept is considered to be a *characteristic of the organism,* and expectations are that tasks which sample the differentiation of various kinds of behaviours should yield estimates of roughly similar levels of differentiation.

However, and in anticipation of later problems to be encountered in the cross-cultural literature, it must be pointed out that some limitations are recognized by Witkin et al. (1962: 16): First, "the widely recognized principle of uneven development" reduces the expectation of unity correlations among measures of differentiation; second, age or brain damage may lead to selective "de-differentiation"; and third, "because any segment of behaviour is the product of many determinants, inevitably, the segment we may consider in seeking concrete evidence of differentiation reflects the influence of other determinants as well" (1962: 16). It is mainly this last qualification which emerges as a concern in the cross-cultural exploration of this concept.

PERCEPTUAL FUNCTIONING

In perception, where the differentiation dimension began as field-dependence/field-independence (FD-FID), a large amount of thought and empirical work has made this "indicator area" the foundation of the work on psychological differentiation. In Witkin's terms, in visual perception:

early in development, the geometrical relationship among the parts of a stimulus field is a dominant determinant of perceptual organization. Stimulus fields in which the parts have little systematic geometrical relationship to each other are perceived as relatively unorganized. During development stimulus objects gain function and meaning as a consequence of continuous, varied dealings with them. This acquired functional significance may contribute to the developing discreteness of objects and may serve as the basis for the formation of nongeometrical integrations of the field. We may refer to the increasing discreteness of objects and to the use of more complex principles of field integration as an increase in the articulateness of experience. The person who experiences in articulated fashion has the ability to perceive items as discrete from their backgrounds, or to reorganize a field, when the field is organized; and to impose structure on a field, and so perceive it as organized, when the field has relatively little inherent structure. In this view the ability to analyze experience and the ability to structure experience are both aspects of increasing articulation [Witkin et al., 1962: 13-14].

In the first book (Witkin et al., 1954), details of perceptual tests were provided, and many of these same tests have been carried through their research until the present time. Three tests have provided the core of their data: the Embedded Figures Test (EFT), the Rod and Frame Test (RFT), and the Body Adjustment Test (BAT). The easiest to use is the EFT which is a "paper-and-pencil" test derived from earlier similar figures used by Gottschaldt (1926). A simple figure is hidden in an organized, complex figure, and the task is to detect the simple one in the complex one. The original version employed twenty-four items with a maximum time level of five minutes for each. A shorter form (Jackson, 1956) employs twelve of these designs with a three-minute limit for each. And the present version (Witkin, Oltman, Raskin and Karp, 1971) employs the first twelve designs as form A and the second twelve as form B, both with a three-minute-per-design time limit. The score is simply the total time needed to detect all of the simple figures. Recently, another form of the EFT has been developed by Witkin, Oltman, Raskin and Karp (1971) for group administration; this form has been termed the GEFT.

The RFT is now also relatively simple to use, with the design and production of a portable version (Oltman, 1968). In this test, the individual is required to orient a rod to the vertical, within the context of a tilted square frame. Over a number of trials, the score is the mean absolute error in degrees from the true vertical on the settings. The task is conceived, as in the case of the EFT, as one which requires the disembedding of a relatively simple stimulus (rod) from a more complex one (frame).

Finally in the Body Adjustment Test (BAT) the task is to adjust the chair to the upright in the context of a tilted room. The score over a number of trials is the mean absolute error in degrees from the true upright. Once again, the task is conceived as one requiring the disembedding of one set of perceptual cues (proprioceptive and visual, both from the body) from another set (visual from the room).

Among all tests of differentiation in the perceptual "indicator area," the correlations are positive (Witkin et al., 1962: 44-45), and Witkin takes this as evidence of differentiation in this area. In his summary (1962: 57) the dimension is referred to as "an analytical, in contrast to a global, way of perceiving" and he argues that it "entails a tendency to experience items as discrete from their backgrounds, and reflects ability to overcome the influence of an embedding context" (1962: 58). A more recent study (Witkin et al., 1967) confirms these relationships and, in addition, demonstrates their stability over time.

The dominant theme during these early studies in the perceptual area was that of "disembedding" some item from its context (or "analyzing" perceptual materials). As we have seen, this was translated into a dimension of "field-dependence/field independence" on which those who were able to disembed or analyze were conceived of as "field-independent" and those who were unable to disembed, or were "global" in perception, were termed "field-dependent" (Witkin, Moore, Goodenough, and Cox, 1975; Witkin et al., 1971: Goodenough, in press). This first level of conceptualization was to be supplemented as data and ideas emerged from the study of cognitive functioning.

COGNITIVE FUNCTIONING

In cognition (where perception is also inevitably implicated) differentiation involves the ability to break up or analyze a problem as a step toward its solution, in addition, of course, to many other components (such as background knowledge, general competence, etc.). Standard psychometric tests, such as block design, picture completion, mazes, object assembly, "appear to involve a capacity to overcome embeddedness" (Goodenough and Karp, 1961). Results from this and other factor-analytic studies indeed show that such tests do load on the same factor as EFT and RFT, and Witkin concludes (1962: 70) that such tests do involve a capacity for analytical functioning.

In addition to these psychometric tests, a number of other kinds of cognitive problems display a relationship to analytic functioning. For example, in some Piagetian conservation tasks, field-independent subjects are more likely to attain weight conservation than field-dependent subjects (Pascual-Leone, 1969). And in concept attainment problems, field-independent subjects tend to employ a hypotheses-testing strategy, while field-dependent subjects use a more intuitive approach (Goodenough, in press).

From these examples, it is apparent that differentiated cognitive functioning requires not only the "disembedding" which we noted in the perceptual domain but also conceptual "analysis" and "restructuring" of cognitive materials. In the former, analysis involves the breaking up of a cognitive problem, while in the latter, restructuring involves its reorganization in such a way that a solution is achieved. These two operations (analysis and restructuring) have been treated by Witkin et al. (in press) as complementary aspects of an earlier term, "articulation" (Witkin et al., 1962). At this level, "articulation" is a counterpart to "global" functioning, and a new dimension "global-articulated" emerged as more encompassing than perceptual "field dependence/independence." Finally, with the inclusion of cognitive functioning in this new dimension, the more general term "cognitive style" came to be used.

Other workers in the area have emphasized different aspects of cognitive differentiation. Bieri (1961, 1966) for example has employed the concept largely to refer to the *number of dimensions* used in making judgments, and this meaning is consistent with the work of Kelly (1955). Harvey et al. (1961) however tend to employ the term in a similar manner to Witkin, defining differentiation as the "breaking of a novel, more undifferentiated situation, into more clearly defined and articulated parts" (1961: 18). Lewin (1951) employs the term to refer to the number of distinct elements in a psychological region, while Scott (1963: 277) uses it to refer to "the distinctiveness of the elements which constitute the set" of cognitive elements. Although it may be argued that these meanings differ one from another, it is possible to discern a common theme which is consistent with the meaning Witkin assigns: All imply the separation of cognitive structures into discrete units whether they be dimensions, spaces, elements, or components.

SOCIAL FUNCTIONING

In the area of social functioning Witkin et al. (1962: 8) are concerned with the attainment of a "sense of separate identity." This term refers to "the outcome of a person's development of awareness of his own needs, feeling, and attributes of others" (1962: 134). This sense of separate identity is considered to manifest itself in at least three ways: First, a person with a developed sense of separate identity should "be capable of functioning with relatively little need for guidance or support from others"; second, he should "maintain more firmly his own direction in the face of contradicting attitudes, judgements and values of others"; and third, he should "have a relatively stable view of himself in varying social contexts" (Witkin et al., 1962: 134-135).

With respect to independent functioning, Witkin provided data from children's TAT response and results from Gordon's (1953) study of dependency attitudes showing that field-independent (FID) subjects (selected on the basis of perceptual differentiation tasks) are less reliant upon external guidance than those who were field-dependent (FD). More recently Witkin (1972) and Witkin et al. (in press) have reviewed the rapidly increasing literature on this question. It is now clear that field-dependent individuals pay more attention to social cues for example by looking at the faces of others (e.g., Ruble and Nakamura, (1972) and by attending more to social aspects of communications (e.g., Eagle, Goldberger, and Breitman, 1969). Further, field-dependent individuals have displayed a greater "social orientation" than those who are field-independent, during attempts at social influence. Evidence presented by Witkin et al. (1962: 149-152) shows field-independent individuals are more able to resist suggestion and influence while making judgements of ambiguous stimulus materials. And many recent studies, employing a variety of techniques (e.g., McFall and Schenken, 1970; Solar, Davenport and Bruehl, 1969) have supported this relationship, while Konstadt and Forman (1965) have extended this finding to include social reinforcement during learning tasks. Finally, recent studies (e.g., Justice, 1969;

Holley, 1972; Greene, 1973) have opened up a new area of study of social behaviour in relation to field-dependence: It is now clear that field-dependent individuals prefer to be physically closer to other persons during a variety of interpersonal encounters. This preference for a smaller social space has been termed a "with-people orientation" by Witkin et al. (in press).

Overall, then, there is accumulating evidence in the area of social functioning that there is a characteristic style which extends beyond perception and cognition to interpersonal behaviour. This evidence has been interpreted by Witkin et al. (in press) as supporting their earlier notion of a "sense of separate identity"; field-independent individuals have "internal frames of reference," which are structured and articulated, while field-dependent individuals "show greater continuity between self and non-self . . . less segregation and less internal structure." which indicate a "more globally experienced self."

AFFECTIVE FUNCTIONING

The fourth and last "indicator area" considered by Witkin et al. (1962: Ch. 9) is that of emotional controls and defenses. For Witkin (1962: 157, n.), "controls" refers to "the adaptive techniques governing the discharge of impulse," while "defenses" refers to "the array of devices which provides protection against the experience of anxiety." Both these characteristics may be inferred from a person's behaviour: "Chaotic activity . . . suggests less structured controls and defenses; specific and directed activity suggests structured controls and defenses" (1962: 158-159).

With respect to "defenses," Witkin argued that "a highly developed defensive system is likely to be characterized by the use of such defenses as intellectualization and isolation, and a less developed system by the use of such defenses as primitive denial and massive repression" (1962: 160). Using TAT responses and scoring them on a five-point scale of structure of defenses, a significant relationship was found with EFT performance. A similar study using Rorschach material is also provided as evidence. Similarly for "controls," EFT and ratings on a three-point control of aggressive impulses scale were significantly related. More recent evidence (Witkin et al., 1968: Schimek, 1968) confirms these earlier relationships between differentiation in the perceptual and affective domains of psychological functioning.

COGNITIVE STYLE

These studies of psychological functioning demonstrate, with a fair degree of conviction, that the consistency of a person's behaviour across at least four areas of psychological activity can be predicted from and understood within a theory of differentiation. It is rare to find a concept which may be inferred from such a wide range of human behaviours and, conversely, from which a wide range of specific behaviours may be predicted. Witkin (1962: 16) clearly favours a point of view which considers differentiation to be a characteristic of the organism, which is manifested in these various behaviours and which assists in "conceptualizing communality in behaviour."

As we noted in Chapter 1, one aspect of the psychological differentiation construct is the notion of "cognitive style." In the earlier work (Witkin et al., 1962) the dimension of "field-dependence" to "field-independence" in perception, and the dimension of "global" to "articulated" functioning in cognition, were clearly spelled out. In that same work (Chapter 6), the notion of "structuring" was also proposed; this term refers to the analysis and restructuring of perceptual and cognitive materials. And in recent statements (Witkin et al., in press, and Goodenough, in press) a broader set of relationships has been outlined:

Looking back over the long research road . . . it can now be seen that field-dependence-independence, with which the journey began, is the analytical-perceptual component of a larger dimension that encompasses analytical and structuring processes in perceptual and intellectual contents [Witkin et al., in press].

The present status of the theory of psychological differentiation (Witkin, personal communication) emphasizes the hierarchical organization among differentiation itself; at a second level, there is a distinction drawn between the "segregation of functions," which was outlined earlier in this chapter, and "self-nonself segregation." This latter notion includes both "restructuring" and "autonomy in interpersonal relations," collectively referred to as the "field-dependent, field-independent cognitive style." This idea of cognitive style, then, is a major component of psychological differentiation, and subsumes such previous notions as disembedding, analysis, restructuring, social distancing, a with-people orientation, and a sense of separate identity. Essentially this cognitive style is defined by a dimension which runs between two poles: at one end, the field-dependent style includes limited analytic and structuring skills in perception and cognition, a with-people orientation and a sensitivity to social situations; at the other end, the field-independent cognitive style includes structuring and an analytical approach to perceptual and cognitive materials, social distancing, and limited social sensitivity.

This theoretical formulation asserts that there is likely to be consistency across these behaviours, and that there should be access to the cognitive style through each of these indicator areas or behavioural domains. Evidence for such consistency was presented in the earlier statement (Witkin et al., 1962) and in many recent studies (reviewed by Witkin et al., in press, and Goodenough, in press) a broader picture of behavioural consistency is emerging. It is indeed the case that those individuals who are field independent tend to have a sense of separate identity, while those who are more field dependent tend to exhibit a with-people orientation.

In addition to these notions, which are included within the concept of cognitive style by Witkin, there are some other notions which may share some features of the style. Other perceptual and cognitive behaviours may require also some restructuring; for example, this may be the case for tests of spatial ability. Tasks designed to assess these behaviours may thus exhibit some covariation with measures of cognitive style at the lowest order of the proposed hierarchical structure.

As the empirical literature has grown, evidence has mounted for a hierarchical organization of these behaviours. This evidence lies both in the pattern of correlations found among the various tests in many studies, and in a few factor-analytic studies which were conducted for the purpose of drawing out these structures. It is common to find sets of low to moderate positive intercorrelations among tests of perceptual and cognitive differentiation, spatial tests, and tests of inference from geometric materials.

That these correlations are far from unity indicates that a wide range of behaviours is being tapped. But higher-order factors are now emerging (e.g., Messick and French, 1975; Vernon, 1972) in culturally homogeneous samples. And other studies (e.g., MacArthur 1975; Defries et al., 1974) suggest that similar factors are emerging across cultures. Although these trends are far from conclusive, it is important to note them here, for they suggest that a conceptualization in "either-or" terms (for example "differentiation" or "spatial skills" or "intelligence") may no longer be the most suitable for proceeding with research in this area. In Chapter 7 a number of tasks, in addition to those outlined in this chapter, will be introduced. At that time consideration will be given to the conceptual relationships which may exist among them, and in particular to the possibility of some hierarchical organization. Since all of these tasks are in the perceptual and cognitive domains, the intermediate level of conceptualization in terms of cognitive style will be employed.

ANTECEDENTS OF PSYCHOLOGICAL DIFFERENTIATION

What factors, experiential, biological, or interactional, lead to relatively low- or high-differentiated psychological systems? Given the biological roots of the concept, it would be frivolous to dismiss the possible role of *genetic* (constitutional) or *physiological* (hormonal, nutritional) factors in the growth of psychological differentiation. However, given the overwhelming emphasis upon experience and learning within the discipline of psychology, it is not surprising to discover that experiential (social and cultural) factors have received the major theoretical and empirical attention.

Genetic and physiological studies are in progress (see Witkin, 1972), but no conclusions have been reached. Hypotheses directing the genetic studies are largely concerned with the role of the x chromosome in normals, and in cases of those with extra (either x or y) chromosomes. Nutritional and hormonal studies are also being carried out (see, for example, Dawson, 1972), with infrahuman samples. And a number of studies have now shown relationships to the central and autonomic nervous systems (see Witkin et al., 1973, for complete references).

The bulk of the work on the antecedents of differentiation has been in the area of child-rearing and socialization. Early work (reported in Witkin et al., 1962: chs. 17, 18, 19) has now been supplemented by more detailed studies by Dyk and Witkin (1965) and by Dyk (1969). A summary article has also appeared (Witkin, 1969) which draws together much of the available material:

Of the social influences likely to affect differentiation, the studies to be reviewed have focused mainly on the influences which may hamper or foster separate, autonomous functioning. Included among these influences have been, first of all, the extent of opportunity and encouragement the child receives while growing up to achieve separation, particularly from the mother—in other words, to move toward self-differentiation. Another social influence considered in these studies, closely related to encouragement of separation, and, like it, affecting development toward autonomous functioning, is the manner of dealing with the child's expression of impulse. Imparting standards for internalization, which become the child's own, and within limits, allowing impulse expression so the child may learn to identify his impulses and to cope with them, are calculated to help the development of autonomous functioning. Some of the studies have also considered characteristics of the mother herself which may aid or hinder her part in the separation process, as well as in imparting standards for internalization and in regulating the child's impulse expression.

These highly interrelated factors—handling of separation, regulation of impulse expression, and characteristics of mother as a person affecting her part in these processes—constitute a "socialization cluster" which influences a child's progress toward separate autonomous functioning [Witkin, 1969: 690].

These three factors were empirically gauged using the following indicators:

(1) Indicators relevant to evaluating separation from mother.

This included five indicators which, stated in terms of discouragement of separation, were:

(a) Physical care of child is inappropriate to his age.
(b) Through fears and anxieties for or ties to her child,

mother markedly limits his activities and his going into the community.

(c) Mother regards child as delicate, in need of special attention or protection, or as irresponsible.

(d) Mother does not accept masculine role for child.

(e) Mother limits curiosity, stresses confirmity.

(2) Indicator relevant to evaluating control of aggressive, assertive behaviour. This indicator was: maternal control is not in the direction of a child's achieving mature goals, or becoming responsible; or is consistently directed against child's asserting himself. Patterns which led to the judgement "indicator present," included: submissive, indulgent maternal behaviour; administration of discipline in arbitrary fashion, "on impulse," and the use of irrational threats to control aggression; maternal wavering between indulgent and coercive behaviour. A mother's inability to set limits for her child, and to offer him and help him absorb a clear set of values interferes with the child's development of controls.

(3) Indicators relevant to evaluating personal characteristics of the mother. Characteristics chosen for consideration were those relevant to the mother's part in the separation process and the impulse-regulation process. The two indicators were:

(a) Mother in rearing child does not have assurance in herself. Lack of self-assurance hampers a mother's ability to define her role as a mother and thereby her ability to help her child define his own role as a separate person. Lack of self-assurance is also likely to make it difficult for a mother to set and maintain limits, thus hurting the child's achievement of self-regulation.

(b) Mother does not have a feeling of self-realization in her own life. We considered that a mother who herself has a sense of self-realization would be better able to allow her child to separate from her and develop as an individual.

Using these specific indicators as guides, ratings were made of the mother-child interaction as to whether in its total impact it has tended to foster the child's development of differentiation (IFD—interactions fostering differentiation) or to interfere with the development of differentiation (IID—interactions interfering with differentiation). These ratings of IID or IFD showed a pattern of significant correlations with measures of differentiation of the children. Boys whose mothers were judged to have interacted with them in ways that fostered differentiation tended to have an articulated body concept, a developed sense of separate identity, and specialized structured defenses [Witkin, 1969: 692-693].

This brief overview should be sufficient to point to a hypothesized source of psychological differentiation and to the fact that Witkin and his colleagues are of the view that they are tapping one of the major antecedent variables.

PSYCHOLOGICAL DIFFERENTIATION ACROSS CULTURES

The psychological system which has just been displayed has drawn largely from theories and research which are based in a Western, Euro-American sociocultural system. We have noted in Chapter 1 that one of the goals of this study is to consider the cross-cultural applicability of a psychological theory. In part, this goal has already been achieved in the large-scale overview of the field by Witkin and Berry (1975). But in part an intensive analysis is required before such a question can be answered, and this analysis will constitute the bulk of our later chapters. To avoid a bias in this later analysis, therefore, both theoretical integrations and supportive empirical material from the overview will be considered later as well.

For the time being, it is sufficient to note that the transportation of a concept across cultural boundaries is fraught with difficulties. The success of the movement will depend in part upon whether the concept is rooted in some pan-human biological or cultural universal—that is, whether there is any basis for "dimensional identity" (Frijda and Jahoda, 1966). Given the biological roots of the concept of differentiation, and given that Witkin is of the opinion that system differentiation is a characteristic of the organism, we are on more reasonable ground here than for many other concepts used cross-culturally. The success of the venture also depends upon the aim of the researcher. As outlined in Chapter 1, we may wish only to test the generality of the theoretical system: whether the socialization antecedents everywhere are implicated in the growth of differentiation, or whether the behaviour which may be sampled from the various indicator areas are everywhere positively related.

This preliminary aim is by no means a simple one as we shall soon see; however greater difficulties lie in our second goal. If, for example, we discover other socialization emphases associated with developed differentiation in other cultures (as did DeVos, 1968, for achievement motivation), or if we find other sociocultural features associated with differentiation, we must deal with the difficult question of attempting to integrate these findings into extant differentiation theory, or of attempting to modify differentiation theory to accommodate these new findings (goal 3). This is, of course, the process of moving from an *imposed etic* through *emic* analyses to *derived etic* concepts (Berry, 1969a).

SOCIOCULTURAL AND PSYCHOLOGICAL DIFFERENTIATION

Over the course of the chapter, a large set of meanings has appeared for the concept of differentiation in both the sociocultural and psychological domains. What do they have in common, how do they differ, and what possibility is there for examining the two domains for meaningful relationships?

It is clear that at least one aspect of the term is common to both domains: Differentiation involves an increase in the number of elements in a system; a more heterogeneous system is a more differentiated system. And in both cases there is also the implication that such increased heterogeneity implies greater organization or integration. However, in the case of psychological differentiation, the single term "differentiation" covers both aspects; indeed both are necessary for the term to be applied, for without concomitant structure, an increase in elements would be considered mere fragmentation. In the case of sociocultural differentiation, though, a second term, *integration,* has been used both historically and in contemporary discourse to refer to the second or organizational aspect. In the sociocultural domain, a third term, *cultural complexity,* has emerged which covers both aspects and appears to be the counterpart to the term "differentiation" in psychological systems.

Thus the appropriate level of comparison, for seeking interrelations among cultural and behavioural variables, seems to exist between cultural complexity and psychological differentiation. A framework for pursuing these relationships is now presented in the form of an ecological, cultural, and behavioural model.

Chapter 4

AN ECOLOGICAL-CULTURAL-BEHAVIOURAL MODEL

In the last two chapters, we have examined some basic theoretical notions about ecology, culture, and psychological differentiation. The purpose of this chapter is to outline a systematic model which structures these three classes of variables and considers some relationships among them. Before such a model can be presented, it will be useful to briefly examine the nature of models (in relation to theories and hypotheses) and to consider the recent use of models, both intraculturally and cross-culturally.

THEORIES, MODELS, AND HYPOTHESES

Relations among the concepts known as theories, models, and hypotheses can be viewed in very complex ways or in rather simple ways. Perhaps the simplest and clearest statement about how these notions relate to each other is the one by Marx and Hillix (1963: 45-53). For them, (1963: 50) a theory is an abstract formal statement to which are appended rules for manipulating these statements and definitions that relate them to the empirical world. They may be established either on the basis of empirical observation or as a result of rational analysis. Hypotheses (1963: 45) are specific empirical predictions which may be derived from the theory and whose accuracy may be checked by empirical observation. Models for Marx and Hillix (1963: 52) constitute a particular subclass of theory and so may also lead to hypotheses.

One way in which models are thought to differ from theories is in the degree of contact they have with the empirical world (Marx and Hillix, 1963: 53). Theory is that which provides "general guidelines," while models provide "specific guidelines for empirical research." Coombs et al. (1970) have extended this idea, noting (1970: 258) that theory provides the *interpretation* while a model provides the *structure*. Guetzkow et al. (1972: 5), as well, argue that theory contributes *explanation* while a model contributes *representation*. And finally a distinction is made (Guetzkow et al., 1972: 4) between a model and a simulation, the latter being considered a subclass of the former: "A simulation is an operating model of a real system." Thus, just as a model is considered to be one step closer to empirical reality than is theory, so a simulation is considered to be a step closer than a model. From a theoretical set of relational statements, we move to a more concrete model of empirical relations, to an actual attempt to put these relations into operation. For our present purposes, we have outlined our theory in Chapters 2 and 3, we are now proposing a concrete model in this chapter, and we will test the model employing empirical data which are to be presented in Chapters 5 to 9.

USE OF MODELS

In recent years the use of models deriving from theory has tended to replace the use of hypotheses. There is no doubt that the classical derivation and testing of hypotheses (with a turning back of data to comment on the hypotheses and the theory) has continued; but the use of models has increased greatly with the arrival of the computer. This new tool has made simulation of models much easier for simple systems and has made it possible for more complex systems. Indeed it has made possible for the first time the exploration of very complex functional systems such as those explored by Forrester (1971a) and his colleagues.

Models may be classified in a number of ways; Rosenberg (1969: 185-186), for example, notes a basic distinction between *prescriptive* (normative) models and *descriptive* ones. A prescriptive model is one which "specifies the behaviour required of an individual or group in order to maximize the value of an explicit criterion" of the model. Game theory falls clearly in this category; these rules specify which strategies should be used and are not necessarily accurate in describing which strategies are actually used. On the other hand, descriptive models more closely approximate actual behaviour. One kind of descriptive model (the *explicational*) "provides an unambiguous language for describing certain empirical relations," while another kind (the *predictive*) "generates propositions about the nature or existence of empirical phenomena not yet examined or observed by the scientist" (Rosenberg, 1969: 186). This latter, of course, approximates the function of the hypothesis in the classical paradigm. Another classification (Rapoport, 1963: 531) distinguishes between descriptive and predictive models. The descriptive model is an empirical description of extant relationships and is employed to gain insight into multiple relationships among sets of data. The predictive model, on the other hand, employs some empirical description to predict other empirical relations and approximates the traditional use of the hypothesis.

In Rapoport's terms, the model to be presented here is both descriptive and predictive. For the ecological and cultural variables, it describes extant and known relationships, but for the behavioural variables, it predicts the kinds and levels of behaviour which are likely to be found in different ecological and cultural settings. As we have noted, then, this latter use of a model is akin to the traditional drawing of hypotheses from extant theoretical and empirical knowledge.

Perhaps the best-known employer of models and simulation techniques is Forrester (1971a, 1971b) and his colleagues (Meadows et al., 1972). In these works, the dynamics of world systems (population, pollution, natural resources, captial investment, and quality of life) and the limits to their growth are explored. The authors use a combination of known empirical relations and a set of assumptions about future relations; their model is thus both descriptive and predictive. There has been a mixed acceptance for the catastrophic nature of some of their predictions, and the enterprise of modeling and simulation has been attacked. However, as Forrester (1971a: 14-15) points out, "mental models" of the surrounding world are an essential part of our everyday understanding of life. To transport these to the computer so that a greater complexity and a wider range of assumptions may be explored is not a novel act; it is simply to apply a new tool to an old problem. Indeed this new tool may enable us to transcend our current pedestrian efforts:

> It's my basic theme that the human mind is not adapted to interpreting how social systems behave. Our social systems belong to the class called multi-loop nonlinear feedback systems. In the long run of evolution it has not been necesary for man to understand these systems until very recent historical times. Evolutionary processes have not given the mental skill needed to properly interpret the dynamic behaviour of the systems of which we have now become a part [Forrester, 1971b: 53].

In Forrester's view, modelling per se should not be attacked; rather critics should attend either to the structure of a particular model (based in part on presently known empirical relations within the system) or to the set of assumptions which are tested in the model. Models, for Forrester, are neither good nor bad, but they can be used either well or poorly.

CROSS-CULTURAL USE OF MODELS

Within the discipline of physical and cultural anthropology, a most useful "model" has been that of somatic and sociocultural evolution. As a descriptive model, with its familiar trunks and branches, it has been an extremely useful tool for the comprehension of human cultural diversity. The success of other models, such as for kinship within a particular sociocultural unit or for sociocultural differentiation (Lomax and Berkowitz, 1972) have also led to the general acceptance of models as a convenient way of handling data in anthropology (cf. Cohen, 1970: 33-42).

And within cross-cultural psychology, we have already noted (Chapter 2) the rise of models as systematic approaches to the complexity of our subject matter. However, this movement has not been without its critics: Frijda and Jahoda (1966: 113) have argued that models have been too simple and "too remote from reality." First, the need in a culture for variety in "adult personality" combined with the complexity of the socialization process both suggest that there will exist a "range of personality types which is not inconsistent with major cultural demands" (1966: 113). Thus, they consider such a "molding into shape" model too simple. Second, given this first element of variability, "the linear deterministic system implied in the scheme becomes inappropriate, since it ignores the feedback from changes in adult personality that may directly affect both the nature of the maintenance system and child rearing practices" (1966: 113). Finally, one must now recognize external elements, such as technical and ideological acculturation which produce changes in most of the constituent elements of the system. All in all, they conclude that such "an intricate system of interlocking variables . . . defies causal analyses by methods at present at our disposal" (1966: 114).

Despite these criticisms and reservations, the use of models (especially where they can handle probabalistic and feedback relationships) may provide the most systematic framework for comprehending the great complexity which confronts the cross-cultural psychologist. If, as Forrester has argued (1971a), we all engage in modeling in any case, then the formal presentation of it may be of some value: At worst it might lead to the reification of lines and diagrams as reality, or to the unmasking of untenable assumptions, but at best it could permit the systematic examination of complex sets of variables in ways which have not been previously attainable.

THE PRESENT MODEL

We have implied, in the previous section, that the present model avoids the "deterministic and linear" faults of previous cross-cultural models: This is accomplished first by treating each of the modelled relationships as probabilistic, to which a correlation coefficient of less than unity may be attached; and second, feedback relationships are recognized for most elements in the model. Earlier versions of the model (Berry, 1966, 1969b, 1971a) were concerned with the same three variables (ecology, culture, and behaviour), and the present model is merely an elaboration and extension of the earlier ones.

Perhaps the best way to introduce the model is to present it graphically and describe it verbally, in terms of its major overall components and relationships. Details of each component will then be provided graphically and verbally, in terms of its constitutent elements and relationships.

There are six major components of the model and nineteen major relationships within it. Of the six components, two *(ecology* and *acculturative influences)* are input variables, and four are variables considered as a function of these inputs. Of the nineteen relationships, eight are considered to be directly influencing (or, conversely, adapting), while eleven are feedback relationships. In addition, there are two components (circles) signifying partial influence.

In broad terms, the *ecology* input component includes both physical environmental and organismic variables, as well as the results of technology fed back from traditional behaviour, and input from acculturative influences. The *traditional culture* component contains a cluster of cultural variables which are considered (by the school of cultural ecology) to be adapted to ecological press. The *traditional behaviour* component is made up of those behaviours which are nurtured in a particular culture by the sociocultural forms adapted to the ecological press. The *acculturative influences* component contains all those variables brought (by large-scale, technologically advanced cultures) to bear on traditional cultures; it also is influenced by feedback from ecology, traditional culture, and traditional behaviour. The

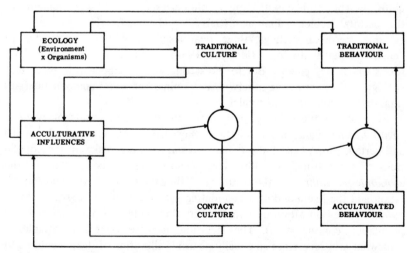

FIGURE 4.1   The Overall Ecological, Cultural, Behavioural Model

contact culture component includes those features of the group's culture which shift in response to the acculturative influences. These changes are partial, with certain elements of traditional culture remaining largely unaltered; the first circle in the model indicates those aspects of traditional culture which are affected, and which become the contact culture component with continued acculturative influence. Finally, the *acculturated behaviour* component contains those behaviours which are modified from traditional behaviour as a result of acculturative influences, and a new set of behaviours which emerges in an attempt to cope with acculturative pressures. The former include those behaviours which are a selection from traditional behaviour; the second circle indicates again that these changes are only partial, with much traditional behaviour remaining. The latter behaviour, which may be termed "acculturative stress" behaviour, includes many problematic behaviours and attitudes, which affect both the remaining traditional behaviour and the acculturative influences.

Each of these six components will now be examined in some detail, so that relationships among elements within each component may become more explicit.

Ecology Component

To avoid the charge of environmental determinism, it may be appropriate to repeat a point of view expressed already in Chapter 2: Cultural and behavioural variables are considered to be in a process of adapting to ecology; these adaptive relationships are probabalistic, not deterministic, and of course are subject to empirical testing. The strength of these relationships may be quite low (but still present); this would correspond to a "weak version" of the cultural ecology approach (Berry, 1971a: 324). However, in more extreme ecological settings, these relationships may be stronger due to "environmental limitations" (Meggars, 1954) on the cultural and behavioural forms which may emerge. But for no setting will the argument be made that ecology molds, forms, or otherwise determines the other components (cultural or behavioural) of the model.

Elements of the ecology component are the major inputs of *physical environmental* characteristics of the setting (mainly temperature and rainfall) and certain properties of the *human organisms* which make up the populations of the setting; two other basic elements in this component are the *economic possibilities* of the setting (including the mode of economic exploitation and the likelihood of accumulating food), and the *demographic distribution* of the population over its territory (including settlement patterns and population concentration). The inclusion of these latter two variables is somewhat arbitrary, since an equally plausible allocation of them would be to the traditional culture component. However since the modelled relationships flow from the ecology to the traditional culture component, the decision is unimportant to the model.

The ecology component is illustrated in Figure 4.2. The relationships illustrated within the component are unidirectional; however as noted previously (Figure 4.1), there are feedbacks to this one from other components of the model. The directionality of the component rests essentially on the fact that such basics as temperature, rainfall, primary human needs, and genetic variability are largely beyond the influence of people and their culture or behaviour. A case might be made for a feedback from "settlement patterns" or "mean size" to "genetic variability," since a low-density, dispersed population may have diminished variability; however for present purposes we will leave this aside.

A foundation for this ecology component is the work of G. P. Murdock and his numerous colleagues, both in the area of cultural ecology (see Chapter 2) and in the Ethnographic Atlas Project (Murdock, 1967). A major review of these specific variables has been presented by Murdock (1969) and our discussion follows his exposition of the relationships. Murdock's primary interest in the relationship between the economic and demographic variables (exploitive patterns and settlement patterns); once this relationship is established, we may consider its relation to the interaction between human organisms and their physical habitat.

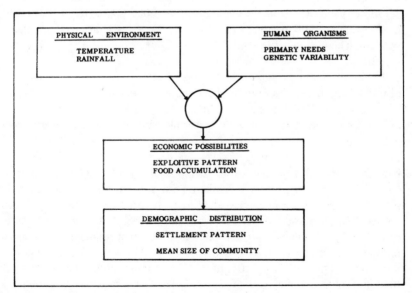

FIGURE 4.2   The Ecology Component of the Model

For Murdock (1969: 130-131) there are three variables of importance: exploitive pattern ("subsistence"), "settlement pattern," and mean size ("average local group"). The fourth variable in Figure 4.2 (food accumulation) will be introduced later in reporting a study of the relationship between subsistence economic activity and socialization practices (Barry, Child, and Bacon, 1959). Employing a sample of 322 societies from the Ethnographic Atlas, Murdock classified them on such exploitative variables as gathering (n = 20 societies), hunting and trapping (n = 30), pastoral (n = 21), fishing (n = 41), and agricultural (n = 210); these agricultural societies were further classified by their emphasis upon root or tree (horticulture, n = 68), cereal grains (swidden agriculture, n = 64) or intensive agriculture (with irrigation, fertilization, and ploughing, n = 78).

These same societies were also rated on settlement patterns, and placed in four categories: *fully nomadic, semi-nomadic, semi-sedentary,* and *fully sedentary.* This dimension and categorization essentially allocates the societies to (respectively) those who move continuously; those who move regularly but occupy a fixed settlement for a single season; those who move less often, but regularly move from one fixed settlement to another fixed settlement; and finally those who occupy a single settlement for a very long period of time (generations).

A final rating was performed, based upon known population concentrations, and included seven categories: (1) less than 50 persons in a settlement unit, (2) 50 to 99 persons, (3) 100 to 199 persons, (4) 200 to 400 persons, (5) more than 400 but in the absence of towns of 5,000 or more, (6) at least one town of 5,000 persons or more, and (7) at least one city of 50,000 persons. These population data were available for only 192 of the 322 societies.

Exploitive patterns appear to be highly related to settlement patterns (Table 4.1), as does the size of local community (Table 4.2)

Gathering and hunting societies are either nomadic or seminomadic (with only 9 exceptions out of 50 societies) while agricultural societies are either semi-sedentary or sedentary (with only 3 exceptions out of 210 societies); pastoral and fishing societies, however, are more evenly divided. These distributions are not random, the relationships being highly significant (X^2 = 321.1, p < .01, df = 2). Similarly, for population concentration, in only 2 of the 34 societies classed as gathering or hunting did population concentrations exceed 200 persons, while in 69 of the 124 societies classed as agricultural, community populations exceeded that number; once again pastoral and fishing communities fall between. These distributions are also not random (X^2 = 96.1, p < .01, df = 2). Even more interesting, however, is that in a large number (30 of 54 or 56%) of those employing intensive agricultural techniques, cities of 50,000 persons or more were found.

TABLE 4.1

SUBSISTENCE ECONOMY AND SETTLEMENT PATTERN (in numbers)

Exploitive Pattern Type of Economy	Nomadic	Semi-nomadic	Semi-sedentary	Sedentary	Totals
Gathering	8	6	3	3	20
Hunting	14	13	3	0	30
Pastoral	10	6	5	0	21
Fishing	4	11	4	22	41
Horticulture	0	1	2	65	68
Extensive cereal cultivation	0	0	5	59	64
Intensive agriculture	0	2	5	71	78
Totals	36	39	27	220	322

Source: From Table 2, p. 144 (Murdock, 1969).

TABLE 4.2
SUBSISTENCE ECONOMY AND SIZE OF LOCAL COMMUNITY (in percentages)

Exploitive Pattern Type of Economy	Mean size of Local Community							Numbers of cases
	<50	50-99	100-199	200-400	<400 no towns	Towns of 5,000	Towns of 50,000	
Gathering	61	23	16	0	0	0	0	13
Hunting	61	29	0	10	0	0	0	21
Pastoral	59	25	8	0	8	0	0	12
Fishing	40	23	27	5	5	0	0	22
Horticulture	18	18	28	16	10	5	5	39
Extensive cereal cultivation	3	16	36	19	23	3	0	31
Intensive agriculture	0	7.5	11	7.5	9	9	56	54

Source: From Table 3, p. 145 (Murdock, 1969).

These significant relationships between the economic exploitive patterns of subsistence societies and both their mean size and their settlement patterns suggest a high probabilistic relationship between these two elements in the ecology component; indeed their distributions do correlate highly (with $X^2 = 182.6$, $p < .01$, df = 2).

With respect to the remaining variable (food accumulation) Barry (Barry, Child, and Bacon, 1959; Barry, 1969) has found a relationship between the degree of food accumulation and socialization (child-rearing) practices within a sample of 104 subsistence-level societies. These societies were classified on an earlier version of Murdock's exploitive dimension (Murdock, 1957) consisting of six levels: hunting, fishing, agricultural (grains important), agricultural (root crops important), pastoral, or agricultural (with animal husbandry important at the same time). Since the degree to which a community could accumulate or store food was considered to be an important variable mediating ecological (subsistence patterns) and cultural (child socialization practices) variables, Barry, Child, and Bacon (1959) *defined* three levels of the accumulation variable in terms of the six subsistence patterns: *High food accumulation* societies are those which are agricultural (with animal husbandry present) or pastoral; *medium food accumulation* societies are those which are either root crop or grain agriculturalists (with animal husbandry unimportant); and *low food accumulation* societies are those which are hunting or fishing. Thus, this final variable is included in our economic possibilities element of the model since it is tied, by definition, to the exploitive pattern variable. However it is not redundant, since this conception of the variable provides a powerful theoretical link to aspects of the traditional culture component.

Finally, in this ecology section, we must define the two major input variables, and their interaction and relations with the economic and demographic elements of the model. The basic argument is that certain levels of the physical environmental variables (temperature and rainfall) will *permit* human organisms (with their needs for sustenance and shelter) to engage in certain economic pursuits; there is no determinism implied. In cases of low rainfall and low temperature (as in the circumpolar regions) agriculture is not possible, and pastoralism, although possible in some areas, is not possible in all; if human beings are to occupy this habitat (in the absence of a massive technology to alter or overcome these physical environmental features) the economic base is limited to hunting or fishing. In cases of low rainfall but higher temperatures (as in many of the temperate zone deserts) agriculture is again not a general possiblility, pastoralism is again marginal, and fishing is impossible; the exploitive pattern appears to be limited to hunting and gathering.

At the other extreme, where there is higher temperature or rainfall, agricultural, pastoral, and hunting/gathering patterns of exploitation are all possibilities. However (and here we must again approach the difficult area of cultural evolution) it is the case that the bulk of those inhabiting areas where cultivation is possible, various forms of agriculture are pursued; without implying that this form of economic exploitation is higher or more advanced, it is indeed the case that where it is possible, societies produce or grow their food rather than gathering or chasing it. Evidence for this assertion is widespread in the literature (e.g., Forde, 1934); however for continuity with the previous discussion we may analyze the data of Murdock (1969: Table 1, p. 132-143) to illustrate the point. For each of the 322 listed societies, latitude and longitude are provided as well as exploitive pattern. Classifying these societies into three categories (cultivation possible, cultivation marginally possible, or cultivation not possible) because of temperature/rainfall (determined from geographic data), the distribution in Table 4.3 emerges. There is an imbalance in the distribution of societies in the three columns as one would expect, since the majority of human beings are unlikely to inhabit areas of low temperature and rainfall by choice. Nevertheless there is a clear relationship between the two variables. All 20 societies in the first column either hunt, gather, fish, or raise animals; this is an obvious state of affairs, since rainfall and temperature are limiting variables. Of the 31 societies in the second column, the bulk (29) pursue these same four activities. Finally, in the third column, a more reasonable test of the relationship may be made: Of the 271 societies inhabiting regions where cultivation is possible, 208 practice horticulture, cereal cultivation, or intensive agriculture, while of the remaining 63, 39 fish or raise animals, and only 24 prefer to hunt or gather. These distributions are not random (X^2 = 87.1, p < .01, df = 1); there is a decided emphasis on cultivation in the vast majority of cases where it is possible.

We may conclude, then, that the physical-environmental factors of temperatures and rainfall provided a clear set of economic possibilities which human organisms, in attempting to meet their primary needs, can pursue. However, these possibilities are not just *limiting* (as in the case of hunting and gathering predominating where cultivation is not possible), but for reasons unknown appear to *encourage* societies to adopt an exploitive pattern involving cultivation, where the possibility exists.

Finally, for this ecology component, it is apparent that the question of the genetic variable input has been hitherto ignored. This has not been for ideological, but for empirical, reasons. First, there are no known data which are able to relate human genetic variation to human behavioural variation *at the, group level*. Certainly, at the level of individual differences, the contribution of behaviour genetics has been great; however these techniques have not yet been applied cross-culturally, perhaps because their use is so difficult in the field. Second, characteristics of the gene pool have been considered (in traditional Darwinian evolutionary theory) to be adapted to the physical

TABLE 4.3
RELATIONSHIP BETWEEN TEMPERATURE/RAINFALL
AND EXPLOITIVE PATTERN IN 322 SOCIETIES

Exploitive Pattern Type of Economy	Physical Environment (temperature and rainfall tolerance for cultivation)			
	Cultivation Not Possible	Cultivation Marginal	Cultivation Possible	Total
Gathering	1	5	14	20
Hunting	8	12	10	30
Pastoral	5	2	14	21
Fishing	6	10	25	41
Horticulture	0	2	66	68
Extensive Cereal Cultivation	0	0	64	64
Intensive Agriculture	0	0	78	78
Totals	20	31	271	322

Source: From Table 1 (Murdock, 1969).

environmental setting which the population inhabits; in a sense the organism and its habitat come as a package to the model, and the study of their prior interrelationships is well beyond the scope of the present study.

Traditional Culture Component

Our main (and focal) interest in this component is in the socio-cultural factors which influence or are associated with the socialization (and hence the behaviour) of organisms coming into the group. Since this component is placed between the traditional behaviour and ecology components, our focus will be further limited to those sociocultural variables which are thought to be adapted to the ecological input (economic and demographic variables) just described. There exist many aspects of society and culture which are ignored here, simply because our purpose is to eventually understand the variation and source of certain behaviours, and not to model the whole sociocultural system. Third, our focus will be restricted to certain aspects of socialization, rather than attempting to describe or account for all of the variables which appear in the sociocultural literature on child training (e.g., Whiting and Child, 1953; Minturn and Lambert, 1964). Specifically our attention will be directed toward those socialization variables which have been implicated by Witkin et al. (1962, 1969) in the development of psychological differentiation.

One rider must be added at this point, since two of the interrelated cultural elements will not appear in the diagram of the traditional culture component. This extra concern is for some *linguistic* and some *arts and crafts* characteristics of a group's culture. These lie largely outside the main arguments to be made in the component which is intended to link ecological, cultural, and socialization elements. Nevertheless they are considered to play some role, and a detailed discussion of them will be provided in Chapter 7.

As before, the component is introduced schematically, and this is followed by a description of each of the elements in it and by a discussion of what is known about their interrelationships. The traditional culture component is illustrated in Figure 4.3.

This traditional cultural component flows mainly from our previous discussion of sociocultural differentiation (Chapter 3). In societies where there is *role diversity* there is the possibility that these roles will become organized in a set of hierarchies, be they political, economic, religious, military, or familial; where no specialization exists, there can be no hierarchical stratification. As Dunning (1960) has pointed out, division of labour is an obvious and the most frequent form. In our previous discussion in Chapter 3 of sociocultural evolution (Naroll, 1956; Freeman and Winch, 1957) we noted the presence of occupational religious or military "specialists" in these two indices.

With respect to the *stratification* of these divisions into status or authority systems, there is evidence (again Naroll, 1956; Freeman and Winch, 1957) that stratification is also an essential element in these indices or scales of sociocultural evolution. Various forms of stratification have been discussed by Nimkoff and Middleton (1960), Ember (1963), and Pelto (1968), involving, respectively, general social stratification and family structure, politi-

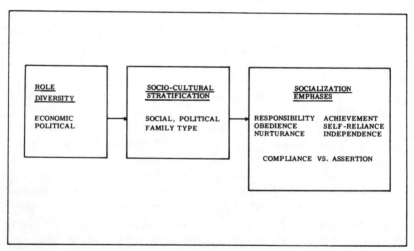

FIGURE 4.3   The Traditional Culture Component of the Model

cal and economic authority, and an overall concept of stratification ("tight" and "loose" social systems).

Finally, with respect to socialization, Barry, Child, and Bacon (1959) and Barry (1969) have examined the socialization emphases in variously stratified societies and noted (1959: Table 3, p. 61) a set of strong relationships among level of stratification and political integration, settlement and exploitive patterns, and pressure toward compliance during socialization.

Following this initial mapping of the traditional culture component, the major task is to provide details of the content of these elements and of their relationships among themselves and to aspects of the ecology component. Beginning with the differentiation of roles, we find repeated and consistent evidence in Naroll (1956), Freeman and Winch (1957), Tatje and Narroll (1970), Carneiro (1970), and McNett (1970) that societies low on measures of sociocultural differentiation and complexity tend to be hunting and gathering peoples, who are migratory and who have low levels of food accumulation and population density. Conversely, those societies high on measures of social differentiation and complexity tend to be agricultural peoples, who are sedentary and who have high levels of food accumulation and population density. There is, of course, a wide range of societies which lies intermediate between these two extremes; consistent with the present argument, these tend to lie intermediate on indices of exploitive patterns (e.g., mixed hunting and cultivation), settlement pattern (e.g., semi-migratory or semi-sedentary), and population density. This broad and general assertion may be supported and illustrated in many ways; perhaps the single best illustration is from McNett (1970), where a range of sociocultural elements which may become differentiated (as opposed to remaining undifferentiated) is related to settlement pattern (see Table 4.4).

Further support derives from Ember (1963), who demonstrated a relationship between the differentiation of economic and political elements (Ember, 1963: Figure 1, p. 243) and then related the latter to population level (Table 5, p. 239; r = +.80 for 24 societies). Pelto as well (1968), in his generalized scale of "tight" versus "loose" societies, supports both the relationships among elements of sociocultural differentiation and stratification, and their overall relationship to ecological variables. To illustrate his dimension, Pelto (1968: Table 1) was able to scale twelve "elements of social structure" with a high (but uncalculated) degree of Guttman reproducibility; very "tight" societies had a "theocracy" and much "corporate ownership of property" and most of the ten lesser elements, while very "loose" societies had only basic elements of "permanent recognized political control" and the "legitimate use of force."

To account for his spread of societies along this general stratification dimension, Pelto (1968: 40) postulates two ecological variables: "high

TABLE 4.4

DIFFERENTIATION OF SOCIOCULTURAL ELEMENTS IN RELATION TO SETTLEMENT PATTERNS

Settlement Pattern	SOCIOCULTURAL CONCOMITANTS		
	Economic	Political	Social
Restricted Wandering (Wander within owned territory)	Personal property primarily for food/getting. Communal ownership of real estate.	Band of related or friendly families headed by advisory leader.	No status differences.
Central-based Wandering (Part of year sedentary at central base)	Surpluses, if any, not used exclusively by any group.	Leader is community symbol.	Status based on ability.
Semi-permanent Sedentary (Move village whenever environment is exhausted)	Family land ownership. Surpluses acquired but redistributed. Some villages specialization if manufacturing.	Clans or moieties generally basis of organization. Headman is agent of community.	Status based upon surplus distribution.
Simple Nuclear Centered (Self-sufficient village)	Private ownership of real estate. Full-time occupational specialization.	Chief with coercive power in a kinship-based system.	Stratification based on property.
Advanced Nuclear Centered (Permanent administrative center)	Larger surplus controlled by the upper class.	Administrative centers with hierarchy controlled by a king. Law and politics supplant kinship organization.	Hereditary classes.
Supra-nuclear Integrated (Components integrated into state, typically by conquest)	Commercialism, large scale circulation of goods, much accumulated wealth, taxes.	Absolute power vested in ruler. Government manipulates population. Professional army.	Large lower class with many slaves

Source: Condensed from McNett (1970), Table 1, P. 873.

reliance on food crops. . . . Growing and harvesting crops on a large scale requires teamwork, and rigid organization may be needed to mobilize and direct the people's efforts toward the common goal of an abundant harvest"; and second, "population density is related to tightness in social structure. In general, it seems that the more people there are in a small area, the more rigid social structure they need to keep them functioning cooperatively, with a minimum of discord and friction."

A third element, that of family and kinship, is also discussed by Pelto (1968: 40), but since this is another sociocultural element, rather than an ecological one, it is internal to this component. However, as Nimkoff and Middleton (1960) had pointed out earlier, this variable is not unimportant, and itself is related to ecological variables. Their basic distinction is between "independent" and "extended" family structure; the former category comprises "nuclear" (husband and wife plus children) or "polygamous" (husband and wives plus children) families, while the latter is composed of families where other relations (such as husband's or wife's parents or siblings) also share the household. The crucial distinction between these two types of family is that, in the "independent family, the head of a family of procreation is neither subject to the authority of any of his relatives nor economically dependent upon them" (Nimkoff and Middleton, 1960: 215).

The arguments advanced by Nimkoff and Middleton (1960) are based upon a further demonstration of a relationship between exploitive pattern and the degree of general social stratification, classified simply as "great" or "little"; Table 4.5 provides these data. Of 364 societies with agriculture present, 274 (76%) of them are classed as highly stratified, while of the 73 societies in this sample with hunting and gathering dominant, 57 (78%) are

TABLE 4.5
RELATIONSHIP BETWEEN EXPLOITIVE PATTERN
AND GENERAL SOCIAL STRATIFICATION

Exploitive Pattern	General Social Stratification	
	Great	Little
Agriculture dominant or co-dominant	274	90
Animal husbandry dominant or co-dominant with fishing, hunting, or gathering	29	14
Fishing dominant or co-dominant with hunting and gathering	31	20
Hunting and gathering dominant	16	57
	340	181

Source: From Nimkoff and Middleton (1960) Table 5, p. 221.

classed as having little stratification. In the same table, these authors indicated that for both "great" and "little" stratification societies, there was a clear trend for the proportion of families which were "extended" to decline as one moved from agricultural to hunting or gathering societies. On the average (from Nimkoff and Middleton, 1960: Table 4), 37% of the 173 societies having "little" stratification had "extended" families, while 64.1% of the 295 societies having "great" stratification had "extended" families.

With respect to relationships between family type and ecological variables, exploitive pattern and family type were clearly related, as were settlement pattern and family type. For exploitive patterns (Nimkoff and Middleton 1960: Table 2, p. 217) in the 260 societies where agriculture was dominant, 64% had "extended" families while in the 54 societies where hunting or gathering was dominant only 22% had "extended" families; in the 225 societies where there was a mixed exploitive pattern, about half (51%) had "extended" families. For settlement pattern (Nimkoff and Middleton, 1960: Table 3, p. 219) in the 410 societies classed as "sedentary," 60% had "extended" families.

These general and impressive trends have been confirmed by more recent analyses by Blumberg and Winch (1973) employing a data base of over nine hundred societies. In addition to confirming these general relationships between family type and many ecological (subsistence pattern, mean size of local community, settlement pattern) and cultural (social and political stratification) variables, they were able to point to a drop in family complexity toward the very "tight" end of the dimension. However this curvilinearity occurs at a point on the dimension beyond which the present study operates, and it need not be incorporated.

The pattern which emerges frőm these studies confirms both the general relationships among a number of sociocultural elements and their relationship to the ecological variables of exploitive pattern and settlement pattern. The demonstration that in sedentary agricultural societies there is a consistent tendency for families to be "extended" to be elements in a stratified social, economic, and familial authority system, may have great import for the techniques of socialization which are employed in such families and societies; it is the final link between the traditional culture and traditional behaviour components, to which we turn now.

This fundamental relationship between child training practices (socialization) and ecological variables (primarily food accumulation defined in terms of exploitive pattern) was first elaborated by Barry, Child, and Bacon in 1959; it was confirmed by Barry in 1969 and again by Barry and Paxson in 1971. Recognizing that child training practices may be viewed both as an antecedent of adult behaviour and as a consequent of adults behaving within a particular cultural framework, Barry et al. (1959: 51) pose the crucial question, "Why does a particular society select child training practices which will tend to produce a particular kind of typical personality? Is it because this kind of typical personality is functional for adult life of the society, and training methods which will produce it are thus also functional?" This functionalist approach to socialization fits well with the present model, and of course with our emphasis upon cultural adaptation to ecological variables.

The basic hypothesis advanced by Barry et al. (1959: 52) is that adult economic roles should be consistent with "the extent to which food must be accumulated and cared for":

> At one extreme is dependance mainly upon *animal husbandry* where the meat that will be eaten in coming months and years, and the animals that will produce the future milk are present on the hoof. In this type of society, future food supply seems to be best assured by faithful adherence to routines designed to maintain the good health of the herd. *Agriculture* perhaps imposes only slightly less pressure toward the same pattern of behaviour. Social rules prescribe the best known way to bring the growing plants to successful harvest, and to protect the stored produce for gradual consumption until the next harvest. Carelessness in performance of routine duties leads to a threat of hunger, not for the day of carelessness itself but for many months to come. Individual initiative in attempts to improve techniques may be feared because no one can tell immediately whether the changes will lead to a greater harvest or to disastrous failure. Under these conditions, there might well be a premium on obedience to the older and wiser, and on responsibility in faithful performance of the routine *laid down* by custom for one's economic role.

> At an opposite extreme is subsistence primarily through hunting or fishing with no means for extended storing of the catch. Here individual initiative and development of high skill seem to be at a premium. Where each day's food comes from that day's catch, variations in the energy and skill exerted in food-getting lead to immediate reward or punishment. Innovation, moreover, seems unlikely to be so generally feared. If a competent hunter tries out some change in technique, and it fails, he may still have time to revert to the established procedures to get his catch. If the change is a good one it may lead to immediate reward [Barry, Child, and Bacon, 1959: 52].

Second, they argue that:

> If economic role tends to be generalized to the rest of behavior, predictions might be made about the typical character or personality of adults in societies with different subsistence economies. In societies with low accumulation of food resources, adults should tend to be . . . individualistic, assertive and venturesome. By parallel reasoning, adults should tend to be . . . conscientious, compliant and conservative in

societies with high accumulation of food resources [Barry, Child, and Bacon, 1959: 53].

Finally, the third step is to argue:

> If economic role and general personality tend to be appropriate for the type of subsistence economy, we may expect the training of children to foreshadow these adaptations. The kind of adult behavior useful to the society is likely to be taught to some extent to the children, in order to assure the appearance of this behavior at the time it is needed. Hence we may predict that the emphases in child training will be toward the development of kinds of behavior especially useful for the adult economy [Barry, Child, and Bacon, 1959: 53].

In order to assess the argument, child-training practices (emphases in socialization) were compared in a sample of 104 societies, with their degree of food accumulation (defined in terms of exploitive patterns); no comparisons were made with "adult personality," since these data were not available to them in the ethnographic literature.

Before examining these ecological-cultural relationships, however, it is useful to note that other cultural elements (such as stratification) and ecological elements (such as population concentration) are strongly related to both variables of food accumulation and pressure in child training toward compliance. For societies extreme on the food accumulation scale, Table 4.6 provides these data. It is apparent that both the food accumulation and socialization variables are related significantly to the other ecological and cultural variables. However, what is the relationship between food accumulation and socialization?

A classification of the seventy nine societies was made on the food accumulation scale as follows: *high food accumulation* societies were those with exploitive patterns combining agriculture with animal husbandry or pastoralism (n = 24); *medium food accumulation* societies were those pre-

TABLE 4.6
RELATIONSHIP BETWEEN DEGREE OF FOOD ACCUMULATION, PRESSURE TOWARD COMPLIANCE AND OTHER SOCIAL STRATIFICATION

Cultural Variable	Degree of Food Accumulation	Pressure Toward Compliance
Size of Permanent Settlement Unit	+.52	+.43
Complexity of Social Stratification	+.74	+.56
Degree of Political Integration	+.76	+.63
Degree of food Accumulation x Compliance	+.94	

Source: Extracted from Barry et al. (1959) Table 3, p. 61, from those societies with extremes of food accumulation; n = 46; statistic is the "coefficient of association."

serving root or grain cultivation with animals unimportant (n = 33); while *low food accumulation* societies were those who relied upon hunting, gathering, or fishing (n = 22). Ratings for socialization emphases were carried out separately for boys and girls by raters (following the procedures employed by Barry, Bacon, and Child, 1957) on six child-training dimensions:

1. Obedience training.
2. Responsibility training, which usually was on the basis of participation in the subsistence or household tasks.
3. Nurturance training, i.e., training the child to be nurturant or helpful towards younger siblings and other dependent people.
4. Achievement training, which was usually on the basis of competition or imposition of standards of excellence in performance.
5. Self-reliance training, defined as training to take care of oneself, to be independent of the assistance of other people in supplying one's needs and wants.
6. General independence training. This was defined more generally through self-reliance training, to include training not only to satisfy one's own needs but also toward all kinds of freedom from control, domination and supervision. Ratings of general independence training were highly correlated with ratings of self-reliance training, but were not identical to them.

For each of these six aspects of training, societies were rated on strength of socialization, which was defined as the combined positive pressure (reward for the behavior) plus negative pressure (punishments for lack of the behavior). The ratings were for the stage of childhood, from age 4 or 5 years until shortly before puberty. Each rating was made by two separate judges, working independently and the sum of their two judgements was used [Barry, Child, and Bacon, 1959: 54].

TABLE 4.7
RELATIONSHIP BETWEEN SIX CHILD-TRAINING PRACTICES AND DEGREE OF FOOD ACCUMULATION

Child-Training Variables	Extremes in Accumulation		Intermediate in Accumulation	
	Boys	*Girls*	*Boys*	*Girls*
Responsibility	+.74**	+.62**	+.33	+.37
Obedience	+.50**	+.59**	+.66**	+.45
Nurturance	−.01	+.10	−.26	+.11
Achievement	−.60**	−.62**	−.32	−.12
Self-Reliance	−.21	−.46*	−.19	−.53
Independence	−.41	−.11	−.21	−.42

Source: From Barry, Child, and Bacon (1959) Table 1, p. 57.
*p <05
**p <01, two-tail, Mann-Whitney U.

Relationships among these two dimensions, calculated separately for extremes of accumulation and for intermediate accumulation are presented in Table 4.7. Of twelve possible correlations in the first group of societies, eight are significant in the predicted direction; and only the ratings on "nurturance" fail to show some relationship with the ecological variable.

When a more global measure of socialization ("pressure toward compliance versus assertion") is employed, these relationships still hold. This global measure, derived from the pattern of results in Table 4.6, combines ratings on "responsibility" and "obedience" on the one hand, and ratings of "achievement" and "self-reliance" on the other. A difference score between the two pairs, if positive, indicates an emphasis upon "compliance," and if negative an emphasis upon "assertion" in socialization. The distribution of societies in Table 4.8 indicates that for both groups of societies (extremes and intermediates in accumulation), there is a significant relationship between this global socialization and degree of food accumulation; of the twenty three societies above the median on the compliance assertion rating, twenty are high food accumulating, while of the twenty three societies below the median, nineteen are low food accumulating.

These ratings, on the generalized socialization dimension bear striking resemblance to two of the three elements of the "socialization cluster" which Witkin et al. (1962, 1969) implicated in the development of differentiation (see Chapter 3). The basic arguments which attempt to relate the "output" from this socialization element of the traditional culture component will be made in our discussion of the traditional behaviour component. However, it is important to note at this time the similarity between the rated "achievement," "self-reliance," and "independence" (assertion) of low food accumulating societies, and the "separation from mother," directed toward "autonomous functioning" variables of Witkin. Conversely it is also important to note the similarity between the rated "responsibility," "obedience," and "nurturance" (compliance) of high food accumulating societies, and the "stress on conformity" and "control of agressive, assertive behaviour" variables of Witkin.

In summary, the traditional culture component has been argued to be in adaption to ecological component variables, and in turn influencing traditional behaviour. Within the component, role differentiation, sociocultural stratification, and socialization emphases have been viewed as an interrelating cluster of sociocultural variables, which are all (in addition) in adaptive relationship with elements of the ecology component. A broad dimension has emerged which places hunting and gathering peoples toward one end and agricultural-pastoral peoples toward the other; a number of sociocultural variables appear to cluster with these peoples at the ends of this exploitive pattern dimension. At the same time, those peoples who are intermediate on

TABLE 4.8
RELATIONSHIP BETWEEN "COMPLIANCE VERSUS ASSERTION" SOCIALIZATION EMPHASES AND DEGREE OF FOOD ACCUMULATION

Compliance versus Assertion	Extremes in Accumulation		Intermediate in Accumulation	
	High (animal husbandry) n	Low (hunting fishing) n	High (agriculture only) n	Low (agriculture and hunting) n
Above Median	20	3	14	6
Below Median	4	19	1	12
	$X^2 = 19.6$ $p < .01$	$df = 1$	$X^2 = 9.95$ $p < .01$	$df = 1$

Source: Extracted from Barry, Child, and Bacon, (1959) Table 2, p. 60.

TABLE 4.9
GENERAL OVERVIEW OF ELEMENT IN
ECOLOGY AND TRADITONAL CULTURE COMPONENTS

Components & Elements	Clustering at Poles of Dimension	
Ecology	◄————————————————————►	
Exploitive Pattern	Hunting & Gathering	Agriculture
Food Accumulation	Low	High
Settlement Pattern	Nomadic	Sedentary
Mean Size	Low	High
Culture		
Role Diversity	Low	High
Sociocultural Stratification	Low	High
Socialization Emphases	Assertion	Compliance

the dimension appear to have intermediate levels of the associated variables. A convenient overview of these relationships is provided, in general terms, in Table 4.9.

Traditional Behaviour Component

In our discussion of the traditional culture component, we noted that not all aspects of culture would be examined, nor would all aspects of socialization be considered. Similarly, in this component, obviously all traditional behaviour cannot be discussed. Our focus here is upon those behaviours which are theoretically linked to the notion of psychological differentiation.

Following closely our discussion of differentiation (in Chapter 3), our traditional behaviour component submodel is illustrated in Figure 4.4. The elements of this component correspond to differentiation in the *perceptual and cognitive* (cognitive style) domains of psychological functioning, supplemented by two elements which are considered to be both logically and psychologically related to cognitive style.

The major input in the model to this organismic state is from the *socialization* element of the traditional culture component. An assumption here is that the socialization-differentiation relationship established by Witkin et al. (1962, 1967, 1969) and by others is a cultural universal; this assumption is of course, open to empirical check. A further input, as already indicated, is in the realm of "other determinants" (Witkin et al., 1962: 16); specifically in our study these involve sociocultural "tightness," linguistic and arts and crafts elements of traditional culture.

The overall expectations are that psychological differentiation will proceed at different rates and to different levels, in different societies, as one moves along the broad dimension outlined in Table 4-9. (At this point, it is

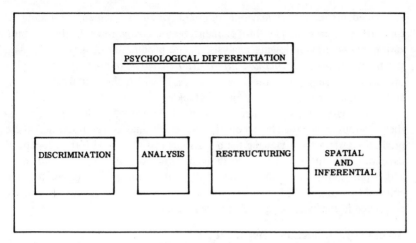

FIGURE 4.4 The Traditional Behaviour Component of the Model

important to recall the discussion in Chapter 3 about the curvilinearity of sociocultural differentiation and integration in relation to the ecology dimension. At the extreme ends, such a general expectation may not hold.) That is, in nomadic hunting and gathering societies, where population density and sociocultural stratification are low, and where socialization emphasizes assertion, we expect to find high levels of psychological differentiation. Conversely, in sedentary agricultural societies, where population density and socio-cultural stratification are high, and where socialization emphasizes compliance, we expect to find low levels of psychological differentiation. And, considering it as a dimension, we expect to find moderate levels in those societies which fall intermediate between these two extremes. Stated very simply, where levels of sociocultural complexity are high, levels of psychological differentiation will be low; and conversely where levels of sociocultural complexity are low, levels of psychological differentiation should be high.

At this point, we may describe each of the elements in general terms, leaving details of both the ethnographic evidence and the psychological testing in the field to Chapters 5 and 7. First, we may note that of the four elements, only two are directly subsumed under the concept of psychological differentiation; the other two are related (both theoretically and empirically), but are not constituents of the concept as employed by Witkin. The first element, *discrimination*, refers to the making of relatively fine visual discriminations from a background which is fairly uniform and homogeneous. It is that behaviour required of individuals in their subsistence activity, where embedding is not involved. The second element, *analysis*, refers to the visual extraction of a small figure from an organized context in which it is embedded. It is that behaviour required when an element of hiding or camouflage is present. The third element, *restructuring,* refers to the reorganization of material following analysis, in the production of new forms. And the fourth element, *spatial and inferential behaviour,* refers to more complex operations subsequent to these earlier ones, in which the spatial relations of, and inferences from, the forms must be tackled.

In summary, this component is essentially a set of predictions or hypotheses about individual behaviour in the traditional cultural setting. These predictions stem from viewing the behaviours (associated with the concept of psychological differentiation) as derived from both the *socialization* input and from some culturally valued "other determinants" specific to each cultural setting. Both ethnographic and psychometric evidence will be employed in the evaluation of these predictions.

Acculturative Influences Component

All cultures are in a process of change; thus our terms "traditional culture" and "contact culture" in Figure 4.1 were relative to a continuing state of rearrangements in cultural characteristics and forms. We have already devoted considerable attention to one form of cultural change—that of adaptation to environmental forces. However a more important source of change in recent history has stemmed from the contact of peoples leading to the diffusion of cultural forms. While it is true that many of these changes have been mutual, with both groups in contact having some influence over each other, it is also true that in most cases of contact involving European expansion, the resultant changes have been far from equal in both cultures.

FIGURE 4.5   The Acculturative Influences Component of the Model

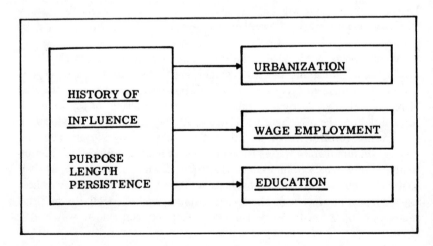

This process of culture change resulting from contact is often referred to as *acculturation,* and in keeping with our observation above, this process has largely involved a one-way flow of cultural characteristics from Western Euro-American societies to non-Western peoples in many parts of the world. Despite this imbalance, we will continue to use the more neutral term "acculturation," rather than the more frequent (and politically loaded) term *westernization;* and we will avoid the use of the term *modernization* as unnecessarily loaded and ethnocentric for our descriptive purposes.

Our discussion of acculturative influences will be limited to those features of Western Euro-American society which are considered to bear some relationship to our eventual goal of understanding behaviour, in both its "traditional" and "acculturated" variations. And second, we will not attempt to deal with characteristics of the more dominant culture (of which there are many) which lie outside the cultural dimensions we have already introduced into the discussion. Keeping these two limitations in mind, we may display the acculturative influences component schematically in Figure 4.5.

A first element to consider is the *history of influence* by the dominant culture; this includes the purpose, length, and persistence of contact. Since our focus is limited to those societies influenced during the period of Euro-American colonial expansion, we may distinguish two main purposes: colonization (settlement) and trade. These purposes have associated with them different degrees of length and persistence of contact; for example, contact persistence has generally been higher where settlement has occurred than where trade (usually with a few voyages a year) has been the purpose of contact.

Three elements stem from this descriptive, historic one. The first two influences *urbanization* and *wage employment* have been general throughout the past two centuries of contact. Wherever groups went for purposes of colonization, the tendency to form settlements, towns, and eventually cities has been apparent, even in those ecological settings where traditional cultures were not sedentary. Thus we may discern a general influence placed upon traditional cultures to become increasingly settled into larger population units and become absorbed into the new wage economy. This tendency has been less, though, where the purpose was merely to trade; however even around trading posts there began a process of settlement and employment which led to the establishment of population units larger than those found in traditional cultures.

A third major influence is that of *education* (both formal and informal) in the skills, values, and technology of the dominant culture. In formal terms, classrooms, compulsory attendence, and deliberate instruction in the language, religion, and knowledge of the dominant society is widespread. In less formal terms, the people in contact are educated by the media and informal interaction with those who have come from the dominant society.

All three elements (among many others) bear acculturative influences which are virtually impossible to resist. Without power to retaliate or resources to withdraw the most likely mode of response is adaptation. Changes occur at both the community and the individual levels, bringing about a contact culture and acculturated behaviour.

Contact Culture Component

In keeping with our limited focus up to this point, the contact culture component will deal only with those variables which may be generated from the topics included within the traditional culture and acculturative influences components. A further limitation is that all of the traditional culture component is not altered by the acculturative influences; very often the culture of a community ranges from very traditional to highly acculturated, both in terms of individuals and in terms of cultural elements. This second limitation was indicated in Figure 4.1 by inserting a circle between the two culture components; acculturation affects only some people and only some aspects of culture, producing a contact culture, which in turn influences those people and aspects remaining traditionally oriented.

The contact culture component is presented schematically in Figure 4.6. Its four elements derive from the last two elements of the ecology component (exploitive pattern and settlement pattern), and two of the elements of the traditional culture component (diversity and stratification, and socialization emphases). These four elements form an interacting cluster of group variables whose levels are altered by the acculturative influences.

Following our discussion of the acculturative influences component, the first element (contact exploitive pattern) largely depends upon the shift from traditional economic (exploitive) patterns to a monetary wage economy. With

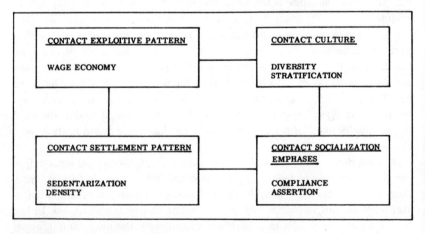

FIGURE 4.6   The Contact Culture Component of the Model

the availability of jobs and technology, money becomes important and trade provides for a new form of food accumulation—on the shelf. With sources of food available from outside the bounds of a particular culture, "subsistence-level" becomes an inappropriate label for the basic economy, and many of the relationships outlined in the ecology and traditional culture component submodels may be reduced in strength.

Nevertheless, the new wage economy, based upon employment and trade, does appear to affect our second element (contact settlement pattern) and result in higher concentrations of populations. As in the ecology component, the economic base again appears to be a limiting variable (population growth not being possible where food is unavailable to sustain life); where food accumulation becomes possible (this time due to the introduction of technology and trade), population concentrations increase.

Evidence for this assertion is largely informal, in the absence of data for this trend which was available for its support within the ecology component (Table 4.2).

Assignment of roles and of status appears in the third element (contact culture diversity and stratification) interposed as previously (traditional culture component) between settlement pattern and socialization. This time, however, the bases for assignment shift radically, so that they now bear strong relationships to the hierarchical systems of the dominant culture. Very often the people in contact are placed at a very low status level in the social, political, and economic spheres; attainment of the higher-status positions appears to be based upon educational success, although in specific circumstances, status may be extended based upon previous rank with the traditional culture (e.g., chief) or upon demonstrated ability in areas essential to the purposes of the dominant culture (e.g., guide, tracker, or culture broker).

Finally, in our fourth element, socialization emphases shift in the direction of those employed in the dominant culture, while at the same time displaying features of impulsiveness and apparent neglect. The first shift appears as a function both of formal education in the ways of the dominant culture and through informal exposure to the mass media; child-rearing practices become more like those which are provided as a model by the dominant culture. The second change may be associated with the peoples' generalized low status (of the previous element), interacting with the uncertainties inherent in all three cultural changes (exploitive pattern, settlement pattern, and stratification). These relationships are not clear; however the increase in difficulties in child rearing during culture contact and an increase in family disorganization are well documented.

Acculturated Behaviour Component

Two major kinds of behaviour are subsumed within this component. One is the fairly general and easy shift in traditional behaviour toward levels found in the dominant culture; as in the case of traditional culture, not all individuals and not all aspects of behaviour make this shift, and this is indicated by the circle in Figure 4.1. Once again we will be attending mainly to those behaviours which have already been considered in the traditional behaviour component (psychological differentiation). However, we will not limit our discussion to these, since some of the most obvious behavioural phenomena during acculturation are those problematic behaviours which have been termed "acculturative stress" behaviours (Berry and Annis, 1974b); these behaviours constitute our second focus.

Elements of the acculturated behaviour component are illustrated in Figure 4.7. There is envisaged a strong interrelationship between our two major elements, and numerous behavioural elements flowing from them. All elements of the traditional behaviour component are expected to shift under the influence of the formal education and wage employment elements, and in response to the changed socialization emphases; most of these cultural changes lead to the expectation that behaviour will change in the direction of the dominant cultural group. Details of these behavioural expectations will be elaborated in the reporting of the studies in Chapters 7 and 8.

With respect to the acculturative stress elements, there is a good deal of background literature which illustrates the personal and social difficulties which are experienced by persons in culture contact situations; these problems do not always occur, but they are reported with such frequency that it is not possible to ignore them, nor their possible relationships with psychological differentiation, when examining behaviour in acculturating settings. First, psychosomatic symptoms of *stress,* usually indexed by short checklists or questionnaires, form a large portion of this background literature; Chance (1965) and Cawte et al. (1968), among others, have given such a measure a prominent place in their empirical analyses of problematic behaviour in communities undergoing acculturation. Its origin may lie in the rapidity of

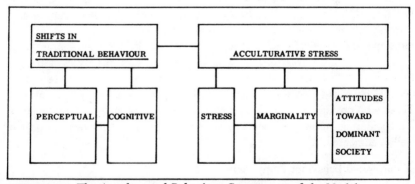

FIGURE 4.7   The Acculturated Behaviour Component of the Model

sociocultural change, in the incongruities between traditional culture and the acculturative influences or in both, interacting with psychological variables; this latter is the set of relationships illustrated in Figure 4.7.

Second, feelings of *marginality* or being "poised in psychological uncertainty" between two sociocultural systems, have often been implicated in the behavioural difficulties apparent in acculturating communities (Park, 1928; Stonequist, 1937). A scale to gauge this dimension has been developed by Mann (1958) and has been found to be useful in relating these feelings to aspects of the sociocultural situation; in addition, Berry (1970) has employed the scale in a similar way, while relating it to the *stress* variable discussed previously.

Finally, an element is considered which is related to stress and marginality (Berry, 1970): *Attitudes* toward modes of relating to the dominant group. These attitudes were first explored by Sommerlad and Berry (1970) in an attempt to understand the variation in response to dominant groups often found in groups undergoing acculturation. Three attitudes are considered: "assimilation," "integration," and "rejection."

The interaction between psychological differentiation and acculturative stress is expected to occur in at least two ways. First, the level of psychological differentiation in the acculturating setting (which is related to its level in traditional culture) may be inconsistent (or partially so) with expectations inherent in the acculturative influences; such inconsistency is expected to induce acculturative stress. Second, attitudes toward the dominant society are likely to be negative where differentiation in the social domain is high; as acculturative influences persist, this negative attitude toward these influences will further induce acculturative stress. In short, where traditional behaviour is inconsistent with acculturative influences, and where attitudes toward these influences from the dominant society are negative, acculturative stress is expected to be high. Again, these expectations will be examined in Chapter 8.

However, before we can explore these behavioural expectations, we must present the ecological, ethnographic, and acculturative background of the communities in the various studies. It is to the description of the cultures and samples that we now turn in Chapter 5.

Chapter 5

THE PEOPLE: CULTURE AND SAMPLE DESCRIPTIONS

The field work was carried out in a number of cultural settings, the selection of which was guided by the ecological and cultural analyses available in the ethnographic literature (primarily the numerous reports stemming from the work of Murdock and his associates). Although details of the experimental design and sampling strategy will be presented in the next chapter, it

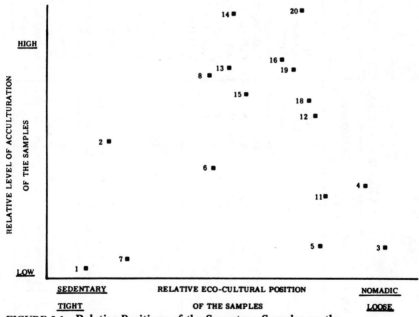

FIGURE 5.1   Relative Positions of the Seventeen Samples on the
Eco-Cultural and Acculturation Dimensions

[69]

TABLE 5.1
OVERVIEW OF FIELD WORK: CULTURES, COMMUNITIES AND PARTICIPANTS

Study	Culture		Community	Traditional Expoitive Patterns	Relative Acculturation	Date of Fieldwork		Number of Participants
1.	Temne	1	Mayola	Agricultural-Animal Husbandry	Low	Aug-Oct	1964	90
	Temne	2	Port Loko	Agricultural-Animal Husbandry	High	Jul-Aug	1964	32
	Eskimo	3	Pond Inlet	Hunting	Low	Mar-May	1965	91
	Eskimo	4	Frobisher Bay	Hunting	High	Mar&Jun	1965	31
	Arunta	5	Santa Teresa	Gathering-Hunting	Low	May-Jun	1967	30
	Koonganji	6	Yarrabah	Gathering-Hunting	High	May-Jun	1969	30
	Telefomin	7	Telefomin	Agricultural-Animal Husbandry	Low	May-Jun	1968	40
	Motu	8	Hanuabada	Hunting-Agriculture	High	May-Jun	1968	30
	Scots	9	Inverkeilor	Agricultural-Industrial	Rural-Village	May-Jun	1964	62
	Scots	10	Edinburgh	Industrial	Urban	Jan-Feb	1965	60
2.	Cree	11	Wemindji	Hunting	Low	Jun-Sep	1971	61
	Cree	12	Fort George	Hunting	High	Jun-Sep	1971	60
	Tsimshian	13	Hartley Bay	Gathering-Hunting	Low	Jun-Sep	1972	56
	Tsimshian	14	Port Simpson	Gathering-Hunting	High	Jun-Sep	1972	59
	Carrier	15	Tachie	Hunting-Gathering	Low	Jun-Sep	1972	60
	Carrier	16	Fort St. James	Hunting-Gathering	High	Jun-Sep	1972	61
	Euro-Canadian	17	Westport	Agricultural-Industrial	Village	May-Jul	1973	48
3.	Ojibway	18	Aroland	Hunting-Gathering	Low	Jun-Aug	1973	39
	Ojibway	19	Longlac	Hunting-Gathering	Medium	Jun-Aug	1973	37
	Ojibway	20	Sioux Lookout	Hunting-Gathering	High	Jun-Aug	1974	31
	Euro-Canadian	21	Sioux Lookout	Industrial	Town	Jun-Aug	1974	40

is appropriate to draw a broad and general outline at this point, before plunging into the specific ecocultural and acculturational characteristics of the groups involved in the study.

Following the two major inputs of our model, cultures and community samples were selected to provide a wide range on the ecocultural and acculturational background variables. Although these two dimensions may not be independent of each other, it is possible (for the sake of displaying the sampling strategy) to indicate the relative position of our samples on these two dimensions; this plotting is shown in Figure 5.1. A listing of the samples is provided in Table 5.1, along with a brief description and chronology of fieldwork. Figure 5.2 indicates the geographical location of the samples.

These samples are spread quite widely, both in terms of their geographical location and in terms of their relative locations on the ecocultural and acculturation dimensions. This spread is essential to the study, for it constitutes the quasi-manipulation of our independent variables. However two important issues are raised in connection with it: How representative are these cultures of world cultural variation, and how can variation of cultural elements which lie outside the model be controlled?

The first of these has been termed "Galton's problem" (Naroll, 1970) and it has plagued the use of archival ethnographic material for comparative survey purposes. This difficulty will be considered in detail in chapter 6 (Experimental Design); in the meantime a simple disclaimer is in order. The cultures and samples in this study do not constitute a representative sample of world cultural variation; nor should they, for they are intended to be an experimental manipulation of, rather than a representative sampling of, "independent" cultural variables.

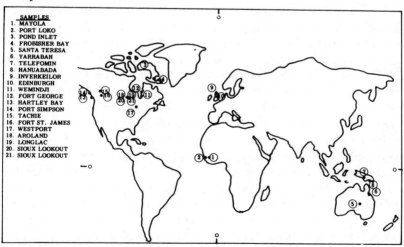

SAMPLES
1. MAYOLA
2. PORT LOKO
3. POND INLET
4. FROBISHER BAY
5. SANTA TERESA
6. YARRABAH
7. TELEFOMIN
8. HANUABADA
9. INVERKEILOR
10. EDINBURGH
11. WEMINDJI
12. FORT GEORGE
13. HARTLEY BAY
14. PORT SIMPSON
15. TACHIE
16. FORT ST. JAMES
17. WESTPORT
18. AROLAND
19. LONGLAC
20. SIOUX LOOKOUT
21. SIOUX LOOKOUT

FIGURE 5.2   Geographical Location of the Seventeen Samples

The second issue will also be taken up in the next chapter, and frequently thereafter in the discussion of results. In essence the problem is one of uncontrolled variation in independent variables as a by-product of sampling across broad sweeps of cultural variation. However, some statistical and sampling controls are available, and these will be considered in the next chapter.

With these two problems set aside for the time being, we may turn to the question of sampling communities within cultures. In general, communities were chosen for their position on the acculturation dimension (one as low as possible, and one in a state of cultural transition), and for practical reasons, such as geographical access and the willingness of local authorities to cooperate.

Following are brief descriptions of the cultures and community samples involved in the study. The order of describing them is not exactly chronological, geographical, or cultural in basis, but is a mixture of these three elements. The research was carried out in three phases (studies 1, 2, and 3). The first took place between 1964 and 1969 and provides the basic set of contrasts in this monograph. A second study (conducted between 1970 and 1973) was designed to obtain a more limited contrast across the ecocultural dimension, staying within a single culture area (Amerindian). And the third study (conducted in 1973 and 1974) was designed to focus more clearly on a single (hunting and gathering) culture under various levels of acculturative influence.

TEMNE OF SIERRA LEONE

The Temne people occupy a territory of about 10,000 square miles in central and coastal Sierra Leone (see Figure 5.2) and numbered over half a million individuals in 1950 (McCulloch, 1950); their population in 1964 when fieldwork was conducted is estimated at perhaps 525,000.

Their designation as a separate cultural group within the West African culture area rests largely with their language, rather than with any other single element or set of cultural elements. Indeed, the cultural continuities across tribal boundaries in this part of the world (such as clans, religion, forms of social organization) are more apparent than the discontinuities which have been used by European ethnographers for classifying the people into various sociopolitical units. Their language is distinct from the Mande-speaking peoples who largely occupy Sierra Leone, suggesting a migration to this area, perhaps in the seventeenth century (McCulloch, 1950: 51). Despite this, there appears to be an internal linguistic division, with those to the north (Sanda Temne) speaking a dialect which is distinct from those in the South (Yonni Temne). Many Temne profess adherence to Islam, following the arrival of

Moslem teachers from further North in the sixteenth century; however, as is usually the case with Islam, traditional religious belief (which includes a variety of deities and practice of witchcraft) continues to be accepted in association with the general features of Moslem belief.

The land which the Temne occupy consists of rain forest and grasslands; this land is used for farming, and to a lesser extent the maintenance of small domesticated animals (usually the goat). Their staple crop is rice, primarily upland rice cultivated on the grasslands, but low land (wet) rice is also cultivated in swampy areas of the rain forest. In addition to rice, ground-nuts (peanuts) and cassava are cultivated, very often in the same fields as the upland rice. Goats (and sheep and fowl) are kept, usually close to the villages, but they are also kept on the farms at the *Kabanka* (or day hut) which is used for shelter while at the fields. Some small fish are extracted from the streams running through their land (usually with traps and nets placed permanently in the stream), but on the coast inshore fishing has become a major source of food. With respect to exploitive pattern, then, we may classify the Temne as agricultural with a secondary emphasis upon small animal husbandry, yielding an estimate of relatively high food accumulation.

Almost all live in permanent farm villages, from which the surrounding land is cultivated. Some large towns now exist, and some Temne have settled in the capital city (Freetown); however the predominant settlement pattern was and remains sedentary communities, with village populations between 300 and 500 persons. With respect to overall population density, the data quoted earlier yield a figure of about 50 persons per square mile. However figures quoted by McCulloch (1950: 49) for those areas where the population tends to concentrate argue for a density far greater than this (80 to 120 persons per square mile). Regardless of the exact figure, it is apparent that their settlement pattern is sedentary and, in keeping with earlier evidence of high food accumulation, their population density is relatively high.

Sociocultural organization and stratification have been outlined by McCulloch (1950: 45-59). Temne country is divided into 44 "chiefdoms," each with a "paramount chief" ruling over it. This person is selected from among the oldest suitable males in the "chiefly families" of the chiefdom. Each village has a lesser chief or headman, while there are intermediate-level chiefs (section chiefs and *santigis*) who are selected by the paramount chiefs for these roles. Authority, thus, is stratified and is held by those born into certain families.

This stratification is further evidenced by the existence of slaves in earlier times and the participation of the Temne in the trading of slaves with Europeans. Within Temne society these were classified as "house" slaves and "ordinary slaves"; the former were born into the household and could not be sold, while the latter were captured during war or in settlement of debt.

Another indication of high stratification in Temne society is the existence of secret societies (*Poro* for men, and *Bundu* for women). These societies provide a relatively separate stratification system, although those with high status in village life tend also to have high status in the secret society. It is not clear how status is acquired, but informants suggest that it is based upon the degree of mystical experience which the initiated youth has during his training and testing in the Poro bush.

In addition to these organizations there are clans which cut across not only the Temne chiefdoms but, as already mentioned, also across cultural groups in Sierra Leone. These clans (*abunas*) were originally exogamous, although within-clan marriage is now often permitted, especially in the larger clans. Marriage is usually polygnous, with wealthy and high-status men having up to twenty-five wives; the modal number, however, is less than three or four. These families are polygynous and may be termed "small extended". Typically, a man and his wives and children (with perhaps some junior brothers and sisters) form a single household. However many or most of these households are headed by a man who is descended from, and has some responsibility to, the village headman or chief; thus the pattern of authority within the village is clear, and most of the families are responsible, by kinship, to another individual in the village.

Socialization practises are characterized by aggressiveness and restrictiveness; indeed a common Temne expression refers to being "held tight" during childhood, implying both physical control and parental restriction on early behaviour. Field observations provide evidence for this view, especially after the age of weaning (around two years); beatings and scoldings grow in frenquency until adolescence. However prior to weaning, there is evidence from field observations for a relatively high degree of warmth and nurturance. As we shall see in Chapter 6, self-reports from participants in the study strongly support this general characterization of restrictiveness.

Finally, in this brief cultural overview, we may examine the history of Western contact experienced by the Temne people. Those on the coast have been in contact longer and with a greater frequency than those in the interior. First contact in Sierra Leone was by Portuguese voyagers in the mid-fifteenth centry (Fyfe, 1962) who named the coast Sierra Lyoa for its lion-looking coastal mountains. Thereafter, the British visited in the 1560s, taking slaves to the West Indies, and a Portuguese Jesuit settled in 1605, baptizing several political leaders. By 1628 there was an English trading post, and in 1663 the Royal Adventurers of England Trading into Africa built forts. Trade increased during the subsequent years, and in the 1780s Freetown was established as a settlement for freed slaves from the West Indies, Nova Scotia, and Britain. Contact increased as the British gradually formed the area into a protectorate and colony, until it finally became part of the British Empire, with full-scale participation in the religious, educational, and economic life of those times. Details of contact for each of the sample communities will be provided in the sample descriptions, to which we now turn.

Mayola

The primary sample is the relatively traditional village of Mayola, located in central Sierra Leone. It is twenty miles from the nearest vehicular road, although four-wheel drive vehicles can travel the path to it if the ferries are operating, and then only in the dry season. When fieldwork was conducted in Mayola, access was by foot only, materials and equipment being carried in by porter. The population was approximately 500 persons, although the exact figure could not be obtained because of some uncertainty about who belonged in Mayola, and who in the many nearby villages.

Like all of these upland villages, the life of the village centered around the rice farms, on which ground-nuts and cassava were also grown. Each day, families would travel the short distance, by well-marked bush paths, to the farming plots asigned by custom to their use. Most families also kept a few goats and chickens, although their eating was not regular, but reserved for special (perhaps twice weekly) meals; eggs, however, were eaten regularly with the evening meal. Bananas and limes were available, but appeared not to be cultivated. Palm wine, briefly fermented from the sap of the oil-palm trees, formed a valued beverage. Many of the men began the day with a good quaff, although its greatest consumption was in the early evening. In summary, the village of Mayola was ordinary and representative in all respects of the majority of villages in Temne country; its selection was based upon an introduction to the headman by a mining company employee who had been born in the area.

With respect to acculturation, all community indices suggest a very low degree of contact. For example, only Temne was spoken, all houses were of the traditional characteristic form, there was no wage employment, nor western school, and the only trade was with other Temne people in the larger provincial centers. Indeed the presence of a white man was clearly unusual in the area, as evidenced by numerous (mainly humourous and enjoyable) personal encouters which served to indicate this minimal degree of contact.

A sample of one hundred persons (stratifed by age and sex) was drawn from a rough census (by households) conducted in the first few days; the intention was to obtain ninety interviews from this sample. This objective was reached, with only four refusals, in nine weeks spent in the village. Interviews, conducted with the assistance of Brima Sebana Kabia (a member of the chiefly family of the Marampa chiefdom), took from two to almost four hours each. Breaks were taken whenever interest or attention waned and interviews were resumed when the participant indicated a wish to proceed.

All interviews were in Temṇe and took place in a single "test center" located in a house rented for the purpose. Conditions of lighting and heating were natural; that is, testing took place beside an open southern-facing window. Not all participants completed all portions of the schedule, and no attempt was made to force those who were reluctant; thus analyses to be reported are made with techniques adapted for missing data.

In summary, it is considered that Mayola is a typical community, drawn from a large number of other fairly traditional upland rice villages, in central Sierra Leone. It is also considered that the sample drawn is representative of the village population, despite the lack of an accurate census. Thus, this sample will be used in our analyses to represent a relatively traditional, sedentary, high food accumulating stratified position on our two dimensions of acculturation and ecocultural adaptation.

Port Loko

The other Temne sample, representing a more acculturated community, was taken from the provincial market town and administrative center of Port Loko. Population was around 20,000, some having been born there, and some having migrated from the surrounding villages. In this part of Temne country (southern) there were no other communities serving these more western functions, and so Port Loko was selected as being representative of a higher degree of contact.

In addition to Temne, Krio (an African language largely derived from English) is widely spoken. Most houses in Port Loko are of a western form, many of the inhabitants are on wage employment, and British mission schools have existed for almost a century. Europeans are frequently seen, mainly in governmental, medical, or educational positions, and many European cultural elements (such as the cinema, newspapers, magazines, and bars) are apparent.

The sample and "test center" were organized with the assistance of Tejan Kamara who was a well-liked and widely known bar owner in central Port Loko. A room to one side of his bar was rented for interviewing, and a sample of forty persons was drawn from the membership list of the *compin* which regularly met there. A "compin" (from "company") is a semi-traditional social and dancing society which cuts across status and clan lines and forms the basis for informal social interaction in many transitional communities in Sierra Leone. It was intended to interview thirty participants from this society; thirty-two were in fact interviewed, with three refusals. Interviews were conducted mainly in Temne, but Krio was used where the participant desired it; once again the work was carried out with the assistance of Kabia.

In summary, it is considered that the town of Port Loko is indicative of the higher contact life emerging in Sierra Leone, although being one of a kind, it represents only itself. The difficulties of drawing a sample in such a setting are obvious, but the use of the "compin" membership is considered to be a useful device for gaining a fairly diverse, if not a representative, sample from the town. Thus this sample will be used to represent a relatively acculturated, sedentary, high food accumulating, stratified position on our two dimensions.

ESKIMO OF BAFFIN ISLAND

The Eskimo (Inuit) people occupy a territory from Alaska in the west to Greenland in the East. Their northern limit is the northernmost limit of land, and their southern limit (with only a few exceptions) is the tree line. In population they total over 100,000 persons of whom about 15,000 are in the Canadian Arctic. Although it is claimed that the Eskimo language can be mutually understood throughout this vast range, there are fairly clear dialectical variations, and fairly clear clusters of people who view themselves as distinct from their neighbours.

One of these cluster is the Eastern Canadian Arctic Eskimo, living on Baffin Island (Driver, 1961; these people (about 2,500 in total) are further fragmented into about half a dozen self-aware groups. Two of these, the *Aggomiut* (from camps near Pond Inlet) and the *Nugumiut* (settled into Frobisher Bay) constitute the population of Eskimo from which this study samples.

The basic exploitive pattern of all Baffin Island Eskimo is hunting and fishing (Driver and Massey, 1957: 177). Hunting is largely for sea mammals (seal, walrus, white whale) and in some areas for land mammals (caribou) and rodents. Fishing is for char (Arctic salmon-trout) and is carried out in estuaries, mainly by spearing. The basic craft for sea hunting is the kayak, in which an individual hunter could travel large distances relatively quickly. In winter, seal hunting takes place from and through the sea ice, and the dogsled is the basic mode of transport. Given the extremely low temperatures and rainfall, cultivation of any kind is not possible, although wild berries (juniper) are occasionally eaten as one of the few non-animal foods. The degree of food accumulation is low, even though freezing for storage is possible for six or seven months of the year; the reason is that the times of plenty are in the warmer months when freeze-storage is not possible, while the times of scarcity occur in the winter.

The Eskimo live in hunting camps, spread around the coast of Baffin Island and each camp is usually composed of relatives. These units rarely exceed twenty-five or thirty persons, since more than this would exhaust the animal resources in their area. Given the extremely low population density implied in the data presented earlier, it is not surprising to discover such a low concentration of population in any one camp. To adequately support even this low population, regular movement of the camps is necessary, both seasonally to exploit different food resources, and every few years to draw from fresh grounds. In addition, of course, hunters travel widely over the territory currently in use. Thus, these people may be classified as migratory (Driver and Massey, 1957: 184).

The Eskimo are perhaps the least stratified of all the world's peoples. Leadership is minimal and depends upon personal qualities such as hunting skill or the ability to deal effectively with social relationships. No permanent chiefs exist, nor is there religious authority. Camp leaders ("camp bosses") possess little authority, and those members of the camp who disagree with it may and frequently do leave with their immediate family and set up camp elsewhere along the shore. Slaves are unknown, as are formal wars involving authority and organization.

Families are independent nuclear (Driver and Massey, 1957: 402) and minimally extended (Murdock, 1967). Polygamy, although permitted, is rare, and could take the form of polyandry as well as polygyny. The role of women is that of a partner in the exploitive activity necessary for the survival of the independent family unit (Giffen, 1930), and they are generally treated with respect; indeed a common saying is that "a man is only as good a hunter as his wife is a seamstress!" Children, too, are respected and are provided with warm and permissive socialization. These practices are well documented, both by Hrdlicka (1941) who notes that "there is but little punishment of the childrem among the Eskimo," and by Butt (1950):

> Children are treated lovingly and every care and consideration is lavished on them. . . . Children are scarcely every subjected to blows or even scolding and cross words, and they do practically as they wish, even to the extent of ordering about their parents and getting their own way in everything.

It is apparent, then, that extreme permissiveness and freedom characterize socialization in Eskimo life. Supporting this view is the rating of Barry, Child, and Bacon (1959) of a Greenland Eskimo sample near the extreme end of the "pressure toward assertion" scale.

First contact with Europeans occurred in the late 1500s with the arrival of Martin Frobisher and John Davis. A long period of exploration, whaling, and trading followed, during which there were no permanent shore bases established, and contact with people was therefore short and spaced, although the traded materials filtered through Eskimo society. Late in the nineteenth century, police, missionaries, and educators established land bases, but it was not really until the 1930s and 1940s that Euro-Canadians made their presence a relatively permanent one. Thus contact has been of long duration, but until recently it has been relatively weak. Details of the contact history of each of the samples will be provided in the sample descriptions which follow.

Pond Inlet Camps

The basic sample of Eskimo participants was drawn from the camps which are spread around the coast of north Baffin Island, near the settlement of Pond Inlet (see Figure 5.2). These people (the Aggomiut) numbered about 300 persons in 1965 and occupied a territory of about 40,000 square miles, yielding an extremely low density (less than one person per hundred square miles). Access to the area at the time of the fieldwork was by single-engine plane, usually chartered by the Department of Northern Affairs (Federal Government of Canada); access to the camps was by dogsled.

The Pond Inlet area was selected because the author's brother was the northern service officer in the area. However camp life in the area was typical of most other eastern Eskimo camps. This life entails the hunting of sea mammals by the men and the preparation of these by the women, who largely remain in camp. Men may be away for long periods (up to a month) on the sea ice, and occasionally for equally long periods inland in search of caribou. However most trips are much shorter, involving only a few days' absence. The women also supervise the children in the camp, but minimal control is exercises. After the age of ten, boys frequently accompany fathers on the hunt, and girls help their mothers in the maintenance of the camp.

With respect to acculturation, contact of the area with non-Eskimos has been minimal. Although traders, policemen, and missionaries had been in the area for over half a century, settlement by others has been very recent. Only in the early 1960s was a school established, and only just prior to that did the federal government establish its presence. Very few persons can speak English, and very few are on wage employment; the balance are unilingual Eskimo speakers largely oriented toward a hunting life. In the camp, houses are sometimes of Eskimo design and materials (snow in winter, sods or skins in summer) and sometimes of introduced materials (packing crate wood or plywood sheets). In the settlement of Pond Inlet itself, however, all houses are of Euro-Canadian design and materials.

A sample of one hundred persons (stratified by age and sex) was drawn from the census list available in the local government office; the intention was to obtain ninety participants from this sample. This objective was reached, with only a single refusal, in seven weeks spent in the area. Interviews were conducted with the assistance of Danielie and Muktah, both bilingual residents of Pond Inlet. All interviews were in Eskimo, and breaks were taken as required by the participant. The location of testing varied: In Pond Inlet itself, a western-style room with heating and lighting was available; in the various camps, testing was carried out in iglus (with natural lighting and temperature) and in a variety of shacks lent for the purpose (again with natural lighting and temperature).

In summary, it is considered that the camps around Pond Inlet are fairly typical of the relatively traditional Eskimo camps in the Eastern Canadian Arctic, and that the sample drawn is representative of the population of these camps. Thus, this sample may be employed in our analyses to represent a relatively traditional, migratory, low food accumulating, low stratification position on our two dimensions of acculturation and ecocultural adaptation.

Frobisher Bay

The other Eskimo sample, representing a more acculturated community, was drawn from the only town of any size in the Eastern Arctic, Frobisher Bay. At the time of the fieldwork, the population was around 1,000 Eskimos and 700 Euro-Canadians (mainly government and military employees). Most of the Eskimos had been born elsewhere and had migrated to the area from hunting camps throughout southern Baffin Island beginning in the 1940s, when a military base was established there. Governmental administrative and military activity increased steadily to the point where a large number of Euro-Canadian (and some U.S. military) personnel dominated the central portion of the town. Schools, hospitals, cinemas, and bars have all been established, and contact, especially for the current generation, has been high (Honigmann and Honigmann, 1965).

The sample was drawn from the subcommunity of Apex Hill, which was located about two miles from the center of Frobisher Bay. The other possible subcommunity (Ikaluit) was avoided because most of its residents were fairly recent arrivals from the camps, while many of those in Apex Hill were pretty well settled into town life, lived in Euro-Canadian houses, and were on wage employment. The test center was established at the Rehabilitation Centre, an institution which provided Eskimos returning from southern hospitalization with new skills if they were unable to remain "on the land." All participants were from the Apex Hill community, and a stratified random sample of forty was drawn from the village list; thirty-four were approached in order to attain the final sample of thirty-one. Interviews were carried out largely in Eskimo, but occasionally in English where this seemed to be natural for the partici-pant. Interview assistance was provided by Bill Allen who was a Western Arctic Eskimo, previously employed as a radio announcer.

In summary, since the town of Frobisher Bay is the only acculturated community in the Eastern Artic, it represents the only possible community from which a sample could be drawn. Whether or not it is representative of future communities in transition, it is not possible to estimate. However we may take it to be the relatively acculturated example of a people who were previously migratory, low food accumulating, and minimally stratified.

Intermediate between those two extreme ecocultural settings (Temne and

Eskimo), two other culture areas were sampled in the first study: Aborigines of Australia and Indigenes of Papua-New Guinea. Unfortunately, these populations have tended to enter into acculturation in an "all or none" fashion. Thus, it is not possible to find relatively traditional and relatively acculturated communities of the same cultural group. This necessitated the sampling of four culturally unrelated communities, two in Australia and two in Papua-New Guinea, such that one in each country was relatively traditional and one was relatively acculturated. In order to keep clear the descriptions and arguments which follow, it is essential to grasp the point. Thus, among these four communities, the traditional migratory hunting and gathering sample is taken from Central Australia (Arunta) while the traditional sedentary, agricultural (and hunting) sample is taken from central New Guinea (Telefomin); however the reverse is true of the other two communities, where the acculturated sample of fishing (with agriculture) people is taken from coastal Papua (Hanuabada) and the acculturated sample of gathering people is taken from the coast of northeastern Australia.

ABORIGINES OF AUSTRALIA

The Aboriginal peoples of Australia are among the most-studied of present-day traditional peoples. As with the Temne and the Eskimo, the Aborigines appear to have migrated to their present locations and to have been settled in these for many centuries (Berndt and Berndt, 1964: ch. 1). Their dispersal across the land is associated with a good deal of physical and cultural heterogeneity. Whether this is due to differing populations arriving at different parts of the country, or due to cultural and physical adaptation to their setting (or indeed to both) is open to dispute. However there are clear lines of division (linguistic, sociocultural, and somatic) which render these people quite diverse.

At the time of first European contact, their total population was around 300,000, and these were divided into about 500 tribal units. Greatest concentrations were on the coast (where water and food were more readily available) and densities were least in the semi-arid interior (Berndt and Berndt, 1964: 26); an estimated population of 18,000 for the 250,000 square miles of the Great Victoria and Western Deserts yields an extremely low density (.00128 persons per square mile). Present population estimates are around 100,000 persons, made up of about 40,000 "full-blood" and 60,000 "part-Aborigines." This population is now increasing, although those who are considered "full-blood" may only be holding their level (Berndt and Berndt, 1964: 27-28).

Their basic economic activity was hunting and gathering, with the addition of fishing among coastal peoples. However there were wide variations within this economic category, with groups in the interior (dry) areas clearly migratory in settlement pattern, while coastal groups were often semi-sedentary, exploiting "natural gardens" and the abundant marine life (Berndt and Berndt, 1964: ch.4). Clearly, population density differences are related to these economic variations within the hunting and gathering category. It is also clear that in these coastal Aborigines we have an exception to the worldwide trend, noted in Chapter 4 (Table 4.3), for deliberate cultivation to appear where the physical environment (in terms of temperature and rainfall) permits it.

Culturally, especially in their ritual life and social organization, the various Aboriginal peoples are very complex (Berndt and Berndt, 1964: 47). In particular, attention to kinship and sections of a tribe appear to be a basic feature of aboriginal life. Although attempts have been made to rate the various tribes on a "simplex-complex" dimension and to relate this to ecological zones, Berndt and Berndt (1964: 59-60) consider that no general relationship can be found. Perhaps this is due to the limited range of exploitive patterns (hunting and gathering) found among these people, or it may be due to other factors.

Despite this generally complex social life, political life was "largely informal and loosely organized" (Berndt and Berndt, 1964: 279). This appears to be consistent with their exploitive pattern and their generally low population density and concentration. The use of authority, too, was limited, with kinship obligations often providing the only basis for responding to the orders of others (Berndt and Berndt, 1964: 302-303). This generally low level of stratification is also consistent with these economic and demographic variables.

The socialization of children tends to be permissive and supportive, with a decided emphasis on informality (Berndt and Berndt, 1964: 127-132). Assertion is also emphasized in many groups; indeed for one (the Arunta) rating on the comliance-assertion dimension (Barry, Child, and Bacon, 1959: Table 2) is fourth from the assertion end, out of forty-six societies they rated.

European contact has generally been more intensive on the coast (especially in the temperate areas where major recent settlement has occurred) than in the desert or tropical areas. The first settlement (in New South Wales) was in 1788, and contact was pushed further and further into the interior as decades went on. Penetrations of the desert and tropical areas were more recent and more sporadic; only Alice Springs and Darwin exist as largely Euro-Australian settlements in these areas. Explorers, missionaries, and traders, however, initiated and maintained contact in the more remote portions of the country, so that today virtually all Aborigines are in Euro-Australian-oriented settlements or towns.

Arunta (Santa Teresa)

In the center of Australia, about sixty miles toward the Simpson Desert, Southeast from Alice Springs, there is a settlement of Arunta people gathered at the Roman Catholic mission station of Santa Teresa. These people were, until recently, desert nomads who gathered and hunted in the southern portion of the Northern Territory. The forefathers of these people had been thoroughly studied by Spencer and Gillen, both in relation to other Central Australian peoples (1899) and in a detailed two-volume study (1927) of the Arunta themselves.

The Arunta is "purely nomadic . . . living entirely on vegetable food and animals that he finds in the bush" (Spencer and Gillen, 1927: 14). Their economic routine consists of "wandering in small parties consisting of one or two families . . . camping at favourite spots, where the presence of water holes, with their accompaniment of vegetable and animal food enables them to supply their wants" (Spencer and Gillen, 1927: 15). In terms of exploitive pattern, it may be argued that these people are somewhat less dependent upon the chance appearance of food than are pure hunters such as the Eskimo; this point has been emphasized by Lee (1968: 40) with respect to the Bushmen. In a sense, food is accumulated naturally in areas which retain water, and to which a nomadic family could return at spaced intervals. Nevertheless, as hunters and gatherers, they may be considered to be lower in the degree of food accumulation than people who cultivate, keep animals, or live in areas of abundant and stable fish resources. Thus the Arunta may be classed as a society between the two extremes already discussed (the Temne and the Eskimo), but at a moderately low food accumulating position.

Given this economic base, it is clear that high concentrations of population could not be maintained. At their height, the Arunta population was estimated to have been around 2,000 persons (in the 1890s), but this had declined to around 400 in the 1920s; these people exploited a territory of about 50,000 square miles. Dispersal across this territory was maintained by convention: "The Arunta tribe is divided into a large number of small local groups, each of which occupies, and is supposed to possess, a given area of country, the boundaries of which are well-known to the natives" (Spencer and Gillen, 1927: 8). Once again, we find that low population density and concentration are associated with a nomadic settlement pattern.

Although sharing in the social and ritual complexity of all Australian Aboriginal peoples, the Arunta possess little social or political stratification. Leadership is exercised by a family head man (*Inkata*) within each nomadic unit, but this minimal authority does not carry over to social encounters with persons outside this small group (Spencer and Gillen, 1927: 9). Indeed, within his group, authority carries little power: "The authority which is wielded by an Inkata is of a somewhat vague nature. He has no definite power over the person of the individuals who are the members of his group" (Spencer and Gillen, 1927: 9). Stratification thus appears to be minimal among the Arunta, and again this is in keeping with the economic and demographic variables already discussed.

Finally, socialization emphasis, as we have already noted, lies strongly toward the "assertion" pole of the compliance-assertion dimension of Barry, Child, and Bacon (1959). In addition, children are nurtured with warmth and permissiveness: "To the children they are, we may say uniformly with very rare exceptions, kind and considerate, carrying them, the men as well as women taking part in this, when they get tired on the march, and always seeing that they get a good share of any food" (Spencer and Gillen, 1927: 38). Similarly, interpersonal relations are marked by minimal toughness: "With regard to their treatment of one another, it may be said that this is marked on the whole by considerable kindness . . . the women are certainly not treated usually with anything which could be called excessive harshness" (Spencer and Gillen, 1927: 38). We find, then, that socialization (indeed all interpersonal relations) is characterized by kindness and the avoidance of harshness (cf. Meggit, 1962: 116, 124).

The sample of Arunta people was drawn from those who had been settled on the Santa Teresa mission station, mostly during the previous decade. This settlement is operated as a mission and incorporates a primary school, a nursing station, and some economic activity in the form of stock-keeping (beef cattle) and small gardens. The population is a shifting one, consisting of about 400 Aborigines and 16 Euro-Australians at the time of the fieldwork (1967). Other Arunta settlements exist, but they are under government control and research permission could not be obtained; representativeness may thus be a problem. In defense, however, there does not appear to have been any special reason for these people to have come to Santa Teresa rather than to a governmental mission, nor are there special features (other than the presence of religious rather than lay personnel) to this settlement which readily distinguish it from a government settlement. We may take this community, then, as being fairly typical of the present-day Arunta, who have only recently settled into a welfare-based community life; in the absence of continuing nomadic bands, these are the most traditional Arunta which are available for study.

The sample was drawn from a community list, but some difficulty was experienced in gaining the cooperation of the persons selected. Older people, especially among the women, were very reluctant to participate in the study, and in the end, younger persons were drawn to supplement the original sample.

Interviewing and testing was carried out with the assistance of Stanislaus

Palmer, a young secondary school graduate from the community. In addition, an elder of the people (George Gorey) was employed to help motivate individuals drawn in the sample to participate. Part of the data was collected by John Dawson, since this particular field trip was a joint research visit. Testing was carried out in a room in the nursing station building, where electrical light was available when natural lighting became limited.

Koonganji (Yarrabah)

As a contrast to the Arunta, within the range of Aboriginal cultures, a society was chosen which inhabited a lush, coastal area of Australia. These people are the Koonganji of Northern Queensland, living in the community of Yarrabah (until recently a mission station operated by the Church of England) about twelve miles from the city of Cairns. The peninsula of Cape Grafton is set aside as an aboriginal reserve, but the proximity of Cairns provides for a relatively high degree of contact.

Little information is available for these people specifically except that which was recorded by early missionaries; however for the North Queensland Cape York Peninsula culture area generally there is enough ethnographic material to draw some broad outlines. The area on the eastern coast is a very wet rain forest (40 to 60 inches of rain per year) and is thus in sharp contrast to the arid central portions of the country (Abbie, 1969: ch. 3).

In such a lush area, vegetable food was abundant, although deliberate cultivation apparently was not carried out. Gathering was the most dominant exploitive pattern, with inshore fishing providing supplementary food resources. Even more than in the case of the Arunta, routine visits to known sources of vegetable foods provided a relatively stable source of sustenance, approaching the moderately high level of food accumulation attained in societies which engage in deliberate cultivation. When stable inshore sources of fish were added to the potential supply, we may judge the society to be in a situation of moderate food accumulation.

No data are available on the traditional levels of population in North Queensland; however one judgement (Abbie, 1969: 62) is that population concentrations were certainly higher on the coast than in the interior. More specifically, Meggit (1962) has estimated coastal population densities to be seven times that of interior tribes; in his view at least thirty-five square miles per person was required in the interior, while five square miles per person would suffice for a coastal gathering economy. Thus while still adhering to the countrywide hunting and gathering exploitive pattern, densities may be considered to be much higher in these coastal areas. In keeping with these estimates, family units while moving regularly within their territory tended to be less widely dispersed and may be judged to be semi-sedentary, in Murdock's (1967) classification.

In summary, the Koonganji people share many of the features of Aboriginal culture, but differ mainly in their degree of food accumulation, their density of population, and in their restricted pattern of migratory behaviour. Within a single racial and sociocultural unit, then, we can contrast these people with the lower food accumulating, lower population density, and more migratory Arunta people.

The sample of Koonganji people was drawn from the settlement of Yarrabah. This community was organized in the 1890s by the Church Missionary Society, under the leadeship of the Reverend J. B. Gribble. The original area was over 50,000 acres (Gribble, 1920), but this has diminished over the years to about 40,000 acres (Long, 1970: 128). During the first few years, only about one hundred persons were induced to settle (Gribble, 1920: 69); however the present population is about 800 persons, having reached this number gradually during the intervening decades (Long, 1970: 130). In 1960, the government obtained control of the community from the Church Missionary Society.

Although only twelve miles from the city of Cairns, a visit may only be made by boat, there being no easy land route over the mountains on the west side of the Grafton Peninsula. However there is a regular movement of people back and forth for shopping, entertainment, work, and secondary school. At the time of the field work there was a primary school in the community (with almost 300 pupils), a community store, and some service jobs available.

A sample of forty was drawn from lists supplied by the community council. With the support of this council, only thirty-two had to be invited to obtain the final sample of thirty. All interviews were conducted in English, the traditional language having been lost by all except the elderly. A room in the school was made available as a test center, and this was provided with electrical light.

INDIGENES OF NEW GUINEA

Even more than in the case of Australia, the people of New Guinea are extremely heterogeneous, both from the point of view of traditional cultures and in the degree of European contact. Thus, the two samples drawn from this setting differ, as we have already noted, on both the traditional and acculturational dimensions. Given these wide variations, it would be impossible to attempt a general cultural characterization which was barely possible in the case of the Aborigines. As a result, specific cultural description will be made at the time of the two sample descriptions and only broad geographical and historical material will be presented at this point.

The island of New Guinea is divided into three areas of political importance: the Western portion (West Irian) is part of the Republic of Indonesia, while at the time of the fieldwork the eastern portion was administered by

Australia. This latter portion is divided into two smaller sections: Papua (the southern part) was historically under British influence, while New Guinea (the northern part) was part of the German Empire. Islands off the north-eastern coast (Manus, New Britain) form a further area, and these too were under German influence.

The people are of Melanesian stock and live in geographical settings which range all the way from coral islands to vast marshes, swamps, and rain forests, and to mile-high mountain valleys. The two settings which are sampled in this study are a set of hamlets in a remote mountain valley (Telefomin) which has had very little contact, and a high-contact coastal community (Hanuabada) which is adjacent to the capital city of Port Moresby. In general, coastal contact has been high, while inland contact has been very low; indeed some areas of the highlands have been visited by outsiders only in the last genera-tion. Although activity during World War II made a concentrated impact on some of the remote groups, most were left with only one or two outsiders in any regular contact with them.

Telefomin

Just to the east of the point where the Indonesian-Australian and Papua-New Guinea borders meet, there is a set of five hamlets in the Telefomin valley (altitude 4,995 feet). The Telefomin people who live here number fewer than 900 and are the only speakers of their language, Telefol. Their territory measures approximately twelve miles wide and fifteen miles long, straddling the headwaters of the Sepik River. The largest hamlet, Kialikmin, has about 350 residents, while the other four range from 65 to 117 persons; all are fairly permanent sites. In terms of overall population, they are not numerous, but in terms of their small territory, their density is fairly high, approximately 6 persons per square mile, which is well above those for the Arunta and Eskimo, but well below that for the Temne (Craig, 1967; Kooijman, 1962).

The people of Telefomin have an extremely varied exploitive pattern: They cultivate gardens for taro and kasava, raise a few pigs, gather on the mountains, and hunt and trap for small animals and birds. Perhaps fifty percent of this economic activity is devoted to the maintenance of the gardens, while the pig-caring, gathering, and hunting share the rest of time. Gardens are rotated, with an average of four being planted each year; there is thus a relatively high degree of food accumulation, three-quarters of it being in the ground (growing stage) at any one time. This judgement is enhanced by their pig-keeping, but detracted from by their hunting activity; on balance they may be judged to be somewhat less food accumulating than the Temne who do not hunt, and who have only a single crop each year which must be stored for ten to eleven months. This evidence of exploitive pattern and food accumulation is consistent with evidence on settlement pattern and population density: Moderately high food accumulation is associated with permanent hamlets (sedentary population) and an intermediate population density and concentration.

Sociocultural stratification in the Highlands area generally is not high; however an organization which coordinated the hamlets in the valley did have some authority over each local group.

With respect to socialization emphasis, there is some noticeable pressure toward compliance, and a moderate level of physical punishment. This generally intermediate placement coincides with the placement of the bulk of societies from New Guinea by Barry et al. (1959).

Contact with the outside world was initiated by a German expedition under the direction of Thurnwald in 1914, and continued by an Australian explorer (Champion) who crossed the island in the 1930s, ascending the Fly River from the south, and descending the Sepik River to the north. Shortly afterward, a small airstrip was made in the Telefomin Valley, and in 1944 gliders were sent in with men and equipment to improve the strip for military purposes. In the postwar period an administrator ((patrol officer), a nursing station (run by the Baptist Mission), and a primary school have all been introduced to the valley. However all these are in a single location (near the airstrip) and the hamlets remain physically uninfluenced by their presence. And culturally the people appear to be relatively uninfluenced as well: Few speak English or pidgin (neo-Melanesian), few over the age of ten or twelve have been to school, and only a few have left the traditional economic pursuits for wage employment.

The sample was drawn randomly from individuals moving back and forth between hamlets and their gardens. The test center (in the hamlet of Angkevip) was central to all the hamlets, and there was a steady movement of individuals and families along the path by the house; when one participant had completed the test battery and interview, the research assistant merely invited the next traveller in to participate; forty-six persons were selected in this way, of which forty agreed to come in.

Prior to the fieldwork, anthropologists (Ruth and Barry Craig of the University of Sydney) had lived in the hamlet for over two years; their house served as a test center, and their earlier informants provided an introduction to the people of the valley. The research assistant (Kamipsep) was twenty years old, had completed primary school, and had worked in the city of Rabaul (New Britain) for a year.

Hanuabada (Motu)

On the south coast of the island, in the Papuan portion of New Guinea, there are a number of villages containing a mixture of Moto- and Koita-speaking peoples. Except for retained linguistic differences, there are no

apparent cultural features which may now be taken to distinguish one group from the other. In addition to this cultural merging, the proximity of the village to the capital of Port Moresby has led to a major level of contact with European and Euro-Australian life.

The meaning of Hanuabada in Motu is "the great village" (Belshaw, 1957); it was a heavily populated settlement even prior to contact, and of course has become even more so now that it is a part of the capital area. The general name Hanuabada is used to refer to five smaller villages which have now all grown together; three of these are Motu and two are Koita (Seligmann, 1910; Belshaw, 1957), At the time of Belshaw's comprehensive study (1950-1951) the population was around 2,500, and by 1968 when the present fieldwork was carried out, these people had increased to about 4,000; in addition there were numerous migrants to this portion of the capital area, but which were not included in the study.

Reports by both Seligmann (1910) and Belshaw (1957: 12, 64) indicate that the Motu were traditionally more oriented toward the land (gardeners with some hunting). Both peoples now engage in land and sea economic activity, as well as in the urban workforce. However, because the rainfall in the area is low, these "gardens are miserable" (Belshaw, 1957: 1), and their primary culture "is largely maritime, bound up with fishing and large-scale trading expeditions" (Belshaw, 1957: 1).

We may judge their exploitive pattern to be basically fishing and secondarily agricultural with some hunting yielding a moderately low degree of food accumulation. Population concentration, even traditionally was relatively high, and settlement pattern was clearly sedentary.

Sociocultural differentiation and stratification is moderately complex (Belshaw, 1957: 12-23, 15). Residence patterns, based upon kinship, are important elements of their social structure; many kin distinctions are made (1957: 18) and these interact with age and sex distinctions to produce a characteristic pattern of social relations. Status (p. 20) is assigned by age within each lineage, and major leaders are selected from primary lineages. Status and authority may also derive from special ability or wealth, and these leaders (such as those of a "canoe crew" or "garden gang") "exercise unquestioned authority, in a quiet democratic manner" (p. 23).

Children seem to be "regarded as a nuisance in early years" but this perceived trouble is "more than counterbalanced by love" (p. 162). Responsibility training is inculcated fairly early:

> Training in correct social behaviour begins when the child is very young, so that the difficult period is cut to the minimum; by the time the child is six or seven, it carries out responsible household duties, knows its rights and obligations, and that it should pay respect to its elders [Belshaw, 1957: 162].

Discipline is largely handled by the father (with the use of spanking or shouting), but both parents surround the child with continual verbal pressure to obey rules (p. 167).

As we have already indicated, the people of Hanubada have had a long and persistent contact with European society. The presence of traders and missionaries (with schools) began a century ago, and their influence has been such that most residents of the village have been to school and speak English well; many live on wage employment and generally exhibit a westernized urban life style. Indeed, "it provides an example of culture change to an extreme degree, for Melanesia. It is the only example we have in this area of a truly urban native community" (Belshaw, 1957: 1-2). Thus the community is one of a kind, and although it cannot represent anything but itself, it is a highly acculturated community of a society that was traditionally sedentary but moderately low food accumulating.

The sample was drawn from two schools (Hagana Primary and Badihagwa Secondary) and from the staff employed by the public service, along with their wives. Apart from the school populations (where numbers and names were known precisely) it was not possible to draw a random sample from such a large and acculturated village. However, in the schools, a random procedure was employed, and for most of the adult males, a random selection was made from employee lists. The balance of the adults (primarily the female sample) was contacted through the male participants. In all, thirty-two persons were invited to participate and thirty agreed; ten of these were pupils released from classes for the purpose. Testing took place in a school office (for the pupils) or an office supplied by the public service (for the older participants).

SCOTLAND

Although they are not considered to be samples directly related to the model (because they are not at the subsistence level), it is important to have Western European peoples included in the study to anchor the other data to the extant psychological literature. Since these people are generally well known, only some broad descriptive characteristics will be provided concentrating on those aspects which differentiate these comparison samples from the ones already described. In keeping with the two samples approach, in Scotland one rural and one urban sample provided the data for the first study.

Inverkeilor

On the northeast coast of Scotland there are numerous villages and towns engaged in farming and fishing economies. Those right on the coast, and with good harbours, have a stronger emphasis on North Sea maritime activity, while those a little inland have a stronger emphasis on farming (mainly potatoes and vegetables). These people are in the mainstream of British culture (unlike some Gaelic-speaking peoples in the West) but are strongly and self-consciously Scottish when dealing with outsiders.

A village, whose resident nurse and headmaster agreed to sponsor the study, was located entirely at random (from the back of a motorscooter). This village, Inverkeilor, is located midway between the two towns of Arbroath and Montrose and has a population of about 1,200 persons mostly farmers and tradesmen. The younger participants were drawn randomly from the school, while the older ones were selected by block sample from a map of the village. A sample of sixty-five was drawn to achieve a total of sixty participants; sixty-two were eventually included. Testing and interviewing took place in the school (for the pupils) and in the Men's Club Hall (for the older participants).

Edinburgh

The urban sample was drawn from the city of Edinburgh, which because of its size posed a serious sampling problem. A procedure similar to that adopted in Port Loko was eventually employed: A clan association (McKenzie), after a year of social contacts, agreed to allow a sample to be drawn from their membership. These associations perform similar cultural and social functions in Scottish (and overseas) cities to those of the West African compins. Like them, their membership cuts across socioeconomic groupings and may be argued to be a reasonably typical cross-section of urban Scottish society. All of the adult participants were drawn from this group, and were tested in the Psychology Department at the University of Edinburgh. Younger participants were from Hunter's Tryst Primary and Firrhill Secondary Schools and were tested in offices in their respective schools. Sixty participants were included in this sample, and there were no refusals.

These ten samples, in four ecocultural settings (plus a Western comparison group) constitute the data source for the first study to be reported. A second and third study are based upon nine samples, drawn from four ecocultural settings within a single (mid-northern Amerindian) culture area, and two comparison villages of non-native Euro-Canadian people in Ontario (one southern and one northern). Two major shifts in sampling strategy characterize the second study: first, by sampling within a single culture area, variation in culture and behaviour due to extraneous (genetic and broad cultural) variables might be minimized; and second, by sampling within a single culture area where all the samples traditionally subsisted on hunting or fishing, but which varied widely on the other ecological and cultural variables, a test case for the relative contributions of special experience (the "other determinants" referred to in Chapter 3) and the modeled cultural variables (differentiation, stratification, and socialization) could be examined. These Amerindian samples are now described.

CREE OF JAMES BAY

Among the Amerindian people of Canada, the Cree are by far the most numerous; in 1969 they numbered over 70,000 persons. However, they are spread from the northern coast of Quebec in the East to the foothills of the Rocky Mountains in' Alberta (a distance of over 2,000 miles) and from the shores of Hudson's Bay in the North to the border of the United States. Unified largely by language, they have adapted themselves to a variety of life styles ranging from northern hunters and fishers to free-moving prairie dwellers (Fisher, 1967). The group of Cree people in this study are those inhabiting the rocky eastern shore of James Bay in the Province of Quebec; these are known as Eastern Cree (Skinner, 1911).

Their language, Cree, is one of the Algonkian family, which includes Maritime (Micmac, Malecite), Ungava (Montagnais, Naskapi), and Northern Ontario (Ojibway, Saulteaux) Indian peoples. With these others included, the whole of the Algonkian family numbers over 150,000 persons or about sixty percent of all Amerindians in Canada.

These Eastern Cree are hunters and fishers, but they now include trapping for marketable furs in their exploitive pattern (Driver and Massey, 1957: 177). Some sea mammals and waterfowl are taken, but primarily moose and caribou are sought. Furs from the beaver, mink, and otter are valued for the cash which may be traded for manufactured goods. Their level of food accumulation is low, since they have no agriculture or domesticated animals to supplement their hunting activities; some meat drying (by smoking) is practiced but this appears to be minimal.

In terms of both daily and seasonal settlement patterns they are fairly migratory (Skinner, 1911; Driver and Massey, 1957: 184). There is a seasonal movement from the coast in the summer to inland camps in the winter and back again. This hunting-migratory pattern implies a low concentration and density of population and this is indeed the case (Driver and Massey, 1957: 186) for all Cree peoples. Eastern Cree specifically have a population of about 5,000 and they cover an area 400 miles north to south and 300 miles east to west, yielding a density of one person for every 24 square miles of exploited territory. The largest concentration is at Fort George where about 1,200 persons congregate, but this is largely due to acculturative factors. Among more traditional bands, populations rarely exceed 600 in a band's territory and perhaps no more than three or four families in a single location in the hunting camps.

In summary, then, we find the Eastern Cree people to have a hunting and fishing exploitive pattern, and an associated low level of food accumulation. Population densities and concentrations are also low, in keeping with their migratory settlement patterns.

Like the Eskimo to the north of them, the Eastern Cree society is remarkably undifferentiated and unstratified (Skinner, 1911). Leadership is in the hands of the older or more able individuals, but authority was minimally exercised (Honigmann, 1968), and individuals are not considered to be under the control of any other person (Hallowell, 1946). Families are independent nuclear (Driver and Massey, 1957: 402) with some influence toward being extended, stemming from other Algonkians to the northeast (Murdock, 1967).

Socialization emphases are toward assertion; the culturally similar Ojibway are rated eleventh from that pole out of forty-six societies (Barry et al., 1959). Field observations confirm such a rating for the Eastern Cree, children being encouraged from an early age to achieve independence. Physical punishment is rarely inflicted on children; indeed "infancy was characterized by strong emphases on indulgence of the child's wants, by manifestations of affection and admiration" (Preston, 1970).

Contact was initiated by the Hudson's Bay Company in 1668, although explorers had been in the area from time to time for almost a hundred years. Charles Fort was opened at what is now Ruperts House, and a few years later Moose Factory was established. Since that time contact has gradually increased, mainly through trade, but in the last hundred years through religious and educational activity as well. No serious accelerations occurred in this process, but at the present time a massive hydroelectric scheme is proceeding in this area.

Wemindji

The Old Factory band was centered about eighty miles south of their present village until 1961; at that time they moved to their present location for better water supply and easier access to the open waters of James Bay. As a result, although still a fairly traditional group of people, their settlement has the appearance of a neat, planned community. The population of the band is close to 600 and, like other Indian communities, is increasing rapidly (3.8% per year on the average).

Along with Eastmain, a band further to the south, Wemindji is the most traditionally oriented of the bands on the coast; it may be judged to be fairly typical and probably resembles the life found in other bands on the coast a generation ago. Only those under the age of thirty speak English or French in addition to Cree, and no one in the band was unable to speak Cree. Many families maintain hunting and trapping as elements in their lives; indeed a recent estimate suggests that as much as eighty percent of their food is still derived directly from the land (Superior Court of Quebec, 1973). A primary school was established at the new site in 1967, although a mission-run school was in operation for a generation at the earlier Old Factory site. Trading (with the Hudson's Bay Company primarly) has been a feature of life for at least two centuries, but a cooperative has recently been formed to provide the community with an alternative retail outlet. This same cooperative has recently organized and constructed a sawmill operation and has obtained a contract to supply the Government of Quebec with rough timber from the marginal tree line forests which fringe their coast.

Contact with the band was originally made in 1959 when the author was a merchant seaman on a biological research vessel operating in James Bay. In 1969, contact was reestablished and agreement reached with the band council to carry out pilot work in the area. Further field work in 1970 permitted the preparation of the interview schedule and tests, and actual data collection took place in 1971. Two persons from the band (Reg Mark and Margery Mark, brother and sister of the then chief) were trained at Queen's University to carry out the actual fieldwork. In the field at the same time was Bob Annis, who acted as a motivator, adviser, and coordinator for the two project assistants.

A sample was drawn from the band list, supplied by the band administrator; this sample was stratified by age and sex, and by three age groups (18 to 25, 26 to 40, and over 40). The intention was to achieve a total of sixty (10 participants in each of the six cells); a final total of sixty-one participated.

Fort George

To the north of Wemindji is Fort George, a regional administrative, educational and medical center. Recent moves by the Government of Quebec to make itself more visible have provided both a new hospital and administrative hierarchy in the two years prior to fieldwork. During 1972 and 1973 (after the study) major changes took place in connection with the hydroelectric project, so that the face of the community has now been changed considerably. Further to the north, another fairly acculturated community exists; Great Whale River, however, was not selected because it is an ethnically mixed (Eskimo and Cree) community which has been studied often for this unique feature. Fort George is fairly typical of an acculturated community in the sub-Arctic, although recent excessive development pressure has probably rendered it much less typical by the present time.

Some of the 1,200 inhabitants are on wage employment, and many (perhaps 60%) speak English or French in addition to Cree. Some younger people, recently returned from school in the South, claim not to speak Cree, but this is very doubtful. Most of the houses are relatively modern although a camp in town belonging to the somewhat more traditional peoples ("the Inlanders") gives the impression of a lesser degree of acculturation. A government primary and secondary school, a hospital, a nursing station, two churches, and an all-weather air strip all have contributed to a fairly high degree of contact. In addition, the usual Hudson's Bay Company store has traded for over two centuries, and there is now a good-sized hotel to accommodate visitors and itinerant government workers.

The sample was drawn as in Wemindji, the Marks again carrying out the interviewing and testing. A total of sixty persons participated although some difficulty was experienced in achieving that number. Reasons for this difficulty are many; the most obvious are that the Marks were nonresidents (belonging to the Wemindji band), and that the community being more acculturated (and fragmented) was less hospitable to an intrusive research effort.

In summary, these two Cree samples, one more traditional and one more acculturated, are taken to represent a low food accumulating, hunting, migratory people within the Amerindian culture area. An even more acculturated sample from the same group (Eastern Cree) was drawn from Moose Factory, but an incomplete sample (of thirty-seven persons) was all that could be drawn before the field personnel had to return to their classes.

TSIMSHIAN OF THE NORTHWEST COAST

Within the same culture area (Amerindian) and at the same exploitive pattern (fishing and hunting) as the Cree, there exists a unique set of peoples on the northwest coast of British Columbia who display very divergent demographic and sociocultural characteristics. These peoples are unique among native peoples in Canada in that they have developed fairly large sedentary villages and a complex stratified society while still engaged in essentially fishing and hunting economic pursuits. So unique is this pattern of cultural development that numerous classic and recent ethnographic studies have been devoted to them. The basic features of these cultures have been outlined by Drucker (1955), and their contemporary life has been examined by Hawthorn, Belshaw, and Jamieson (1960); for our purposes, these general accounts, among the wealth of available literature, will sufice.

The Tsimshian constitute a fair portion of these northwest coastal people; of the 45,000 Indians in British Columbia, the Tsimshian number over 8,000. They are divided into three geographically distinct groups, of approximately equal population: the Tsimshian proper (or coastal Tsimshian) number around 3,000; the more northerly Niska (on the Nass River) number around

2,500; and the more easterly Gitksan number over 2,500 persons.

As Drucker (1955: 1-6) points out, there very few cases of a nonagricultural, nonpastoral people achieving such cultural complexity. Rarely does a fishing and gathering economic base supply the continuity and stability of food supply upon which to create sedentary communities, with differentiation of roles and stratification of positions (both economic and political).

> That they were able to attain their high level of civilization is due largely to the amazing wealth of the natural resources of their area. From the sea and rivers, fish—five species of Pacific salmon, halibut, cod, herring, smelt and the famous olachen or "candlefish" (this last being so rich in oil that a dried one with a wick threaded through it burns like a candle), and other species too numerous to mention—could be taken in abundance. Some of these fish appeared only seasonally, but were easy to preserve. The sea also provided a tremendous quantity of edible mollusks; "when the tide goes out the table is set," as the saying goes. More spectacular was the marine game: hair seal, sea lion, sea otter, porpoise, and even whale. On shore, land game too abounded. Vegetable foods were less plentiful, although many species of wild berries were abundant in their season. In other words, the bounty of nature provided that which in most other parts of the world must supply for himself through agriculture and stock raising: a surplus of foodstuffs so great that even a dense population had an abundance of leisure to devote to the improvement and elaboration of its cultural heritage [Drucker, 1955: 2].

In summary we may judge their exploitive pattern to be a gathering and fishing (but primarily the latter) one. However, the usual tying (by definition) of food accumulation to exploitive pattern does not hold in this case; the stability and abundance of marine resources (often referred to colloquially as "marine agriculture") permitted a high degree of food accumulation, both in nature, and through their art of salmon preservation by smoking.

In this case, although based on an economy similar to that of the Cree, Eskimo, and Arunta, the northwest coast peoples are able to congregate in fairly large population centers, which are basically permanent. Thus in terms of *settlement pattern,* we find large sedentary villages maintained as a home base, but with fishing camps scattered, usually within a half-day's journey, along the shores of the numerous bays and fjords. Traditional population levels are difficult to ascertain; however Tsimshian villages probably averaged 200 to 300 persons congregated in a single place at a single time (Drucker, 1955: ch. 4). Although this number is not large in absolute terms, it is large when we consider that all these people were permanent residents of a single site, rather than dispersed in small family units over a large territory of exploitation. Thus, summarizing their demographic characteristics, we find the Tsimshian to be remarkably sedentary, with a relatively high degree of population concentration, for a society based upon fishing and gathering.

Sociocultural differentiation and stratification of the northwest coast peoples has been the subject of a great deal of ethnographic work (e.g., Boas, 1895; Sapir, 1915). The potlatch, the most obvious feature of their social life, by itself has been the subject of innumerable monographs (McFeat, 1965: part 3). The notion of status differentiation is clearly developed among the coastal peoples:

> All these tribes are characterized by a clear development of the idea of rank; indeed, it may be said that nowhere north of Mexico is the distinction betwen those of high and those of low birth to sharply drawn as in the West Coast tribes. Three classes of society may be recognized—the nobility, the commoners and the slaves [Sapir, 1915: 357].

Authority is exercised by the chiefs over all people in the village; few are permitted the freedom so often encountered in Amerindian society:

> A necessary consequence of the division of the village community into a number of large house-groups is that, associated with each chief, there is, besides the immediate members of his own family, a group of commoners and slaves, who form his retainers. The slaves are immediately subject to his authority and may be disposed of in any manner that he sees fit. The commoners also, however, while possessing a much greater measure of independence, cannot be considered as unattached. Everything clustered about a number of house-groups headed by titled individuals, and in West Coast society, as in that of mediaeval feudalism, there was no place for the social freelance [Sapir, 1915: 358].

The purpose of examining these details is to document the high degree of sociocultural differentiation and stratification, and not to provide a complete ethnography of these people; there is thus little need to go further, except to note that the predominant family type is extended (Driver and Massey, 1957: 402).

There are few ethnographic observations on socialization emphases in traditional life on the coast; two contemporary works (Hawthorn et al., 1960; Lewis, 1970) contain some useful material, but little of it relates either to the Tsimishian specifically or to traditional emphases. Evidence does suggest, though, that the extreme emphases upon compliance, transmitted with a relatively high degree of severity which characterizes other stratified societies does not hold on the coast. For example, Hawthorn et al. (1960: 284-285) refers to the fondness and warmth with which children are treated; this appears to be common to most Indian peoples. In their rating of compliance and assertion, Barry et al. (1959: 60) place the Kwakiutl (a culturally similar group on the coast) toward the middle of the dimension. We judge, then, the emphases in Tsimshian life to be intermediate between the two poles which have been used to characterize the practice of extremely low and extremely high food accumulating societies.

European contact with coastal peoples was initiated by Bering and by Perez in the early 1770s, and by James Cook in 1778 (Drucker, 1959: 19). The fur of the sea otter immediately attracted attention, and companies were formed specifically to engage in this trade. British, Americans, and Russians all competed for trade and influence on the coast until eventually the sea otter was virtually wiped out, and the native peoples were provided with a large array of forts and trading posts on their lands. In 1792 Vancouver explored and mapped the coast and in 1793 the Northwest Company dispatched Alexander MacKenzie overland to the west coast. This latter effort led the way for a land-oriented trade from then on, and in the 1800s numerous Hudson's Bay Company forts were established close to the Indian population centers. By the 1860s, the territory joined the emergent Canadian Federation, and full government services (primarily education) became increasingly available to these people. At the present time, no bands exist which are very traditional, and to some degree all communities have shifted to a wage economy which articulates with the larger Canadian society.

Hartley Bay (Kitkiatak)

Located about ninety-five miles south of the city of Prince Rupert, the Tsimshian village of Hartley Bay is relatively isolated and has remained (considering it is on the coast) relatively traditional. Its present band population is 360, although only 200 live permanently in the village; the balance are away for employment or education. Access to the village is by air or sea; no road exists because of the rugged terrain. Permission to land planes or dock boats at the village must be sought, prior to departure, from the Band Council, and by statute they deny the use of alcohol in the village. It is apparent, then, that the people of Hartley Bay prefer to control any likely influence from the outside; just as apparent is the neatness and social order which is maintained among them.

Although the site was a fishing camp in traditional life, its use for a permanent village is relatively recent. Around 1920, twenty-seven families from further north decided, mainly for religious reasons, to set up a new community. It is possible that the order which does prevail in the village is due in part to the fact that the people were motivated to come as a group and to start a new settlement. In one sense, then, this community is not representative of most coastal villages; it is in better shape socially, with few signs of poverty or deviant behaviour. On the other hand, it may be representative of villages a generation ago, before the process of acculturation became so swift. Thus the village of Hartley Bay is taken for the purpose of this study to represent a more traditional community of Tsimshian people.

The sample was drawn in the usual way from the band list; as a large number of persons were temporarily away for seasonal employment (salmon fishing and processing) only fifty-six participants were interviewed. Testing was done by Ted Wilson, a university student originally from Hartley Bay, and by Shirley Reece, a current resident. Both were trained by the author and Robert Annis, and the latter supervised the work in the community.

Port Simpson (Lachwalamish)

To the north of Prince Rupert, twenty-five miles by sea, is the Tsimshian village of Port Simpson. Founded in 1834 as Fort Simpson by the Hudson's Bay Company, it was named after Captain Aemilius Simpson, former chief factor at Fort Nass a few miles further to the north. As a Tsimshian village in earlier years, it was known as Lachwalamish or the "place of wild roses." Its present band population is about 2,000, with 800 of these actually living on the site. No road connects it overland to Prince Rupert, but one is in the process of being built. However, the short distance by sea, and frequent air, radio, and telephone contact have made it more highly acculturated than Hartley Bay.

The town has a number of small stores, a nurse, a school (with twelve teachers) and three churches. Most of the people fish during the salmon season (summer) and a logging operation is proceeding nearby on reserve lands. The harbour has a large man-made pier which is partly sheltered by an island just off its shore; as many as forty fishing boats may be tied up at one time. During the period of fieldwork, a major agreement was reached between the band council and the government to establish a salmon processing and canning factory in Port Simpson. This should raise the level of prosperity, as well as increase the proportion of band members living in the town.

Contact was initiated in the early 1800s, and in 1857 William Duncan arrived to begin his missionary endeavours on the coast. By 1862 alcohol was a sufficiently serious problem that Duncan took fifty families to a new settlement fifteen miles south toward Prince Rupert (to Metlakatla), but after further disputes in 1881 he left with these people once again to New Metlakatla just inside the border of Alaska (which is twelve miles north of Port Simpson). Thus it is apparent that early contact was highly disruptive, alcohol and religious factors causing major shifts in population (Barbeau, 1940). Despite these, Port Simpson maintained its balance and grew to become a fairly stable and economically sound community. The well-known carver, painter, and spiritual leader Charles Dudoward resides at Port Simpson, and maintains a very traditional focus to his own life and those of his adherents (many of them young). Partly inspired by the cultural center at

Ksan (a village of the Gitksan Tsimshian people further inland), there are signs of cultural reaffirmation taking place after a long period of acculturative influence. As a high-contact community, it is considered that Port Simpson is representative of the more acculturated Tsimshian peoples.

The sample was drawn in the usual way from the band list; again because of absences from the community less than the exact number of participants was tested; in the end fifty-nine were included. Testing and interviewing were done by Ted Wilson (of Hartley Bay) and Laurie Price (of Port Simpson) under the supervision of Bob Annis.

CARRIER OF THE ROCKY MOUNTAIN PLATEAU

On a plateau, in the interior of northern British Columbia there is a unique group of Athapascan-speaking people, the Carrier. They are unique because although they are similar to other Athapascan-speakers (fairly migratory hunting and fishing people), they have adopted a large portion of the sociocultural differentiation and stratification from coastal peoples such as the Tsimshian. According to Steward (1963: ch. 10) the Carrier were originally culturally adapted to these exploitive patterns, in ways similar to all sub-Arctic hunters. "The original type of Carrier society was some kind of simple hunting band" (1963: 175), with a single difference that the salmon at the headwaters of rivers running to the coast provided a good source of food, and their villages were "fairly permanent" (p. 175). At an unspecified date, the northwest coast cultural patterns spread up the rivers and the Carrier adopted many features of the stratified societies we have seen, including the potlatch and a nobility: "The common people lived, hunted and fished as before, but from time to time they had to hand over the surplus to their moiety chief for a potlatch ceremony" (p. 175). However, the minimal wealth of the Carrier clearly exposed the limitation: "The Carrier pattern of moieties, nobles and potlatches was a rather shabby imitation of the Northwest Coast system" (p. 176). Thus we have a group of people whose culture does not fit the ecological analyses which has guided the research up to this point; we have, in a sense, a test case where some of the sociocultural forms are due more to diffusion and borrowing, rather than to ecological adaptation. This borrowing was made possible and viable by the salmon at the height of the streams; in the absence of this it is unlikely that these cultural elements could have been introduced.

In summary, we have a society whose exploitive and settlement patterns are intermediate between those found among the Cree and Tsimshian, but whose sociocultural differentiation and stratification are closer to (since derived from) the Tsimshian and other northwest coastal cultures. As a case somewhat discordant with the model, it should provide us with the possibility of teasing out the relative contributions to the development of psychological differentiation of sociocultural factors and the "special experience" factors inherent in a hunting society.

As with the Tsimshian, there is no record of traditional socialization emphases; however observations of contemporary Carrier life (Hawthorne et al., 1960: 285-290) support the general description of child rearing as being warm, supportive, and with a moderate pressure toward assertion. This latter point is based upon Barry et al. (1959: 60) where the Kaska (culturally related to the Carrier) are rated thirteenth from the assertion pole out of forty-six societies and between the Ojibway (related to the Cree) and Kwakiutl (related to the Tsimishian); in the absence of precise and specific ratings, these data provide a general picture, which is open to verification by the interview and test data.

Contact with the Carrier was initiated by Alexander MacKenzie in 1793 on his way overland to the Pacific coast. In 1806 Fort St. James was established as a trading post, and missionary work was begun in 1843 by Roman Catholic priests. Contact increased gradually, with no steep increase or decrease in rate. Prince George became a major town in the late 1800s and in the early part of this century the transcontinental railroad was pushed through Carrier country to the new estern terminus at Prince Rupert.

Tachie (Stuart-Trembleur)

This fairly isolated band occupies the northern shores of Stuart Lake, about one hundred miles from Prince George and thirty-five miles north of Fort St. James. Over 600 persons are on the band list, but only 500 live on the site. The community is fairly typical of isolated bands in northern British Columbia, but change is occurring at an accelerating pace; a road was constructed in 1968 linking Tachie to Fort St. James; a weekly bus service commenced in 1972; and electricity was installed the same year. However there are no phones, mail, or plane service.

A church was built in 1941 and a government school (grades 1 to 7) was constructed in 1964; kindergarten was added·in 1972. Students who wish to attend high school must go to Prince George and board there.

Fishing (for trout and salmon) and hunting and trapping still provide every man a fair proportion of his subsistence; however wage employment (logging camps, sawmills, and guiding) also forms a portion, and this is increasing rapidly. All people speak Carrier, although the very young ones claim some difficulty; those under thirty years of age are usually bilingual.

The sample was drawn from the band list in the usual way; sixty persons were interviewed. Rose Pierre and Alec Pierre, both members of the band, carried out the testing under the field supervision of Bob Annis. Rose Pierre was also the band secretary, and a sister of the Chief Harry Pierre, who welcomed the project in the community.

Fort St. James (Necoslie)

Founded by Simon Fraser in 1806 as a trading post for the Northwest Company, Fort St. James became the capital of what was then New Caledonia. At the present time the Necoslie Band lives in a community which may be described as a suburb of Fort St. James. Although almost 600 persons are on the band list, only about 400 live there at the present time. This is small in comparison to the 3,500 non-native people living in Fort St. James.

The houses are all fairly modern bungalows and provide few visual cues to its status as a reserve. A government school was built in 1920, and electricity was introduced in 1952. Many of the men are on wage-employment (mainly lumbering and guiding) but many of the jobs are short-term or seasonal (such as the recent railway construction to the town from Prince George). Trapping and hunting, however, are still pursued, especially on weekends and holidays.

The sample was drawn, as usual, from the band list; sixty-one persons participated. Two band members, Brenda Prince and Fred Sam, carried out the interviews and were supervised by Bob Annis.

WESTPORT

As an anchor to the Amerindian study (similar to the function the Scots had for the Temme-Eskimo study) the village of Westport in southern Ontario was selected.

Its population is 700 and it is located about forty miles north of Kingston. It is not on a main highway and is considered to be a fairly traditional country village. Settlers moved into the area between 1810 and 1820, and Westport soon became a thriving market and manufacturing center. In its prime, the village was serviced by both railway and ferry, however these have gone and now not even a bus route passes through. In the summer, many tourists and cottage owners come to the village for supplies, but there is little industry at the present time other than dairy farming and beef cattle raising. In a sense, Westport has passed its prime and gives the impression of an attractive backwater where nothing very much happens. For these reasons it was selected as a comparison village for the Amerindian communities already described.

The sample was drawn from the 1971 census lists and forty-eight persons were tested. Interviewing and testing were carried out by John Kane, a student at Queen's University who "belonged to" the village. Testing took place in a hall rented for the purpose.

The third study which has been carried out selected a single culture (the Ojibway) which represents neither extreme in the Amerindian exploitive pattern range. This was done so that a group which is "typical" of those in contact with Euro-Canadians might be studied more intensively. In particular, the acculturation dimension was the major focus, and so three levels were selected from Ojibway villages.

OJIBWAY OF NORTHWESTERN ONTARIO

Stretching from northeastern Ontario through the Northwest and into Manitoba is a group of Algonkian-speaking people who are variously known as Ojibway, Algonquin, Chippewa, and Saulteaux; the latter two subgroups also extend southward into the northern United States. Their population is approximately 12,000 in Canada, most of them concentrated in the area north of Lake Superior.

Traditionally these peoples were hunting, fishing, and gathering; moose, deer, and smaller animals were shot or trapped, fish were netted or speared, and vegetable foods (particularly wild rice) were gathered. They are thus fairly low in food accumulation, but because of the availability of a starch (rice) as a supplement to the chase, they are not considered to be as extreme as the Cree or the Eskimo in the exploitive pattern.

With respect to settlement pattern, the Ojibway were fairly nomadic pursuing resources according to their movements and seasonal locations. The size of each band varied from fifty to one hundred individuals (Rogers, 1969) although during gathering and fishing periods this number may have been larger. Population density was low, ranging from six to twenty-two square miles per person (Rogers 1969: 34).

In keeping with this relatively migratory, lów population pattern, sociocultural stratification is low, with chiefs having little authority and there being no social classes apparent (Murdock, 1967). And in terms of family organization, they are independent nuclear. Finally as we have already noted, their socialization emphases lie slightly toward the assertion pole (Barry et al., 1959) among the ratings for forty-six societies.

We may conclude, then, that the Ojibway are a fairly typical, moderately low food accumulating group of Amerindian peoples, who maintain a fairly conventional relationship between exploitive pattern, settlement pattern, sociocultural stratification, and socialization emphases. This typically is important, for in this third study we are not crossing any of the ecological dimension, but rather are examining in greater detail the factors involved in the acculturation dimension. Thus, extremity on the one dimension would have reduced the generality of our focal examination of the other.

This northwest corner of Ontario lay in the path of the early fur traders who were pushing further to the west. However, being part of the rocky Laurentian Shield, land settlement by non-native people has been minimal in the area, and that which does exist is concentrated around mining sites. Thus, although voyageurs traded through the area as much as 200 years ago, and indeed traded with the people of the area, really significant acculturation has taken place only in this century, and then only in centers of non-native population.

Three Ojibway communities were selected for study: one (Aroland) is a relatively traditional rural community, although it is clearly within the Euro-Canadian acculturation network; another (Longlac) is a reserve adjacent to a moderate-sized town, and a third (Sioux Lookout) is a sample drawn from those Ojibway who have settled into the Euro-Canadian town of the same name. In addition, a non-native sample was drawn from Sioux Lookout, to provide cultural and behavioural norms with respect to the acculturative influences in the northwestern Ontario region.

Aroland

The relatively traditional community has a population of approximately three hundred people. The Ojibway language is usually spoken in the community although all except the oldest residents can speak some English. There is a Department of Indian Affairs day school in the village attended solely by children of the village. Two teaching sisters and two male teachers, all non-Ojibway, teach there and live in the village. A Catholic priest also lives in the village. Students are taken by bus to the regional high school fifty miles away; however, at the time the study was carried out, there were no students from the village attending it.

Until 1962, the only transportation in and out of the village was by a weekly train; there is now a good all-weather gravel road. The nearest non-native communities are fifteen and fifty miles away. The community fifty miles away is the center for health care, government services, shopping and entertainment. Travel to either community is by private vehicle; no public transport is available.

There is some wage employment available in the nearby foresting operation and pulp mills; many Aroland males participated in these wage activities.

Longlac

This transitional community is an Indian reserve situated two miles from a white community of approximately 1,000 people. It has a population of around 450. Ojibway is spoken by some of the older people; the young speak only English although some do claim a passive knowledge of Ojibway. Everyone on the reserve speaks at least some English. The children attend school in the white community, and the high school students are taken by bus to the regional high school. The community is on a major highway and the white community two miles away has a regular daily train and bus service.

Although jobs are available in the adjacent town, manh people of Longlac are unable to find employment. Consequently there is much unemployment and welfare is a major source of income. In both Aroland and Longlac, sampling and testing were carried out by John Kane (a project assistant) and by Nora Atlooken and Lawrence Longpeter, residents of the two communities.

The large northern community of Sioux Lookout has a population of nearly 3,000 people. It has one public hospital and one government "Zone Hospital," serving native peoples living in a large area to the north. There are three public schools and one high school within the community. A good paved road links the town to the Trans-Canada Highway, and there is daily railroad service, in addition to two charter and one schedule/charter air companies.

Sioux Lookout (Ojibway)

For the native sample, a list of the Ojibway residents of the town was compiled by consulting with various individuals and agencies. The estimates of the numbers of native individuals in the town ranged between 150 and 200. The list compiled included approximately 60 families, and so was probably close to exhaustive. The whole list was used as a sample pool, and an effort was made to interview a sample of individuals balanced by age and sex. The number of people in the oldest category (over forty years) living in the community was relatively small, most older Ojibway people preferring to remain on their reserves. Because of this circumstance, it was impossible to obtain a full sample in this age category.

Almost all respondents were on wage employment and appeared to be well-integrated into the life of the town. Clearly motivational and attitudinal factors contributed to the movement of these people into the town. Thus they constitute a special group, in a psychological sense, and they represent no other population.

The sampling and testing were carried out by Tom Mawhinney (a project assistant) and Irene Papassay (an Ojibway, resident in Sioux Lookout). A test center was established in the local community center for the duration of the project.

Sioux Lookout (Euro-Canadian)

The Euro-Canadian sample pool was composed of 103 families selected by random means by the most recent assessment list for the community. From these families, a sample of individuals balanced by age and sex was interviewed. Most were employed in local industry (railway maintenance, forestry, mining) and may be considered to represent a fairly typical northern Ontario town.

The testing was carried out by Tom Mawhinney and Robert Cosco, the latter being a resident of Sioux Lookout.

TABLE 5.2
COMMUNITY SAMPLES BY CULTURE, SEX AND AGE

Community Sample	Culture and Location	Total Number of Individuals	Sex		Age				
			Males	Females	10-15	16-20	21-30	31-40	40+
Study No. 1									
1. Mayola	Temne	90	45	45	20	20	20	20	10
2. Port Loko	(Sierra Leone)	32	20	12	6	7	11	5	3
3. Pond Inlet	Eskimo	91	46	45	19	17	20	20	15
4. Frobisher Bay	(Baffin Island)	31	16	15	6	6	7	6	6
5. Santa Teresa	Arunta) (Australia)	30	21	9	12	3	9	4	2
6. Yarrabah	Koonganji)	30	14	16	7	6	6	7	4
7. Telefomin	Telefomin) New	40	20	20	8	8	8	8	8
8. Hanuabada	Motu) Guinea	30	18	12	6	6	10	4	4
9. Inverkeilor	Scots	62	27	35	12	15	15	7	11
10. Edinburgh	(Northeast Coast)	60	31	29	12	12	12	12	12

						18-25	26-40	40+
Study No. 2								
11.	Wemindji	Cree	61	31	30	21	21	19
12.	Fort George	(James Bay)	60	31	29	22	19	19
13.	Hartley Bay	Tsimshian	56	28	28	24	17	15
14.	Port Simpson	(N.W. British Columbia)	59	28	31	21	20	18
15.	Tachie	Carrier	60	29	31	20	20	20
16.	Fort St. James	(Rocky Mountains)	61	26	35	22	19	20
17.	Westport	Euro-Canadian (Southern Ontario)	48	23	25	16	16	16
Study No. 3								
18.	Aroland	Ojibway) N.W.	39	20	19	14	12	13
19.	Longlac	Ojibway) Ontario	37	17	20	13	12	12
20.	Sioux Lookout	Ojibway)	31	13	18	13	15	3
21.	Sioux Lookout	Euro-Canadian (N.W. Ontario)	40	19	21	13	14	13
TOTALS			1048	523	525			

An overview of these twenty-one samples is provided in Table 5.2 along with details of numbers and age-sex distributions.

These brief ethnographic sketches have served to introduce the basic ecological, cultural, and acculturational features of the cultures and samples on this study. Obviously, no attempt has been made to present a comprehensive ethnographic account, but sufficient detail to assess cultural and sample placement in the model has been displayed. We turn now to a consideration of the design of the study, including an attempt to quantify many of these culture and sample details.

Chapter 6

EXPERIMENTAL DESIGN AND METHODOLOGY

In this chapter, we will elaborate the overall experimental design of these studies and consider some fundamental methodological issues which have confronted cross-cultural research in psychology. We also begin to operationalize the model by quantifying the independent (ecocultural and acculturational) variables. This is followed by a statement of the predictions which emanate from the model and the design, and these in turn set the stage for the presentation of our behavioural findings in Chapters 7 and 8.

EXPERIMENTAL DESIGN

The use of the term "experimental" in the title of this chapter is deliberate. Rather than simply referring to the "design" of the studies, the choice reflects a growing concern with the nature of research which attempts to relate cultural and psychological variables (e.g., Triandis et al., 1971; Edgerton, 1974; Price-Williams, 1974). In Edgerton's terms, the approach taken by anthropology is one of "naturalism": "Anthropologists are naturalists whose commitment is to the phenomena themselves" (1974: 63). On the other hand, he argues, the approach taken by psychology is one of "experimentalism," which, as seen by many anthropologists, "ignores context and creates reactions" (p. 64). Edgerton's purpose in making these observations appears to be one not of maintaining disciplinary separation, but of providing a basis for pursuing a methodological convergence.

Edgerton is not alone in his concern for bridging the two fields. One strategy, which has been attempted by many psychologists in field settings, is to engage in psychological experimentation within the context of the culture; this has been referred to as "experimental anthropology" by Cole et al. (1971). However both Edgerton and Cole employ the term "experimental" in only one of its two possible meanings in the cross-cultural enterprise: control over the independent variables in a specialized setting within a particular culture. More precisely, it means establishing a behavioural situation in a culture through control over the immediate independent variables, made up of the task setting, the instructions, or the stimulus. This, of course, is the basic meaning of the term in western laboratory psychological science. Its disadvantages and advantages are well known; on the one hand it is unnatural (contrived and artificial) and reactive, while on the other hand it permits precise observation under standard, controlled conditions.

Although the studies reported in this volume are "experimental" in this first sense, they are also "experimental" in a second, and perhaps more important, sense. That is, the present experimental design considers a variety of background cultural variables as the independent variables, and systematically varies them by selection from extant cultural variation. Dependent behavioural variables are then examined as a function of these independent cultural variables, and relationships are extracted. This second sense of the term is in fact only "quasi-experimental" (Campbell and Stanley, 1966); however this constitutes the best approximation to a true experimental design available for cross-cultural research.

Many sources of independent specification of cultural variables are available; in fact the whole of the ethnographic literature is such a resource. The most accessible and structured sources are those systematic inventories and cultural samples stemming from the pioneering work of G. P. Murdock: the Human Relations Area Files, the Ethnographic Atlas, and the Cross-Cultural Cumulative Code. Of course these will be of value only if they include the cultural variables which are theoretically linked to the behaviour being studied.

The quasi-experimental strategy employed is to select for actual field study those cultural groups in the Atlas (or other file) which exhibit some variation on the independent cultural variables of interest. Then the psychologist engages in fieldwork, using both ethnographic methods (to complete whatever missing cultural material is still required) and psychological methods (including both unobtrusive methods and the "experimental" methods in the first sense of the term). Given that the two levels of data are essentially independent of each other (that is, one is derived from cultural archival material, and the other is collected from individuals being tested in the field), both correlational and experimental analyses may be attempted.

By going to the ethnographic files for a systematic treatment of the independent cultural variables, the psychologist is confronted by two issues. The first is the problem of independence of observation within the files, and the second is the representativeness of the cultural sample drawn from the files.

Although very sophisticated treatments of archival data have been developed in recent years (see, e.g., Naroll and Cohen, 1970), the first problem continues to be bothersome, especially for those who wish to comment on psychological questions. From the point of view of psychology, the aim of these archival studies is to relate cultural and behavioural variables. To some extent codings and ratings of cultural and behavioural variables in the archives may lack independence; to this extent, correlations between these two levels would be spurious. To overcome this problem estimates of the degree of non-independence may be made by "data quality control" tests (Naroll, Michik, and Naroll, 1974), and fieldwork employing psychological methods may be conducted to provide relatively independent behavioural data.

The second problem facing the users of the various cultural archives is one of representativeness of the the cultural sample which is drawn from them. In general, anthropologists who have used the files have been attempting to gain an overall understanding of human cultural variation; which variables relate with each other, and under what conditions? The sample of cultures which is drawn for such an analysis is of crucial importance to their enterprise, for if it is not representative, no generalizations may be made about worldwide cultural variation in general (Naroll, 1970: 891). And of course if the cultural groups in the sample are not independent of each other (the famous "Galton's Problem"; Naroll, 1970) generalizations are even more difficult. The reason for considering this problem here is to distinguish this conventional use of the files in anthropology from the use made in the present study. In the former, since worldwide generalizations are the aim, a representative sample of cultural variation must be the source. However, in the latter, such generalization is not the immediate aim, rather the files are used only to provide a basis for selecting the independent cultural variables. Thus representativeness is not a requirement, at least not for this experimental goal of systematically relating cultural and behavioural variables.

While the representativeness aspect of Galton's Problem is not at issue in pursuing the quasi-experimental strategy, it may still be a problem with respect to the question of sample independence. In the present study, since two samples are usually drawn from each culture, it will be necessary to consider this issue when examining overall cultural and behavioural relationships.

However a more general goal of cross-cultural psychology has been to increase the relevance of the science to problems of behaviour outside the laboratory and beyond the limits of western culture. The cross-cultural method has been employed to increase the range of independent variables normally available to us (cf. Whiting, 1968) and to provide some perspective to the study of behaviour. In one sense, then, an eventual goal is to *test* the generality of a particular phenomenon or relationship, and if this is found to be limited, to *increase* it by exploring further cultural manifestations of it (Berry, 1969a). Thus some representativeness is required if some generality is to be inferred. To the extent that *variation* is present in the independent cultural variables, quasi-experimental manipulation will have been achieved; but to the extent that the variation is *representative*, generality will have, in addition, been gained.

By employing both uses of the term "experimental," some headway may be made in bridging the gap, at least in terms of design. In one sense, it is possible to employ the great contribution of anthropology (the specification and systematization of cultural variables) for experimental manipulation, and in the other sense it is possible to enter the selected fields to employ the great contribution of psychology (the standardization of behavioural data collection) for experimental control. However this strategy does not alleviate the reactive difficulties which concern the anthropologist, nor does it ease the concern of the psychologist for possible loss of experimental control in such field settings.

DESIGN OF THE STUDIES

The studies in this volume have followed the basic strategy which has just been outlined: selection of a set of cultural groups (guided by data available in the ethnographic archives) which vary on cultural variables which are theoretically linked to the behaviour of interest (psychological differentiation). This cultural selection has been followed by a period of fieldwork in which testing and interviewing took place with samples of individuals drawn from the cultural group.

As we have seen, there have been twenty-one such samples (four of them in Western settings) over a period of ten years. Given the span of these studies, they were carried out in phases, each one with a specific goal. In the first study a basic contrast was sought between an agricultural and a hunting society; this contrast was reported in Berry (1966). As part of this first study, two further groups were included to fit into the design at cultural positions intermediate between the original contrast; this was reported in Berry (1971a). At this point, the literature based upon studies with agriculturalists was well documented (e.g., Dawson, 1967; Okonji, 1969; Wober, 1966; MacArthur, 1970; Baran, 1971), and so a decision was made to concentrate thereafter on hunters and gatherers.

This decision led to the second study which concentrated on variation within a single culture area of hunting and gathering groups. Another reason for this limited focus was a concern for the problem of uncontrolled cultural variation which attended the broad cultural sweep in the first study. When the manipulation of the independent cultural variable is gross, effects are likely to be found, but the source of these effects cannot be pinned down with much certainty; large variations in culture not only vary the variables of interest to the study, but also, potentially, extraneous variables of which the investigator may not even be aware. Thus, in the second study, the decision was to manipulate the independent cultural variable within the confines of a single culture area, in an attempt to reduce this uncontrolled cultural variation. This strategy, of course, creates risks for the investigator; if the variation is so limited, the effects may disappear altogether. It is similar to the testing of the limits of sensitivity of a model, or to the laboratory experimenter's reduction in manipulation to discover the point where the effect can no longer be observed (Berry and Annis, 1974a).

In the third study, the focus was on a single cultural group within the hunting and gathering category. Here the manipulation was along an acculturational rather than a cultural dimension. Over the course of the second study this acculturation dimension had grown in importance, and this led to a decision to focus on it exclusively in a single cultural group of hunters and gatherers.

The designs of these three studies are presented in Table 6.1. Classification by ecological-cultural and acculturation levels were made, prior to fieldwork, on the basis of ethnographic descriptions (including the Ethnographic Atlas). Later in this chapter detailed quantifications will be provided for these two variables; for the purposes of illustrating the design, however, general ordinal classifications are sufficient.

Overall, then, the three studies have progressed from a very broad cross-cultural sweep, through a more limited cross-section, to a more focused examination of the cultural-behavioural interactions. They are unifed by a common set of independent cultural and dependent behavioural variables. However they differ from each other not only in features of design, but also in some content areas. Thus, in the chapters which present the results of the studies, some separations are maintained, as well as some integrations being attempted. Specifically, the material will be presented and analyzed in two ways: The first is a hypothesis-testing analysis, and the second is a *model* analysis.

In the first analysis, the behavioural data are employed to test the predictions which stem from the model. This is done in three ways. First, *within* each of the three studies, the experimental design permits an analysis of variance to be carried out by ecological-cultural and acculturation levels. Second, *across* the three studies, behavioural means will be examined as a function of the independent variables by means of correlational analyses. And third, *within* cultures and samples, individual differences in behaviour are considered as a function of a variety of cultural variables. In all of these

TABLE 6.1
DESIGNS OF THE THREE STUDIES: CLASSIFICATON OF SEVENTEEN SAMPLES

Study I

Acculturation Level	Ecological-Cultural Level			
	Low	*Low Medium*	*High Medium*	*High*
Relatively Low Relatively High	Mayola Port Loko	Telefomin Yarrabah	Santa Teresa Hanuabada	Pond Inlet Frobisher Bay

Study II

Acculturation Level	Ecological-Cultural Level		
	Low	*Medium*	*High*
Relatively Low Relatively High	Hartley Bay Port Simpson	Tachie Fort St. James	Wemindji Fort George

Study III

Acculturation Level	Ecological-Cultural Level
	High
Relatively Low Medium Relatively High	Aroland Longlac Sioux Lookout

presentations in Chapters 7 and 8, the strategy is to check the hypotheses stemming from the model, against the behavioural data.

However, in Chapter 9, the strategy is turned around. The question is not whether the behavioural data confirm or support the model, but "What is the best fit of the behavioural and cultural data among themselves?" That is, how is it possible to model the observed relationships better than in the model which had guided the study? Here a multiple regression analysis will be employed in a search for the best fit among the ecological, cultural, accultura-tional, and behavioural data.

METHODOLOGY

Before turning to the quantification of our independent (ecological and cultural) variables, it is necessary to consider some methodological features of these studies. In particular, two issues will be considered: The first concerns the focus of the studies (in terms of *emic* and *etic* analyses; Berry, 1969a; Price-Williams, 1974), and the second concerns the source of the data (in terms of the multimethod-multitrait strategy recommended by Campbell and Fiske, 1959).

In pursuing psychology cross-culturally it is essential to consider the nature of the cultural biases of the investigation. Apart from the question of sheer ethnocentrism, the major concern of a cross-cultural methodology is whether the focus of the study is on the generality of a phenomenon or on its specific manifestation within a particular culture. In the former, an etic framework is adopted, in which some universals are assumed to provide a basis for comparative study; this approach has been termed an "imposed etic" by Berry (1969a) and a "pseudo etic" by Triandis, Malpass, and Davidson (1971). In the latter, an emic exploration of the local cultural and behav-ioural characteristics of the phenomenon is attempted, within the assumptive framework of the people themselves. In contrast to the imposed etic strategy, where the investigator arrives with his concepts, his tools, and his assump-tions, the emic approach is essentially one of discovery. Eventually, of course, the task of the psychologist is to attempt an integration, to create a "derived etic" (Berry, 1969a) framework which is able to deal comparatively with both sets, without either sacrificing some of the universal characters of the etic or destroying the local character of the emic. This integration is achieved by allowing these two strategies to play back and forth, in a process of continuous mutual modification, until the emic is absorbed into the altered etic, and the new derived etic emerges.

As we have already noted, the focus in these three studies is upon a presumed universal dimension of behavioural development—psychological differentiation. The theory and previous research which were outlined in Chapter 3, then, constitutes one imposed etic for the studies. However, because we are attempting to relate behavioural to cultural variables, we also have an imposed etic in the theory of cultural ecology as outlined in Chapter 2. And finally, because of its central position in both the behavioural and cultural theoretical systems, socialization constitutes a third imposed etic.

One may begin research cross-culturally by simply and blindly imposing a theoretical system on a particular cultural situation; however, given the costs involved in cross-cultural research, this would be foolhardy. On the other hand, the researcher may attempt to justify some of the assumptions in his imposed etics, to establish a reasonable basis for proceeding. In the present research, a good deal of evidence was available in support of the assumptions.

In the theory of psychological differentiation, as we have already noted in Chapter 3, there are some universal elements in the system. First, as a theory analogous to biological differentiation, it may be relevant to all mankind; that is, since all human beings share a common biology, differentiation may be reasonably expected to occur in the psychology of all peoples. Second, as a developmental system, since progressive age-related changes in behaviour are apparent in all peoples, psychological differentiation may be a reasonable conception of these changes in behaviour in other cultural systems. And third, with respect to socialization practices (which are themselves universal; Aberle et al., 1950), there is evidence for some stable cross-cultural dimensions of socialization (e.g., Minturn-Triandis and Lambert, 1961) relevant to differentiation, and some evidence that these dimensions are systematically related to cultural ecology (e.g., Barry, Child, and Bacon, 1959). Finally, with respect to cultural adaptation, there is now widespread evidence of such adaptation as a universal process, at least at the subsistence level (e.g., Damas, 1969; Murdock and Morrow, 1970). Thus we may conclude from this brief recapitulation of earlier material that some reasonable bases exist for the imposed etics in these studies.

Turning now to the emic focus, we have already noted that hunting and gathering peoples constitute the major interest of this research; there is thus relatively higher emic attention paid to these people than to agriculturalists. In part this focus developed because of the shortage of psychological work with hunters and gathered in relation to the attention paid to agriculturalists in Africa and elsewhere. In one sense it has been a catching-up operation paralleling the recent anthropological interest in such a life style (Lee and Devore, 1968; Bicchieri, 1972). Emic discussions of all these variables will be presented in Chapters 7 and 8. And in part, work with hunters and gatherers offers potentially the most challenging opportunity for applying psychological knowledge in their service; this latter point will be elaborated in Chapters 8 and 10 in our discussions of applications and implications.

Our second methodological issue is the multiple nature of methods and tasks in these studies. In the case of data-gathering methods, three separate strategies have been employed. Following the argument of Campbell and Fiske (1959), if the results are independent of the method used to obtain them, then the interpretations of the findings may be made with some confidence. In addition, in cross-cultural work, if some control over the ethnicity of the investigator can be obtained, then even greater confidence may be warranted (Campbell, 1970: 71).

In the first strategy, an interpreter-assistant, who is indigenous to the cultural group, works along with the researcher during testing and interviewing conducted in the local language. This strategy was used primarily in Study 1, and to a lesser extent in Study 3. Its advantages are that a constant element (the researcher) is maintained throughout the work, and a variable element (the interpreter-assistant) provides the necessary cultural contact. In this strategy, the researcher knows the hypotheses, but the interpreter-assistant does not.

The second strategy, used less frequently in Studies 1 and 3, was· to employ English as the medium of communication where the participant preferred to operate in that language. In this case, the interpreter-assistant was usually not present during the interview and testing, but was available in case of communication difficulties. This strategy is closest to the conventional research setting in intracultural work, with the researcher knowing the hypotheses, and conducting the work alone.

A third research strategy, which was employed in Study 2, relied upon indigenous research workers to collect the behavioural data. These workers were trained by the researcher and supervised in the field by a university assistant. They worked mainly in the indigenous language, but in English where this was preferred by the participant. And, although the workers were trained in interview and test methods, they were not aware of any of the hypotheses.

In these three methods, there are differences in research skills, in language of communication, in ethnicity of the researcher, and in knowledge of the hypotheses. From one point of view, this may appear terribly unsystematic and potentially dangerous. But from another, such a multimethod approach permits an essential check on patterning of cross-cultural data; if the material which is collected by these various methods exhibits stable patterns within samples and clear trends across samples, then interpretations are possible which are free of methods bias.

In addition to a multimethod strategy, Campbell and Fiske (1959) have also recommended the use of multiple tasks to pursue multiple traits. To a certain extent, this suggestion, too, has been followed. In all the behavioural measures to be considered in Chapters 7 and 8, more than a single measure is used for each area of behavioural functioning, and in addition, tasks which are conceptually distinct from the core area of pyschological differentiation are employed. For example in the area of perceptual functioning, three different tasks are used in various samples to assess perceptual differentiation, and three others are employed as non-differentiation tasks. Thus, if measurers of differentiation cohere within a particular domain, or indeed across domains of psychological functioning, then we have achieved a multiple index of psychological differentiation. However, as an empirical question, the internal coherence of differentiated behaviour will be examined in Chapter 9. And, of course, only then will it be possible to check the efficacy of three various methodological controls.

INDEPENDENT VARIABLES: QUANTITATIVE INDICES

In order to operationalize the model and to develop and assess hypotheses, it·is necessary to establish quantitative indices for our independent variables. Although a rough estimate of the background features of each sample may be derived from the ethnographic material reported in Chapter 5, it is essential now to quantify these variables with some degree of precision.

Fortunately most of the cultures included in the three studies are' included in a variety of cultural ratings of exploitive patterns and other variables. Most significantly, all (except two) of the traditional cultures appear in Murdock's (1967) Ethnographic Atlas, and the two which do not (the Telefomin and Koonganji peoples) are culturally related to other groups which are included (that is, they are located in the same cultural area and province). In addition, many of these cultural groups are also listed in the codings of Driver and Massey (1957), and of Murdock and Morrow (1970). Since the most comprehensive listing is the Murdock (1967) Ethnographic Atlas, this forms the basis for our quantification of the ecological setting. Similarly, for the demographic and cultural variables of interest, ratings are provided in these same ethnographic materials. But for socialization emphases, only some coded ratings are provided in Barry, Child, and Bacon (1959) and in Barry and Paxson (1971) for these cultures; these data are supplemented by other ethnographic material and by self-reports from the respondents themselves.

In all, three quantified indices are developed and reported in this section: ecological, cultural, and acculturation. The first two of these are then combined to yield a joint ecocultural index and will be used as the first major independent variable. The acculturation index is an estimate of the second major input variable in the model—the degree to which nontraditional influences have affected the life of a particular group of people in the study.

Ecological Index

Three elements from the model are coded and rated in this index: exploitive pattern, settlement pattern, and mean size of local community. The patterning of data from these subsistence and demographic codes is shown in Table 6.2. The upper line for each cultural group provides the ratings directly from Murdock (1967), and the lower lines provides the ratings employed in the three studies. In some cases, the Murdock ratings are slightly discrepant from ethnographic sources or from observations made while carrying out the fieldwork; in these cases alterations are made. And in some cases missing ratings are provided on the basis of the ethnographic material reported in Chapter 5.

Of particular importance is the change made to the "fishing" ratings in Table 6.2. This is necessitated because this exploitive pattern is ambiguous with respect to the model: Some "fishing," in the Murdock codings, refers to the hunting of sea mammals; some refers to the catching of fish by spears or by hooks in the open sea; some refers to the catching of fish by placing traps or nets in rivers or streams; and some refers to the taking of shellfish along tidal flats. In keeping with the arguments of Lee (1968: 41), it is considered that the first (hunting of sea mammals) should be classified as "hunting," and the last (taking of shellfish) should be classified as "gathering"; this is more in keeping with the nature of the subsistence activity involved in each case. This re-allocation leaves two activities in the "fishing" code, which are themselves closely related to the arguments used by Lee; thus for our purposes fishing by spear or hook in the open sea is also allocated to the "hunting" classification, and fishing by leaving stationary nets in rivers or streams is allocated to the "gathering" classification. These recodings eliminate the ambiguity of the "fishing" classification and permit a much clearer quantification.

The coding and quantification for each element requires some discussion. For *exploitive pattern*, each numeral indicates the percentage reliance (divided by 10) upon each subsistence activity. Weights are then assigned, with animal husbandry receiving 1, agriculture 2, gathering 3, and hunting 4. The total score is the sum of the percentages times the weights. This yields a subindex which approximates the "food-accumulation" score of Barry et al. (1959). For *settlement pattern*, "complex settlement" (X in the Atlas) is scored 1, "relatively permanent" (V) is scored 2, "semi-sedentary" (T) is scored 3, "semi-nomadic" (S) is scored 4, and "nomadic" (B) is scored 5. And for *mean size* of settlement unit, an average population of 400-1,000 is scored 1, of 200-399 is 2; 100-199 is 3, 50-99 is 4, and less than 50 is 5.

Thus three elements have been included in the ecological index. Although many others might have been included, on the basis of the model and on the basis of decisions of others (e.g., Tatje and Narroll, 1970; Carneiro, 1970; and McNett, 1970) regarding essential components, these three were considered

TABLE 6.2
ECOLOGICAL INDEX FOR TEN CULTURES

Culture	Atlas number	Ecological Ratings — Exploitive Pattern: animal husbandry	agriculture	gathering	fishing	hunting	settlement pattern	mean size of local community	Ecological Scores: exploitive pattern	settlement pattern	mean size of local community	Standardized Scores: exploitive pattern	settlement pattern	mean size of local community	Ecological Index: Total
Temne	957	2 2	6 6	0 2	2 0	0 0	X X	5	20	1	1	-2.01	-1.92	-1.34	-1.98
Eskimo	462	0 0	0 0	0 0	8 0	2 10	S S	1 1	40	4	5	+1.06	+0.73	+1.19	+1.09
Arunta	56	0 0	0 0	6 6	0 0	4 4	B B	1 1	34	5	5	+0.14	+1.61	+1.19	+0.52
Koonganji	—	. 0	. 0	. 9	. 0	. 1	. T	. 3	31	3	3	-0.32	-0.16	-0.07	-0.27
Telefol	—	. 2	. 5	. 2	. 0	. 1	. V	. 4	22	2	2	-1.71	-1.04	-0.71	-1.53
Motu	631	0 0	5 3	1 1	4 0	0 6	V V	5 5	33	2	1	-0.02	-1.04	-1.34	-0.39
Cree	494	0 0	0 0	2 2	3 0	5 8	S S	1	38	4	5	+0.75	+0.73	+1.19	+0.86
Tsimshian	378	0 0	0 0	2 8	6 0	2 2	T T	4	32	3	2	-0.17	-0.16	-0.71	-0.27
Carrier	468	0 0	0 0	2 4	4 0	4 6	T T	4 4	36	3	2	+0.44	-0.16	-0.71	+0.18
Ojibway	502	0 0	0 0	3 3	4 0	3 7	S S	2 2	37	4	4	+0.59	+0.73	+0.56	+0.64

the most likely to be involved in the prediction of psychological differentiation. In addition, one very practical reason exists for the selection of these three variables: The most complete ratings exist for them in the ethnographic files and are thus least affected by supplementary data gathered within the framework of this particular study—that is, they may be considered the most "independent" variables of the set of potential independent variables in the study.

In the ecology component of the model (Chapter 4), exploitive pattern was considered as one element, and settlement pattern and mean size were treated together as another element. In Table 6.2, the ecological scores are summed (after standardization) to yield the ecological index; this index incorporates the elements in proportions 1 to .5 to .5, respectively.

Cultural Index

Two further elements from the model are included in the cultural index: sociocultural tightness and socialization emphases. In each case, the element is composed of more elementary units. For the former, three equal units from Murdock (1967) are employed: political stratification, social stratification, and family organization. In codings in Table 6.3 for *political stratification,* 1 represents two or more political levels above the local community level, 2 represents one level, and 3 represents no level above the community. For *social stratification,* a hereditary aristocracy (D) is scored 1, the existence of wealth distinction (W) is scored 2, and "no class" distinctions (0) is scored 3. And for *family organization,* large extended families (E) received 1, small extended families (F) 2, minimal extended families (G) 3, and independent families (N) are scored 4.

Once again, other elements might have been included, but for the same reasons as for our choice of elements in the ecological index, these three were finally selected. Moreover, these elements come closest to the basic meaning of the dimension "tight" to "loose" which has been developed by Pelto (1968). Finally, these elements are conceptually closest to the social practices which were originally isolated by Witkin et al. (1962) as fostering the development of differentiation.

For socialization emphases, two equal units enter into the codings in Table 6.4. The first is derived from the "compliance-assertion" ratings made by Barry et al. (1959), for each culture, and the second resides in the self-ratings each participant made of the severity with which he was brought up. It is important to note here that these are entirely separate indices, one being a set of ratings made of cultural practices available in the ethnographic literature, and the other being a set of self-ratings by participants collected during fieldwork; to the extent that these two ratings covary across our samples, we have an indication of their concurrent validity. Note also that since the

TABLE 6.3
SOCIOCULTURAL TIGHTNESS SCORES FOR THE CULTURAL INDEX

| Culture | Atlas number | Cultural Ratings | | | Cultural Scores | | | Standard Scores | | | Tightness |
		political stratification	social stratification	family organization	political stratification	social stratification	family organization	political stratification	social stratification	family organization	Total
Temne	957	32 / 32	. D	Fp / F	1	1	2	−2.13	−1.27	−0.58	−1.42
Eskimo	462	20 / 20	0 0	Gr / G	3	3	3	+0.66	+0.79	+0.32	+0.66
Arunta	56	20 / 20	0 0	R R	3	3	4	+0.66	+0.79	+1.21	+1.08
Kbonganji	–	.31	. 0	. F	2	3	2	−0.74	+0.79	−0.58	−0.17
Telefol	–	.31	. 0	. E	2	3	1	−0.74	+0.79	−1.48	−0.59
Motu	631	40 / 40	W W	N N	3	2	4	+0.66	−0.24	+1.21	+0.66
Cree	494	20 / 20	0 0	G G	3	3	3	+0.66	+0.79	+0.32	+0.66
Tsimshian	378	41 / 41	D D	Ep / E	2	1	1	−0.74	−1.27	−1.48	−1.42
Carrier	468	30 / 30	D D	Fr / F	3	1	2	+0.66	−1.27	−0.58	−0.59
Ojibway	502	20 / 20	0 0	N N	3	3	4	+0.66	+0.79	+1.21	+1.08

TABLE 6.4
SOCIALIZATION SCORES FOR THE CULTURAL INDEX

Culture	Sample	Traditional Cultural Compliance-Assertion Index	Self-ratings, Sample Distributions "Mother"			"Father"			Compliance-Assertion: Standard Scores	Self-ratings: Standard Scores	Socialization Total: Standard Scores
			VS %	FS %	NSS %	VS %	FS %	NSS %			
Temne	1. Mayola	8.0	98.9	0	1.1	98.9	0	1.1	−1.76	−1.91	−1.91
	2. Port Loko	8.0	81.2	0	18.8	81.2	0	18.1	−1.76	−1.16	−1.42
Eskimo	3. Pond Inlet	−11.0	1.1	4.4	94.5	1.1	4.4	94.5	+1.33	+1.75	+1.65
	4. Frobisher Bay	−11.0	0	12.9	87.1	0	12.9	87.1	+1.33	+1.51	+1.52
Arunta	5. Santa Teresa	−12.0	23.3	33.3	43.3	26.7	33.3	40.0	+1.49	+0.25	+0.73
Koonganji	6. Yarrabah	2.0	36.7	36.7	26.6	50.0	30.0	20.0	−0.78	−0.41	−0.56
Telefol	7. Telefomin	4.0	90.0	2.5	7.5	97.5	0	2.5	−1.11	−1.73	−1.54
Motu	8. Hanuabada	2.0	63.3	6.7	30.0	53.3	16.6	30.0	−0.78	−0.59	−0.69
Cree	11. Wemindji	− 8.0	10.0	61.7	28.3	10.3	60.3	29.3	+0.84	+0.63	+0.73
	12 Fort George	− 8.0	8.6	48.3	43.1	21.4	41.1	37.5	+0.84	+0.44	+0.60
Tsimshian	13. Hartley Bay	− 2.0	32.7	43.6	23.6	37.3	39.2	23.2	−0.13	−0.22	−0.19
	14. Port Simpson	− 2.0	17.5	64.9	17.5	30.2	52.8	17.0	−0.13	−0.13	−0.13
Carrier	15. Tachie	− 2.5	43.3	38.3	18.3	41.4	29.3	29.3	+0.03	−0.13	−0.19
	16. Fort St. James	− 2.5	18.6	35.6	45.8	19.7	14.8	65.5	+0.03	+0.72	+0.48
Ojibway	18. Aroland	− 2.5	7.8	45.6	46.8	8.6	45.7	45.7	+0.03	+0.72	+0.48
	19 Longlac	− 2.5	16.2	54.2	29.6	17.7	57.2	25.1	+0.03	+0.06	+0.11
	20. Sioux Lookout	− 2.5	22.6	32.3	45.1	22.6	32.3	45.1	+0.03	+0.34	+0.30

second of these ratings applies at the sample level, the listing in Table 6.4 is by sample.

In the Barry et al. (1959) paper, ratings were available for only two of the ten cultures in the present study (for the Ojibway and Arunta, at −2.5 and −12 respectively). However, for three other cultures, ratings are available for adjacent groups within the same culture area, and these have been employed as "best estimates" in the present study (Kwakiutl at −2, for the Tsimshian; Kaska at −2.5, for the Carrier; and Greenland Eskimo at −11, for the Baffin Island Eskimo). In addition, a number of other compliance-assertion ratings were available for nonadjacent but culturally similar groups; in these cases, original ethnographic sources (those referred to in Chapter 5) were employed to modify, if necessary, the available ratings. In this way, ratings were made within the framework of those cultures for which independent estimates were already available according to the scoring of Barry et al. (1957). Thus of ten cultures, seven may be considered reliable and independent of the present investigation, while the other three (Telefomin, Koonganji, and Motu) may be contaminated. However, since these three do not lie at the extreme ends of the scale, serious distortions of relationships are considered to be unlikely.

With respect to our second source of data, a basic three-point scale was employed with each participant, which read in English: "When you were growing up, did your mother (father) treat you very strict, fairly strict or not so strict?" In some samples, this question was asked in various ways to suit the local phrasing; but in all cases, the three-point alternative was provided. And in some samples the question was asked for "mother" and "father" separately, while in others it was asked for "parents" alone (Temne, Eskimo, and Scottish samples). These self-ratings are also provided in Table 6.4. Note that the compliance-assertion index is allocated by culture, while the self-ratings index is allocated by sample. In the latter case, a single index, which is characteristic of the sample as a whole, was generated by assigning a weight of 1 for "very strict," 2 for "fairly strict," and 3 for "not so strict," and adding across parents.

These two sources of data on socialization emphases are considered to be approximations only, in two senses. In the first, the socialization factors isolated by Witkin as antecedent to psychological differentiation are only partially represented in these data; "compliance" and "strictness," although components, are not identical with his socialization cluster. And in the second sense, these two sets of data only approximate the actual socialization phenomenon. In the case of compliance-assertion, ratings are based upon childhood and not upon infancy; ideally both should be represented in any complete description of socialization. And in the case of the self-ratings, there is the possibility that variations in the phrasing of the question, and the three alternatives might have contributed to the distribution of responses. Moreover, they are retrospective (and susceptible to memory error), and the large degree of skew for some samples (Table 6.4) indicates a lack of discriminability in the scale.

Despite these numerous weaknesses, the patterning of responses across samples appears to be remarkably consistent, with those claiming a "strict" socialization largely residing on those cultures rated as "compliant" by Barry et al. (1959). The value of this approach to estimating socialization experience is, of course, an empirical question. If these two estimates prove to be consistently related to each other and if they prove to be predictive of behavioural variation, then this first approximation will have performed satisfactorily. However, in future study, it is clear that better ethnographic, family, and individual study of socialization will be required.

Ecocultural Index

With the two component elements of the cultural index now elaborated, we may present the overall index itself. In Table 6.5, the sociocultural tightness scores and the socialization emphasis scores, combined and restandardized with equal weight, yield the cultural index. In the same table the ecology index is brought forward from Table 6.2 and combined equally with the cultural index to produce a more general ecocultural index, which corresponds to the first major set of inputs in our overall model.

Since our general view is that culture is adaptive to the ecological setting of the group, we would expect to find a strong set of relationships between these two sets of variables. Similarly, since we view ecology and culture, both conceptually and empirically, as clusters, we would also expect to find strong relationships among elements within each index. In Table 6.6, these interrelationships are presented for the two indices and their constituent elements.

This pattern of intercorrelations is clear. Within the ecological index, the three elements hold together very well, with a minimum correlation of +.74. However, within the cultural index, particularly for some of the "tightness" elements, correlations range down to +.53. For the "socialization" elements, correlations are very high with the ecology elements, displaying in these samples the same relationships found by Barry et al. (1959). Even more noteworthy is the correlation of +.89 found between the two socialization scores; these two elements are derived from relatively independent sources (cultural archives and self-rating), and this coefficient may be considered as an estimate of the concurrent validity of these elements.

Between the two indices there is also a pattern of substantial intercorrelation. First, the two total indices themselves correlate +.84, confirming our decision to combine them into a single more general ecocultural index. And second, the relationship between constituent elements of one index and the other index are all substantial, ranging from +.92 to +.56.

At this point it is necessary to consider the sample independence aspect of Galton's Problem. As we noted earlier, the statistical interrelationships among ecological and cultural elements are enhanced because, from most cultures, two samples have been drawn, and they have been entered into the correlation matrix in Table 6.6. To examine the statistical effect, the seventeen samples were divided into two subsets of eight samples each. This was accomplished by separating the eight "relatively traditional" samples from the eight "relatively acculturated" samples and by eliminating the medium acculturated sample from the one culture (Ojibway) which provided three samples. In general, the relationships are not altered substantially. The global correlation between the ecological and the cultural indices which was +.84

TABLE 6.5
COMBINED ECOCULTURAL INDEX FOR THE TEN CULTURES

Culture	Sample		Ecological Index	Cultural Index	Ecocultural Index
			Standard Score	*Standard Score*	*Standard Score*
Temne	1.	Mayola	−1.98	−1.93	−1.96
	2.	Port Lòko	−1.98	−1.48	−1.66
Eskimo	3.	Pond Inlet	+1.09	+1.58	+1.43
	4.	Frobisher Bay	+1.09	+1.57	+1.36
Arunta	5.	Santa Teresa	+0.52	+0.80	+0.72
Koonganji	6.	Yarrabah	−0.27	−0.53	−0.45
Telefòl	7.	Telefomin	−1.53	−1.48	−1.51
Motu	8.	Hanuabada	−0.39	−0.53	−0.49
Cree	11.	Wemindji	+0.86	+0.75	+0.79
	12.	Fort George	+0.86	+0.64	+0.72
Tsimshian	13.	Hartley Bay	−0.27	−0.37	−0.34
	14.	Port Simpson	−0.27	−0.31	−0.30
Carrier	15.	Tachie	+0.18	−0.26	−0.11
	16.	Fort St. James	+0.18	+0.36	+0.30
Ojibway	18.	Aroland	+0.64	+0.64	+0.64
	19.	Longlac	+0.64	+0.25	+0.38
	20.	Sioux Lookout	+0.64	+0.41	+0.49

TABLE 6.6
INTERCORRELATION AMONG ECOLOGICAL AND CULTURAL INDICES ACROSS THE SEVENTEEN SAMPLES

Variables	1	2	3	4	5	6	7	8	9	10
1. Exploitive pattern	–									
2. Settlement pattern	.85	–								
3. Mean size	.74	.90	–							
4. Political stratification	.91	.80	.66	–						
5. Social stratification	.45	.64	.80	.53	–					
6. Family organization	.53	.55	.56	.64	.60	–				
7. Socialization: compliance-assertion	.87	.93	.89	.80	.53	.46	–			
8. Socialization: self-ratings	.91	.80	.77	.75	.44	.47	.89	–		
9. Ecological Index Total	–	–	–	.89	.56	.56	.92	.91	–	
10. Cultural Index Total	.70	.76	.78	–	–	–	–	–	.84	–

Note: all coefficients are positive.   For n=17, r $<$ .40,   p $<$ .05.

across the seventeen samples rises to +.88 across the eight relatively traditional samples and drops to +.78 across the eight relatively acculturated
samples. And individual correlations among the constituent elements exhibit
similar minimal variation. Thus we may conclude that the general patterning
among these index elements is a stable one and does not rely upon sample
non- independence for the magnitude of their intercorrelations.

Overall, then, our first set of independent variables has exhibited a high
degree of internal consistency. This is not surprising given the earlier analysis
of, for example, McNett (1970). What is noteworthy at this point, though is
that *our selection of samples fits the hypothesized relationships.* That is, our
sample of cultural groups has observed the parameters of the model; without
this, prediction to the behavioural levels of the model would not be possible.

Acculturation Index

An index of acculturation for each sample is provided in Table 6.7. There
are three elements to this index which are derived from the central features of
the *acculturative influences* and *contact culture* components of the model:
western education, wage employment, and *urbanization.* As a single measure,
western education is perhaps the best, because it represents a deliberate
attempt to influence the behaviour of a group of people. It is also a good
measure for the present study because it exists as an individual as well as a
group measure. In Table 6.7 the mean years of education for each sample are
indicated; in all cases, this number represents fairly closely the relative
availability of western education in each community as judged from historical
and ethnographic viewpoints as well. The second element is a judgment from
"5" through to "1" of the relative availability and use of wage employment
by the community. It is included to permit the description of a situation
where wage employment is available (and provides a working norm) but is not
taken up either through disinterest on the part of the community or through
discrimination on the part of the employer. Finally, for urbanization, 1 is
defined as a situation of traditional housing and community layout and no
"services" (running water, sewage, electricity), and 5 is a situation of western
housing and layout, with "services," with relative ratings in between.

These three scores are standardized, and a total acculturation index is
calculated. On the assumption that experience of education and a general
experience of town life should both contribute, the wage employment and
urbanization elements were first combined (equally), and this new "town
life" element was then combined (equally) with education to produce the
acculturation index.

Once again there is a general expectation that these constituent elements
should cluster among themselves. This is borne out, with correlations of +.79
and +.76 between education, and wage employment and urbanization respec-

TABLE 6.7
ACCULTURATION INDEX FOR SEVENTEEN SAMPLES

Culture	Sample	Mean Education in Sample	Wage Employment Ratings	Urbanization Ratings	Standard Scores			Acculturation Index Total
					Education	Wage	Urbanization	
Temne	1. Mayola	0.0	1	1	-1.59	-1.69	-1.42	-1.68
	2. Port Loko	3.0	3	4	-0.58	+0.44	+0.91	-0.02
Eskimo	3. Pond Inlet	0.4	2	2	-1.49	-0.62	-0.64	-1.20
	4. Frobisher Bay	3.0	2	3	-0.58	-0.62	+0.14	-0.44
Arunta	5. Santa Teresa	2.1	1	1	-0.89	-1.69	-1.42	-1.26
Koonganji	6. Yarrabah	4.3	2	2	-0.13	-0.62	-0.64	-0.38
Telefol	7. Telefomin	0.0	2	1	-1.59	-0.62	-1.42	-1.47
Motu	8. Hanuabada	5.3	4	4	+0.22	+1.50	+0.91	+0.68
Cree	11. Wemindji	3.8	2	1	-0.30	-0.62	-1.42	-0.69
	12. Fort George	6.3	2	3	+0.57	-0.62	+0.14	+0.26
Tsimshian	13. Hartley Bay	7.6	3	3	+1.02	+0.44	+0.14	+0.74
	14. Port Simpson	8.8	4	4	+1.44	+1.50	+0.91	+1.42
Carrier	15. Tachie	6.3	3	3	+0.57	+0.44	+0.14	+0.47
	16. Fort St. James	7.6	3	4	+1.02	+0.44	+0.91	+0.95
Ojibway	18. Aroland	5.7	3	3	+0.36	+0.44	+0.14	+0.34
	19. Long Lac	6.9	3	4	+0.78	+0.44	+0.91	+0.80
	20. Sioux Lookout	8.1	4	5	+1.20	+1.50	+1.69	+1.48

tively, and +.87 between the latter two scores. This degree of coherence supports the decision to incorporate these three elements into a single index. Interestingly, these coefficients do not vary substantially when subsamples (which are divided by acculturation level) are examined separately; whether high or low in acculturation, education wage employment and urbanization appear to covary in a similar fashion.

RELATIONSHIPS AMONG THE INDICES

In the model presented in Chapter 4, two general levels of input were considered: ecocultural and acculturational. Since our aim is to understand the distribution of behaviour as a function of these two sets of variables, ideally they should be independent of each other. At this point, it is useful to consider their interrelationships, for if a moderate or strong covariation were present, it would be fruitless to present our hypotheses for both sets of independent variables or to consider the distribution of behaviour in relation to their independent contributions. In Table 6.8, coefficients are presented among all constituent elements and indices which bear upon this question.

In strong contrast to the high levels of consistent positive intercorrelation *within* each of the three indices (Table 6.6), there is a diffuse and nonsignificant set of relationships *between* indices and all their constituent elements. The key indicator is the low overall correlation (+.16) between the combined ecocultural index and the acculturation index; this correlation rises to +.24

TABLE 6.8
INTERCORRELATIONS AMONG INDICES ACROSS SEVENTEEN SAMPLES

Eco-Cultural Variables		Acculturation Variables			
		Education	*Wage*	*Urban*	*Acculturation Index*
1.	Exploitive Pattern	+.42	+.17	+.24	+.35
2.	Settlement Pattern	+.25	−.10	−.02	+.12
3.	Mean Size	−.06	−.35	−.20	−.16
4.	Political Stratification	+.32	+.16	+.18	+.27
5.	Social Stratification	−.25	−.29	−.26	−.29
6.	Family Organization	+.04	+.03	+.17	+.07
7.	Socn: Compliance-Assertion	+.11	−.18	−.08	+.01
8.	Socn: Self-Rating	+.22	+.05	+.18	+.19
9.	Ecological Index	+.33	+.05	+.14	+.25
10.	Cultural Index	+.17	−.04	+.09	+.12
11.	Ecocultural Index	+.23	−.01	+.10	+.16

Note: For n = 17, r   .40, p < .05

TABLE 6.9
ECOCULTURAL AND ACCULTURATION INDICES COMBINED

Culture	Sample		Ecocultural Index	Acculturation Index	Ecocultural + Acculturation Index
Temne	1.	Mayola	−1.96	−1.68	−2.27
	2.	Port Loko	−1.66	−0.02	−0.77
Eskimo	3.	Pond Inlet	+1.43	−1.20	−0.33
	4.	Frobisher Bay	+1.36	−0.44	+0.26
Arunta	5.	Santa Teresa	+0.72	−1.26	−0.70
Koonganji	6.	Yarrabah	−0.45	−0.38	−0.51
Telefol	7.	Telefomin	−1.51	−1.47	−1.89
Motu	8.	Hanuabada	−0.49	+0.68	+0.33
Cree	11.	Wemindji	+0.79	−0.69	−0.20
	12.	Fort George	+0.72	+0.26	+0.54
Tsimshian	13.	Hartley Bay	−0.34	+0.74	+0.45
	14.	Port Simpson	−0.30	+1.42	+1.02
Carrier	15.	Tachie	−0.11	+0.47	+0.33
	16.	Fort St. James	+0.30	+0.95	+0.92
Ojibway	18.	Aroland	+0.64	+0.34	+0.57
	19.	Long Lac	+0.38	+0.80	+0.83
	20.	Sioux Lookout	+0.49	+1.48	+1.43

across the eight relatively traditional samples, but drops to -.04 across the eight relatively acculturated samples. Throughout Table 6.8, coefficients are scattered,. with the strongest positive relationship being between exploitive pattern and education (+.42), and the strongest negative one between mean size and wage employment (-.35). Thus our attempt to sample from communities with relative independence of the major input variables appears to have been achieved. Although there is some positive covariation, it is small, permitting the examination of the independent contributions of each to the distribution of behaviour across the samples. Additionally, of course, we are interested in the joint contribution of the independent variables. In our presentation of the model in Chapter 4, it was argued that both ecocultural and acculturational factors should be predictive of differentiated behaviour. For this reason, a final combined index is presented in Table 6.9, with the ecocultural and acculturational indices restandardized and contributing equally. This ecocultural plus acculturational index will be employed in the graphic display of the distribution of the various behaviours across the seventeen samples, and in the testing of our hypotheses, to which we now turn.

GENERAL HYPOTHESES

On the basis of the model outlined in Chapter 4, the cultural material presented in Chapter 5 and the indices developed in this chapter, some

TABLE 6.10
CLASSIFICATION OF THE HYPOTHESES

Level	Independent Variable	Behavioural Domain	
		Differentiation	Acculturative Stress
Sample	Ecocultural Index	S:EC-1	S:EC-2
	Acculturation Index	S:AC-1	S:AC-2
	Ecocultural + Acculturation Index	S:EC+AC-1	–
Individual	Ecocultural Index	I:EC-1	I:EC-2
	Socialization (S-R)	I:SN-1	–
	Acculturation Index	I:AC-1	I:AC-2
	Education	I:ED-1	I:ED-2
	Interaction	I:INT-1	

general hypotheses emerge in each of the two areas of behavioural functioning. These may be stated in general terms to provide an overview, before
being immersed in the details of the chapters to follow; however, each will be
elaborated in the appropriate chapter. These general hypotheses are classified
according to their sample (S) or individual (I) status (that is, whether they
will be tested across groups or across individuals), and according to their
derivation from the ecocultural (EC) independent variable, the acculturation
(AC) variable, or their combination (EC+AC). In Table 6.10 an overview of
the hypotheses is presented, while the text contains a listing of them.

SAMPLE HYPOTHESES (about differences across samples)

S:EC-1   On tasks of *differentiation*, mean performance of samples
will be most differentiated at the nomadic, loose end of
the ecocultural dimension.

S:EC-2   On scales of *acculturative stress*, mean scores of samples
will be highest at the nomadic, loose end of the ecocultural dimension.

S:AC-1   On tasks of *differentiation*, mean performance of samples
which have experienced more acculturation will be more
similar than those with less acculturation, to the norms of
the community providing acculturative influences.

S:AC-2   On scales of *acculturative stress*, mean scores of samples
which have experienced more acculturation will be more
similar than those with less acculturation, to the norms of
the community providing acculturative influences.

S:EC+AC-1 On tasks of *differentiation*, mean performance of those
samples with the highest (nomadic + acculturated) EC+AC
index will be most differentiated.

INDIVIDUAL HYPOTHESES (about correlations across individuals)

I:EC-1   On tasks of *differentiation*, those individuals will be most
differentiated who reside in samples at the nomadic loose
end of the ecocultural dimension.

I:EC-2   On scales of *acculturative stress* those individuals will
score highest who reside in samples at the nomadic, loose
end of the ecocultural dimension.

I:SN:1   On tasks of *differentiation*, those individuals with greatest
socialization for assertion will score most differentiated.

I:AC-1   On tasks of *differentiation*, those individuals will be most
differentiated who reside in samples at the more acculturated end of the acculturation dimension.

I:AC-2   On scales of *acculturative stress*, those individuals will
score lowest who reside in samples at the more acculturated end of the acculturation dimension.

I:ED 1   On tasks of *differentiation,* those individuals with greatest
            formal education will score highest.
I:ED-2   On scales of *acculturative* stress, those individuals with
            greatest formal education will have lower scores.
I:INT-1   On scales of *acculturative stress,* those individuals with
            highest levels of differentiation will have lower scores.

In some instances, no hypotheses have been advanced. In the case of relationships between the combined index and acculturative stress, an overall prediction is not possible, since the direction of the relationships with each of the constituent indices (the ecocultural and the acculturation) are hypothesized to be in opposite directions. And in the case of relationships between socialization self-ratings and acculturative stress, there are no theoretical grounds upon which to base a prediction.

We may now turn to the description and anlayses of the behavioural data, and to the testing of these hypotheses. As we have already noted, in Chapters 7 and 8, these tests will take the form of analyses of variance within each of the three studies, and correlational analyses across all seventeen samples for the "sample" hypotheses, and by correlational analyses within samples for the "individual" hypotheses. In addition, an examination of interrelationships and regression analyses as a test of the model will be carried out in Chapter 9.

Chapter 7

ADAPTATION AND DIFFERENTIATION

In this chapter and the next, we will consider the distribution of behaviour in the samples as a function of the ecological, cultural, and acculturational variables which have been outlined in the last chapter. Our primary emphasis in this chapter is upon the behaviours which have developed in adaptation to the ecocultural setting of the group, while in the next chapter it will be upon the response to acculturation.

Although the theory of psychological differentiation which was outlined in Chapter 3 encompassed perceptual, cognitive, social, and emotional behaviour, our focus in this study is primarily upon perceptual-cognitive functioning. Some cross-cultural work has been carried out within the present framework upon social and emotional variables (see Berry 1967, 1974a; Berry and Annis, 1974a), but theoretical and measurement problems and some sampling limitations have emphasized the exploratory nature of this work. For this reason, studies which lie outside the perceptual-cognitive area have not been included.

It is appropriate that this cross-cultural examination of differentiated behaviour concentrates upon perceptual and cognitive functioning, where the enterprise began and where theoretical, empirical, and measurement problems, are best understood. As we have seen, at the core of the concept is the notion of disembedding; an individual who is perceptually differentiated is one who is able to isolate, analyze, or abstract a small chunk of the environment from its context in the larger world. The extraordinarily simple beginning to our study started with the idea that hunters had to do this for sheer survival, but farmers need not (Berry, 1966; 211-212). A basic functional question about ecological demands upon behaviour led to the expectation that hunters would be good at disembedding, while farmers would not necessarily be so. Although very sophisticated role analyses for hunters have been prepared (see, for example, Laughlin, 1968), the basic element remains that of disembedding.

However, the notion of disembedding involves more than mere fragmentation; Witkin et al. (1962) have argued that integration is also essential to the concept of differentiation. In behavioural terms, for a hunter to develop the ability only to fragment his perceptual world would be dysfunctional: Survival requires putting it back together again in a variety of ways. First, perceptual cues (tracks, vapour, sounds, smells) must be organized to provide information about the probable existence of food, and about the nature of the beast. Second, other perceptual cues (hills, clouds, sun, stars, wind direction) must be organized to provide information about the hunter's location not only in relation his quarry but also to his place of residence (for an elaborate analysis of these navigation techniques for a seafaring group, see Gladwin, 1970).

Thus the two key features of the concept of perceptual differentiation match two essential functional behaviours required of a hunter in his ecological setting. As a group, then, we should be surprised to discover hunters who are perceptually undifferentiated (field-dependent), although we might expect to find individual differences which tend to appear in any sample. Conversely, we should be surprised to find high levels of perceptual differentiation among groups who have no functional requirement for disembedding, although it is quite possible that for other reasons (for example, from cultural diffusion from other groups) such behaviour might be apparent.

Following the original argument further (Berry, 1966: 212-214), it was considered that environmental press is a necessary (but not sufficient) condition for the development of adaptive behaviours: Mechanisms of a biological, cultural, and/or psychological nature are required before such behaviours may appear. Environmental press may simply extinguish the life of individuals or the group, or it may force migration to settings where extant behaviours are more suitable. Thus mechanisms to bring about behavioural adaptation must be considered in addition to mere press.

For biological mechanisms, two have been suggested: genetic selection and protein availability. In an early review and commentary on the present study, Witkin (1967) suggested that if there is any connection between field independence and genetic action, then it is quite possible that those who are field-dependent in a hunting band would die out naturally, thereby altering the gene pool. In addition, two cultural mechanisms may operate on the gene pool: Field-dependent persons may die out as a result of group pressure (ostracism, homicide), or the genes may diminish in frequency through marriage restriction or prevention. All these are possible, but no genetic evidence is available to permit a decision at this time. The second biological proposal, concerning protein availability, has been advanced by Dawson (1966, 1969, 1972). In this work with those suffering from the effects of low protein intake in childhood (kwashiorkor), he has found lower levels of perceptual differentiation in a small sample (of ten persons) in West Africa. More recently, with rats, he has demonstrated lower spatial (maze-running) ability for those animals injected with estrogens, which substance is associated with kwashiorkor. Once again, interpretation is difficult; the low numbers of human subjects (combined with inferential problems of getting from kwashiorkor to estrogen) and the presence of the phylogenetic gap make the application of such arguments difficult to assess.

For cultural mechanisms, all those which were discussed in the traditional culture component of the model may be operating as pressures toward the development (learning) of psychological differentiation; these include both socialization emphases and sociocultural stratification. However, other cultural features may be implicated, and two of these were advanced in the original argument (Berry, 1966: 213-214): language distinctions, and arts and crafts. Although these factors have not been subjected to systematic assessment in Studies 2 and 3, their variation in Study 1 was highly associated with the presence of perceptual differentiation. Specifically for language distinction, Whorfian analysis suggests that a group will employ language which reflects the environment and their relationship with it (Whorf, 1956); the innumerable Eskimo terms for snow and Arab terms for camels are the usual clichés offered in support of this statement. However, it is possible to carry out language analyses specifically in any behavioural domain of interest, and this was done in the first study for "geometric spatial" terms. The argument is, very simply, that if such features of the environment are important for disembedding in one's ecological setting, they will appear in the linguistic distinctions made by the group; if not important, these distinctions may not appear.

A second cultural mechanism which was originally proposed is that of training and development in the arts and crafts. In particular, if paintings, sculpture, maps, and other representations of the physical environment are well developed in a group, they could provide a further cultural mechanism. In the case of both linguistic distinctions and developed arts and crafts, it was argued that they provided the necessary conceptual and practical tools and context for the acquisition of perceptual differentiation. With these "cultural aids," higher levels might be attained, but without them, lower levels only may be possible.

The final class of mechanism to be considered is behavioural or psychological. One, which was originally the sole mechanism considered is *perceptual learning;* the other, which has recently been suggested, is *early perceptual tuning* (Annis and Frost, 1973). For the first, the argument is that the cluster of ecological and cultural features, including those in our model (as well as linguistic and craft activity) all provide settings, models, and reinforcement for the development of perceptual differentiation. Based upon the established relationships, primarily with socialization (Witkin et al., 1962; Dyk and Witkin, 1965) and with social conformity (Witkin et al., 1974), it was expected that the traditional culture component of the model would be predictive of the level of differentiation of a group in adaptation to a particular ecological setting. In addition, direct interaction with aspects of the ecological setting were expected to provide learning situations which would also lead to the development of an adaptive level of differentiation. Thus both ecology and traditional culture components were expected to lead, by way of perceptual learning, to a characteristic level of psychological differentiation in different populations. For the second mechanism the argument has been advanced that *learning* may not account for all adaptive behaviour in the visual domain; *early tuning* of the visual system to some features of the visual environment may be important adaptations, not only because they occur early in life but also because they are irreversible. However, given the small range of phenomena considered (mainly line orientation) and the small number of studies, this factor remains as a potential alternative mechanism. In any case, tuning phenomena appear far more relevant to studies of illusion susceptibility cross-culturally (e.g., Segall, Campbell, and Herskovits, 1966) than to studies of psychological differentiation.

These arguments were originally presented in the context of a sharp contrast between the hunting Eskimo and the agricultural Temne. The question arises about their applicability to groups which occupy other positions on the ecocultural dimension. First, although more extreme in terms of our model, a purely pastoral sample has never been assessed; such a study needs to be carried out, especially in view of the findings of Edgerton (1971) that psychological differences (in personality) are apparent between agricultural and pastoral peoples. Our prediction from the model would be, considering settlement pattern and the variables of tightness, that low levels of perceptual differentiation would be found, especially if they are sedentary or semi-sedentary.

Two other exploitive patterns are coded by Murdock (1967) in his Ethnographic Atlas: gathering and fishing. For gathering, a role analysis suggests less ecological demand for perceptual differentiation than for hunting, but more than for farming: The detection of foods in places where they have not been planted is more demanding than returning to one's fields at harvest time, but less demanding than the pursuit of moving game. In the extreme case of hunting, both food resource and human consumer are in a constantly moving relationship with one another, changing cues and contexts minute by minute, while in the case of farming, both resource and consumer are in stable settings. For gathering, though, the resource is more or less stable and in predictable places, while the consumer must navigate to find it.

For fishing, as we have already seen (Chapter 6), activities may be allocated to either the hunting or the gathering classification: If fishing involves hunting of sea mammals or true fishing in open water, then it shares the double mutual movement characteristic with hunting. However, if it involves the collection of marine foods on tidal flats or the placement of nets in streams or rivers, then it shares a skill pattern with gathering. By allocating fishing activity to these two other subsistence activities, a fundamental ambiguity may be removed—at least for the prediction of psychological developmental consequences.

In a traditional group, behavioural adaptation to the ecological setting may be fairly close: Our hypotheses, indeed, are that sample means of tests of differentiation will range consistently with the ecocultural index. However, all groups are influenced by culture contact, thus introducing another source of behavioural patterning. And·so our second concern is with the nature of acculturative influences and with their consequences for differentiation. The argument is relatively simple: If one group is being influenced in systematic and powerful ways by another group, then the former will acquire some behavioural characteristics of the latter; the taught will generally become more like the teacher. However, given the many generations of previous interactions with a particular ecological setting, and the numerous experiences during the period of psychological development, the expectation is that behaviour which is adapted to the traditional ecological and cultural features of life will persist well into an acculturating situation. That is, the basic patterning of differentiation will derive from its adaptation to traditional ecological and cultural settings; changes due to acculturation are·likely to be no more than variations on the theme.

Since the major form of acculturation in all our samples has been, and still is, westernization from a Western cultural tradition, we may expect that all groups in the study are being influenced to assume behaviours which are characteristic of this tradition. For our present discussion, we may ask what the levels of differentiation which are characteristic of this tradition are. Two answers are possible, one based upon a consideration of the life style and one based upon an examination of typical test results. For the former, living and learning in a technical, industrial society involves deliberate instruction in analytic skills, both of the figural and logical variety. Of course not all persons develop these skills, but the rewards (in both education and the·work world) are clearly directed toward those who gain the ability to operate in the analytic mode. And it is in these two areas of education and work where the most forceful and deliberate acculturative influences are placed upon peoples in contact with the Western cultural tradition. Thus based upon this analysis, we expect that levels of differentiation will rise as a consequence of acculturation.

Our second answer may be provided by an advanced reference to test norms for our European-derived samples; in most cases their performance on tasks of perceptual differentiation is higher than for the other samples in the studies. This norm is provided for the sole purpose of indicating the nature and level of the acculturative influence. They are not intended to enter into the comparative framework for the simple reason that the tasks are all derived from Western systems, and hence are biased in that direction. On the grounds that "he who makes the test does best," caution demands that the testmaker stand well back!

Finally, since both ecocultural and acculturational factors are considered to be predictive of levels of differentiation, we expect that even more accurate prediction may be possible from a simultaneous consideration of both variables. Thus, a combined index is employed to display the patterning of group mean scores.

Since both predictors are considered to operate in the same direction (higher ecocultural index, higher scores; higher acculturation, higher scores), the two indices are combined to yield a single predictor of performance on the tasks.

INTERVIEW QUESTIONS

Over the period of research, many interview questions have been asked, scales employed, and tests administered. Those which are common to the adaptation and acculturation aspects of the study are discussed here, along with the differentiation tasks; those which are unique to the study of acculturation will be discussed later (in Chapter 8).

For all samples in the studies, basic personal and demographic questions were posed. These included age, sex, education, and self-rating on compliant socialization. In some samples, these questions were supplemented, where they made sense, with questions on occupation, place of birth, travel experience, literacy, ownership of various possessions obtainable through contact, marital status, number of wives, number of children, and number of fathers' wives. These supplementary questions were largely related to level of acculturation or to socialization. Since these questions were not universally asked (or applicable), and since where they were asked, they tended to cohere with the responses to the basic questions, we will not be concerned with them in this monograph.

In general the interview questions were used at the beginning of the sessions. None is threatening, and as a group they served to loosen up the relationship and to establish communication. For some questions, precise answers are never possible in certain samples: For example, the age of Temne adolescents was established by asking the parents to "count farms" since the child was born, while the ages of adult Eskimo respondents had to be estimated by the researcher and his assistants, and then checked for relative accuracy with community elders or administrative officers. And for other questions, efficient communication requires circumlocution to the point where comparability may be lost: For example, the question on compliant socialization was phrased as being "held tight" (i.e., physical or social restraint of independence) in the Temne samples, and as "very strict" in the Scottish samples.

In an attempt to assess level of acculturation through education, we limited the definition of education to "formal western education." Of course, all groups provide education to their offspring, and do so in varying ways, from relatively simple opportunities for imitation or observational learning to highly structured institutions for formal teaching and learning. In four of our cultural areas, there was some deliberate, but nonwestern, instruction. In the two Temne samples, Koranic schools operated to provide instruction in Koranic texts, which were learned by rote, while in Telefomin, a quasi-Christian catechist provided some basic biblical materials in the form of pamphlets which could be deciphered to varying degrees by peoples in the village. In two cases (Eskimo and Cree) some degree of literacy had been acquired prior to formal schools being introduced; here, the "syllabic" script spread from band to band and from person to person (sometimes with the assistance of a missionary), so that these two peoples had some of the skills associated with formal western education even though no school had been attended. In summary, then, education is recorded as the number of years an individual had attended a western institution of formal instruction.

With respect to compliant socialization, as we have already noted in Chapter 6, a basic three-point scale was employed, which read in English: "When you were growing up, did your mother (father) treat you very strict, fairly strict or not so strict?" In some samples this question was asked in various ways to suit the local phrasing; but in all cases, the three-point alternative was provided. Finally, in some samples, the question was asked for "mother" and "father" separately, while in others, it was asked for "parents" alone; these differences will be indicated when the data are presented.

PSYCHOLOGICAL TESTS

Tasks were selected which were considered to tap the skills associated with ecological adaptation and to be influenced by the hypothesized cultural variables. Of the six tasks employed, two are clearly tasks of perceptual differentiation (Embedded Figures Test and Portable Rod and Frame Test), and one is a cognitive differentiation task (Kohs Blocks). Of the other three tasks, one (discrimination) does not appear to involve disembedding or analysis, but was intended to represent a simple, ecologically relevant perceptual skill. The other two were a task of spatial ability (Morrisby Shapes), and inferential ability (Ravens Matrices). At this point it is useful to recall the hierarchical relationships which were proposed in Chapter 3, and the traditional behaviour component of the model (Figure 4.4). In those discussions, there was allowance for tasks which are not a part of the psychological differentiation constellation to be related to differentiation at different levels. That is, although not involving an act of disembedding, spatial and inferential tasks may involve analysis and restructuring; if this is the case, then such tasks may be related to the cognitive style of the peoples in this study.

Kohs Blocks

The test developed by Kohs in 1923 was designed to assess basic intelligence; indeed, Wechsler includes a modified version of this task in his Intelligence Tests, as do McElwain, Kearney, and Ord (1967) in their Queensland Intelligence Test. Despite this, the task conceptually involves analyzing a design, selecting block surfaces which match the components, and assembling them to create the total design; and empirically (Goodenough and Karp, 1961) it loads consistently on the same factor as tests of perceptual differentiation. Although we will return to this issue in our discussion of Raven Matrices, and again in our chapter on "Implications," let us note for the present that on both conceptual and empirical grounds the Kohs Blocks Test appears to be a test of differentiation, no matter what else is claimed for it.

The original version of the test (and the one employed throughout these studies) consists of seventeen designs. These designs are printed on cards, and a set of sixteen blocks is provided. On both the cards and the blocks, four colours are used (red, white, blue, and yellow). Each colour is represented on one full face of each block, while the other two faces are in red-white and blue-yellow, divided on the diagonal. The test itself is preceded by a relatively simple four-block design in two colours; if this is mastered (as it almost always is), then the seventeen designs of the test itself are administered in a standard sequence. Of these seventeen, nine are for four blocks, two are for nine blocks, and six are for all sixteen blocks.

Administration of the test was always individual, so that the maximum performance that an individual is capable of might be attained. Verbal reinforcement was provided after each correct production, but none was offered after incorrect ones. The test was terminated after three incorrect or incomplete productions.

Timing of tests is always a difficulty in field testing. On the one hand, most psychological tests are timed as a basic requirement of their design and administration, while on the other hand most people in the world appear not to share our western concern for time (e.g., Doob, 1972). Given this basic conflict, it was decided to retain timing as a feature of the Kohs test, but to extend the time limits so that those who were obviously able to do a particular design had more time in which to complete it. And in cases of obvious ability, but of slow and deliberate design construction, these time limits were extended for the last block or two to be put in place. The time limits were decided after pilot testing in Scotland with children and relatively uneducated adults. Increases of thirty seconds were allowed on designs one to six, and design ten; increases of sixty seconds were allowed on designs seven, eight, and nine, while none was allowed for designs eleven to seventeen.

Scoring followed the original procedure by assigning points for correct design construction, and none for failure. In later designs, points are subtracted if an intermediate time barrier is exceeded. However, unlike the original scoring, no points were subtracted for too numerous moves during the construction of the designs. The maximum possible score is 131 over the seventeen designs.

In a sense, both the use of the original seventeen designs and the increase of time allowed on some of them "spread the task out," so that initial unfamiliarity could be overcome during the course of the test. It was considered that the use of the shorter Wechsler version, or the retention of the shorter time limits, would make the test too abrupt and create leaps of too great difficulty from one design to another. Impressions gained from administering the task to hundreds of participants from many cultural settings are that an individual was brought along to maximum performance by the smooth gradations of the test as used in the study.

Finally, mention should be made of the motivational issue in cross-cultural testing, as it relates to Kohs Blocks. Of all tests used in a decade of research, no other test has been so obviously enjoyable. It has been variously perceived as a "toy," a "game," and as "great fun" by participants in the field. Indeed, in one community (Mayola), people selected in the sample would present themselves at the test center to "play the game"; upon enquiry, it was clear that word about the blocks had got around!

Embedded Figures Test (EFT)

One of the central tests to the concept of perceptual differentiation is the Embedded Figures Test developed by Witkin in 1950. The task is to locate a small design embedded in the organized context of a larger design, and is thus a direct representation of the notion of disembedding.

In the original version, twenty-four designs were included, each with a time limit of five minutes. Witkin et al. (1971) now employ the first twelve of these designs as Form A and the second twelve as Form B, each design with a three-minute time limit (cf. Jackson, 1956). For the field purposes of this study, it was considered that twelve designs were too long, and so six of the Jackson twelve were selected for use. And to provide an introduction to the task, two practice designs were employed. Thus the version used in this study is a subset of the original test. (The designs used are: for practice, P-X and 7-F; and for the actual test: 10-G, 15-D, 11-A, 3-C, 4-D and 9-C).

Scoring of EFT followed the original procedure: The number of seconds required to locate the figure was noted and summed for the six designs. In case of failure to locate, the maximum time (180 seconds) was assigned. Thus the total possible score was 1080 (6 x 180 seconds). However, since this produces a high score indicative of low differentiation, scores are reported in reversed form in this study; these are achieved by subtracting the actual score from 1080 to yield a score positive in direction.

Serious problems arise in the field with the use of the EFT. First, there is little apparent fun in attempting the task, at least in comparison with Kohs Blocks; with inherent motivation low, it becomes difficult to keep the participant at the task. Second, no overt movements are required during the search for the figure; visual scanning is carried out by the participant, but short of monitoring his eye movements, it is not possible to decide whether the task is being performed or not. And third, since the instructions require visual scanning only, the participant must hold in check his tendency to trace the various lines of the complex figure during his search; this requires constant reminding, leading to a reduction in rapport.

All these problems led to the decision not to employ EFT beyond Study 1. Although the Kohs Blocks Test is conceptually and empirically a part of the differentiation idea, it is neverthelsss not a task which was developed specifically to assess it. Thus Study 2 is without benefit of a deliberately designed differentiation task; however, in Study 3, a portable rod and frame apparatus became available, to rectify this lack.

Portable Rod and Frame Test (PRFT)

This portable version of the original task (Witkin et al., 1962) was developed by Oltman (1968) for use in settings where the larger test could not be employed. It is a standard instrument with simple instructions, which may be transported from one field setting to another. The development of the PRFT has made a differentiation task once again a possibility in cross-cultural research.

The basic task in the PRFT is to adjust a black rod to the upright, while viewing it in the context of a tilted square black frame. The task is performed with vision entirely blocked off at the sides and top, except for the long box at the end of which are the rod and the frame. Thus the requirement is to disembed one visual element from another, but this time with the assistance of bodily cues for the true vertical.

Eight trials are presented (after familiarization practice), two trials each for four different combinations of frame setting (28° left, 28° right). A score is assigned by summing the degrees away from true vertical for each of the eight rod settings; the larger the score, the less differentiated the performance. Thus, scores on PRFT are also reversed (by substructing from a constant) to yield scores consistent in direction with scores on the other tasks.

In addition to these three tasks, which are clearly related to the concept of differentiation, three other tests were employed. The first of these, Raven Matrices, has been employed in cross-cultural research very often (see reviews by Irvine, 1969b; Wober, 1969) and thus provides an excellent point of comparison for any cross-cultural investigation. The task in its elementary version (Raven, 1963) involves visual perceptual detection skills, although not necessarily of a disembedding nature (see Witkin and Berry, 1975: 74-75). It also involves an inferential task subsequent to the perceptual one, before the correct answer can be indicated. MacArthur (1973) refers to it as a test of ability to infer from nonverbal stimuli, and considers it (on the basis of factor-analytic study) to be intermediate in content between the cluster of verbal inferential tasks and a cluster of disembedding and spatial-type tasks.

As used in the three studies, the test involves three sets (A, Ab, B) of twelve items. Each set is more difficult than the one prior to it: set A is largely a pattern completion task involving visual detection with little inference required; set Ab is also a pattern completion task, but may be solved either by "gestalt" completion (global) or by "inferential" completion (analytic); and set B may be solved only by inferential completion from perceptual material.

Original conceptions of the test, were that it was a pure measure of "g" and might even be "culture-free" (Raven, 1963). And so for this reason there are grounds for including this test in any large-scale cross-cultural study; is it really free of cultural influences or is it patterned in some systematic way?

The test was not timed in the studies and was administered individually. Each item is followed by six possible answers, and the participant is encouraged to consider all possible answers before indicating a choice. Scoring in the standard way for the correct answer was carried out, so that a maximum score of thirty-six was possible. However, nonstandard scoring, by giving partial value to "better" or "worse" incorrect responses, may be carried out; indeed data from Study 1 have been reanalyzed by Jacobs (1968), and a high correlation was found between the two methods of assigning scores. ·

A second task, one designed to assess spatial ability, was employed in Study 1; this was the Morrisby Shapes (Morrisby, 1955). In addition to the conceptual reasons outlined in Chapter 3 in relation to differentiation theory, the primary reason for employing this task was that, on both functional and popular grounds, hunters should have a well-developed spatial ability: Spatial organization of one's surroundings is necessary for successful hunting, and in the case of some hunters (e.g., the Eskimo) popular stereotypes ascribe high spatial and mechanical (or applied spatial) skills to them.

Morrisby Shapes are extremely difficult to do well; they are sufficiently hard to permit selection of university graduates for postgraduate training! However, if spatial abilities of hunters are thought to be high, then a simple test would not be of much use. The test contains sixty items and has a ten-minute time limit. Each item contains three printed quadrilaterals (ranging from near squares to near rectangles to near parallelograms and trapezoids), and each quadrilateral has a small circular hole. Two of the quadrilaterals would "fit" (i.e., be exactly congruent, including the hole) one of top of the other, if they were given the same orientation; however, the third must be turned over and reoriented for it to "fit." The task is to indicate, for each of the sixty sets, which one quadrilateral is not able to "fit" without also being turned over. Training is provided by Morrisby through the use of obvious, printed examples. For Study1, even earlier training was provided by making cutouts of plastic and administering these so that the "turn over" and "orienting" manipulations could be experienced. Scoring was done with a correction for guessing, so that the final score was the total correct less one half those wrong, with a maximum possible of sixty.

Since the basic perceptual discrimination is prior to disembedding (and separate from it; Karp, 1966; Houston, 1969; Sack and Rice, 1974), it was considered that a task of discrimination might be employed as well. None was available in the standard test materials, and so a task was developed using a portable tachistoscope. (The speed was set at 20 MS using a camera shutter, and light was provided by a 0.25 amp./2.2 volt bulb powered by a 2.5 volt mercury cell. A black head cloth restricted extraneous light.) This task required a participant to draw what he had seen in the brief presentation. The targets were geometric shapes (squares, rectangles, triangles) with progressively large (from 0 to 15 mm.) gaps in one of their sides. At this speed and for very small gaps, none was detected and drawn; however, participants began to detect and reproduce larger gaps. A score was assigned (from 1 to 15) which was the size of gap first detected and drawn; a score of twenty was awarded those not detecting even the largest gap. One difficulty with this task was that not all participants were able to draw. Thus a prior screening task was used, which requested the pencil-and-paper reproduction of a variety of shapes while they were in full and continuous view. Those who could not draw these were not administered the test of discrimination in the tachistoscope.

Finally, tasks which are perceptually very basic were administered for screening purposes. These include tests of acuity (near at 2.5 cm, and far at 6

m) using the Landolt Rings, and checks for colour defects, using the Ishihara. In no case where these tests were used was a decision to include or exclude a potential participant based on acuity or colour tests results different from a brief question concerning problems of seeing; thus in Studies 2 and 3, these tests were dropped and replaced with a simple enquiry for the purposes of screening.

The bases for referring to a task as one of differentiation (or not) are both conceptual and empirical. And one must be in a position to establish the assertion both intraculturally and cross-culturally. First, within Western psychological study, Witkin et al. (1954, 1962) have clearly identified the Embedded Figures Test as the conceptual and empirical exemplar of differentiation; the Rod and Frame Test (and its portable version) also qualifies on this basis. The other task which we term one of differentiation is Kohs Blocks. On conceptual grounds, the task is appropriate, involving the analysis of complex visual designs; and the empirical evidence (e.g., Goodenough and Karp, 1961) is that the task loads on the same factor as differentiation tests. Thus we may conclude that these tasks are valid for the estimation of perceptual differentiation within Western cultural settings.

The three tasks which have been outlined, but which do not usually appear in the relation to psychological differentiation, are distinct on either conceptual or empirical grounds or on both. For Discrimination disembedding of a simple element from a complex organized context is not involved; rather the task is to detect an element from a fairly simple gestalt and was intended as an experimental analogy to the task facing the hunter. And although empirically it may correlate with differentiation tasks, we have already noted that it represents a different ability in factorial studies. For the other two tasks, the skills required may be more complex. For the Shapes, which were designed as a test of spatial ability by Morrisby, the task is to *orient* and *relate* geometric shapes, after they have been apprehended, and for the Matrices, the task is to make *inferences* geometric designs to complete a cognitive problem. On conceptual grounds, both do not involve disembedding. Once again, though, one mightreasonably expect to find higher-order relations, although matrices and spatial tasks do not generally load on the same factor as differentiation tasks (e.g., MacArthur, 1975; Witkin and Berry, 1975).

Turning to the cross-cultural use of these tests, how do we know whether they retain their conceptual and empirical meanings in other cultural settings? Both functional and conceptual equivalence (Berry, 1969) may be established by analyzing the nature of the tasks in relation to the ecological and cultural settings in which they are employed. And empirical meaning (metric equivalence, as discussed by Berry and Dasen, 1974: 18-19) may be established by examining such things as similarity of factor loadings of a test in differing cultural settings.

For the three differentiation tasks, conceptual equivalence was ensured through appropriate instruction and demonstration of the tasks, as well as by occasional probes for the participants' understanding of what they were supposed to be doing. Functional equivalence was also present for the tasks, in that in all ecocultural settings the task of disembedding was present in everyday life, although (as our model has considered it) to very different degrees.

In an earlier study, Dawson (1967) showed that EFT and Kohs Blocks loaded on one factor in two West African cultures, and MacArthur (1973) has confirmed this for other African samples and extended it to Eskimo samples as well. Since these two studies demonstrate metric equivalence for the two extremes of our own sample range, there is little reason to doubt that it is a fairly constant feature of the ecocultural dimension as a whole.

For the three other tasks, some evidence of empirical separation exists as well. MacArthur (1973) has shown that the Matrices load on a different factor than do Kohs Blocks or EFT in African and Eskimo samples, and we may conclude as before that this may be characteristic of the whole dimension. But there is no direct information available on the other two tasks' metric equivalence (or lack of it) with differentiation tasks. It would be somewhat surprising, however, to find such equivalence cross-culturally when it is generally absent intraculturally.

Overall, then, our classification of the six tasks can be supported on both conceptual and empirical grounds. Empirical tests by factor analysis on the present data, however, are not warranted, given the relatively small and heterogeneous samples gathered for the purposes of this study.

HYPOTHESES

As we argued in the presentation of the model (Chapter 4) and in the section on hypotheses (Chapter 6), the general expectation is (S:EC-1) for levels of differentiation to increase along the ecocultural dimension, from the "tight" sedentary end to the "loose" migratory end. Thus we expect performance on Kohs Blocks and the Embedded Figures Test to be patterned in that way, and for performance on the Portable Rod and Frame Test to be high in relation to established norms. Of the three other tasks, two are intimately related to ecological pressures experienced by hunters and gatherers; we thus expect performance on the Discrimination and Morrisby Shapes tasks to also range in a similar way with the ecocultural dimension. And finally, given the figural nature of Ravens Matrices, there is the expectation that test performance will be similarly patterned here as well; the restructuring of perceptual information, and making appropriate inferences to new geometric forms, are both conceptually related to the general cognitive style which has been outlined.

With respect to changes in perceptual differentiation test scores with acculturation, we outlined a general expectation (S:AC-1) that these would tend to become more like those in the culture exerting the Acculturative Influences. Given the generally high levels of Western performance found in the cross-cultural literature for these tasks, the expectation is that scores on all tasks would move in the direction of greater differentiation. Whether this anticipated change is indicative of greater differentiation or of greater test sophistication, or indeed of something else, is difficult to discuss at this point; and so we will be returning to it in Chapters 9 and 10.

Remaining at the group level, our expectation is that since ecocultural and acculturational factors are considered to operate in the same direction, a combined ecocultural plus acculturational index would be predictive of the distribution of differentiation scores (S:EC+AC-1).

Finally, turning to the individual level, hypotheses were advanced (I:EC-1 and I:AC-1) which predicted that individuals who reside in communities at the upper end of the ecocultural dimension, and in communities which have higher levels of acculturation, would exhibit higher scores on these tasks. Further, looking at individual predictions within samples, it was considered (I:SN-1 and I:ED-1) that those with greater self-reported socialization for assertion and those with higher levels of education would score higher.

RESULTS

For the three tests of differentiation, means and standard deviations are provided in Table 7.1. As we have already indicated, only the Kohs Blocks task was employed throughout: EFT was dropped after Study 1, while PRFT was added only in Study 3. Note that for EFT and PRFT scores are reported in nonstandard form. For EFT, means are subtracted from 1,080 (the theoretical maximum) and for PRFT means are subtracted from 50 (the approximate norm provided in Oltman, 1968); this was done so that a higher score would be indicative of higher differentiation.

Other test results are also reported in Table 7.1. Matrices, which were used throughout, are reported first, followed by Morrisby Shapes and the Discrimination task, which were used in only in Study 1. Note that for Discrimination, scores are reversed; means are subtracted from 15, which is the largest gap actually presented during the task.

Finally, for visual acuity, using the Landolt Rings, there were no differences apparent in any of the samples in Study 1 for either far (6 m) or near (25 cm) acuity: Over 90% of each sample scored better than 6/9 in far acuity and A.7 on near acuity. And for colour vision, using the Ishihara, only eight

TABLE 7.1
SAMPLE MEANS: SIX PERCEPTUAL TASKS

Study	No.	Name	Number	Kohs Blocks		Embedded Figures Test[1]		Portable Rod and Frame Test[2]		Raven Matrices		Morrisby Shapes Discrimination[3]			
				Mean	Sd	Mean	Sd	Mean	Sd	Mean	Sd	Mean	Sd	Mean	Sd
1.	1	Mayola	90	6.4	6.9	27.7	92.4			13.1	2.4	0.9	6.3	1.2	6.9
	2	Port Loko	32	15.6	14.6	148.9	234.0			13.9	3.8	0.2	5.2	3.2	7.1
	3	Pond Inlet	91	78.6	30.6	737.1	213.7			26.8	3.2	15.1	10.2	8.5	6.0
	4	Frobisher Bay	31	89.9	28.2	795.8	148.1			28.9	3.1	22.0	12.9	7.7	6.5
	5	Santa Teresa	30	39.9	17.3	588.6	235.5			23.2	4.4	7.2	8.0	6.2	5.9
	6	Yarrabah	30	50.7	19.6	624.8	276.2			24.7	5.4	11.6	9.7	6.2	5.3
	7	Telefomin	40	9.5	8.6	28.2	63.0			14.7	4.1	1.1	5.9	3.5	6.2
	8	Hanuabada	30	62.6	21.8	681.3	185.2			26.1	5.8	20.8	10.3	9.6	3.9
	9	Inverkeilor	62	90.2	33.2	744.3	237.7			29.5	4.9	16.4	14.2	6.7	5.8
	10	Edinburgh	60	90.3	31.6	813.5	208.8			31.0	4.2	14.2	14.3	5.9	6.5
2.	11	Wemindji	61	96.6	27.9					24.2	6.9				
	12	Fort George	60	96.3	35.6					25.3	7.9				
	13	Hartley Bay	56	81.8	27.1					27.7	5.4				
	14	Port Simpson	59	95.1	28.1					31.1	3.6				
	15	Tachie	60	115.3	20.1					28.1	6.8				
	16	Fort St James	61	92.4	29.2					26.2	4.8				
	17	Westport	48	101.6	24.0			22.8	8.7	30.5	3.4				
3.	18	Aroland	39	101.1	32.9			33.5	15.4	27.3	5.4				
	19	Longlac	37	99.1	29.0			34.0	9.3	27.2	5.4				
	20	Sioux Lookout	31	106.1	28.9			33.3	10.0	28.7	5.2				
	21	Sioux Lookout (Eurocanadian)	40	94.1	29.8			31.1	13.9	29.7	5.9				

Notes 1 Scores reversed by subtracting from 1080
       2 Scores reversed by subtracting from 50
       3 Scores reversed by subtracting from 15

partial defectives were found in the samples: three in Inverkeilor, two in Mayola, one each in Edinburgh, Yarrabah, and Frobisher Bay, and none in the other samples. Thus, on these basic sensory dimensions, no differences of importance were found.

Among these six tests, intercorrelations show consistent positive relationships as shown in Tables 7.2 and 7.3.

Relationships between these six tests and the variables of compliant socialization and western formal education are provided below. In Table 7.4 correlations between test performance and self-ratings on compliant socialization are indicated, while in Table 7.5, correlations are provided for years of formal education.

For our sample-level hypotheses, two distinct modes of evaluation are available: analyses of variance within each of the three studies (following the ANOVA designs outlined in Table 6.1), and correlational analyses over all samples in the three studies. The first mode permits the examination of variance within the three studies as they developed chronologically, respecting the integrity of the design of each study. The second mode recognizes that with the development of the two major indices (ecocultural and acculturational), a broader analytical strategy becomes possible.

When the eight samples of Study 1 are considered as four ecocultural settings by two levels of acculturation, analyses of variance yield a significant F-ratio on all tests for both ecocultural and acculturational level; these values are reported in Table 7.6. In the same table, F-ratios are reported for Study 2 (where the six samples are considered as three ecocultural settings by two levels of acculturation), and for Study 3 (where three levels of acculturation are considered within a single ecocultural setting). In all cases, significant F-ratios appear for the ecocultural independent variable, while in four of the analyses no significant effect was found for the acculturational variable.

Considering further the sample-level hypotheses over all samples in the three studies, data are presented graphically in Figures 7.1 through 7.5 and correlationally in Table 7.7.

In the five figures, sample means are plotted as a function of the ecocultural plus acculturational indices, and the value of these correlation coefficients which are indicated in Table 7.7 range from +.94 for Embedded Figures to +.76 for Raven Matrices. (Since PRFT was employed only in the third study, which did not range on the ecocultural dimension, data from it cannot be presented graphically or correlationally across samples.) These, of course, are based upon material aggregated to the sample level, where coefficients of such magnitude are not uncommon.

In the case of the other coefficients, all ecocultural correlations are significant and account for over fifty percent of the variance across samples. However coefficients with the acculturational variable are generally lower and

(text continued on page 162)

TABLE 7.2
TASK INTERCORRELATIONS: STUDY 1

No.	Name	KOHS	EFT	MATS	Shapes	Significance Levels
				Variables		
Study 1						
1.	Mayola					n=90
	EFT	.45	—			
	MATS	.37	.15	—		r>.17
	Shapes[a]	—	—	—	—	
	Disc	.07	.02	.11	—	p<.05
2.	Port Loko					n=32
	EFT	.59	—			
	MATS	.58	.55	—		r>.29
	Shapes[a]	—	—	—		
	Disc	.27	.22	.14	—	p<.05
3.	Pond Inlet					n=91
	EFT	.68	—			
	MATS	.60	.51	—		r>.17
	Shapes	.64	.48	.45	—	
	Disc	.34	.08	.15	.18	p<.05
4.	Frobisher Bay					n=31
	EFT	.66	—			
	MATS	.62	.54	—		r>.28
	Shapes	.57	.52	.38	—	
	Disc	.24	.38	.47	.29	p≤.05

5. Santa Teresa						
EFT	.68	—				n=30
MATS	.41	.46	—			r > .30
Shapes	.46	.44	.39	—		p < .05
Disc	.26	.10	.33	.21		

6. Yarrabah						
EFT	.79	—				n=30
MATS	.70	.78	—			r > .30
Shapes	.58	.51	.56	—		p < .05
Disc	.37	.40	.27	.24		

7. Telefomin						
EFT	.80	—				n=40
MATS	.58	.51	—			r > .25
Shapes	.61	.52	.58	—		p < .05
Disc	.85	.84	.81	.57		

8. Hanuabada						
EFT	.86	—				n=30
MATS	.48	.44	—			r > .30
Shapes	.43	.36	.38	—		p < .05
Disc	.14	.23	.12	.17		

9. Inverkeilor						
EFT	.84	—				n=62
MATS	.81	.70	—			r > .21
Shapes	.66	.51	.67	—		p < .05
Disc	.19	.13	.22	.15		

10. Edinburgh						
EFT	.72	—				n=60
MATS	.70	.62	—			r > .21
Shapes	.69	.54	.63	—		p < .05
Disc	.04	.02	.10	.11		

Note: All correlations are positive.

a. Insufficient variance for Shapes in Mayola and Port Loko.

TABLE 7.3
TASK INTERCORRELATIONS: STUDY 2 AND 3

| Sample | | Variables | | | Significance |
No.	Name		KOHS	MAT	PRFT	Levels
	Study 2					
11.	Wemindji	MAT	.36	–	–	n=61 r >.21 p <.05
12.	Fort George	MAT	.56	–	–	n=60
13.	Hartley Bay	MAT	.50	–	–	n=56
14.	Port Simpson	MAT	.54	–	–	n=59
15.	Tachie	MAT	.66	–	–	n=60
16.	Fort St James	MAT	.36	–	–	n=61
17.	Westport	MAT	.64	–	.28	n=48
		KOHS	–	–	.65	
	Study 3					
18.	Aroland	MAT	.73	–		n=39
		PRFT	.52	.48	–	
19.	Longlac	MAT	.23	–		n=37
		PRFT	.26	.37	–	
20.	Sioux Lookout	MAT	.57	–		n=31
		PRFT	.43	.32	–	r .27 p .05
21.	Sioux Lookout	MAT	.64	–		n=40
	(Eurocanadian)	PRFT	.36	.21	–	r .25 p .05

Note: All correlations are positive.

TABLE 7.4
TASK INTERCORRELATIONS WITH COMPLAINT SOCIALIZATION SELF-RATINGS[a]

Study	Sample		Variables					
	No.	Name	KOHS	EFT	PRFT	MAT	Shapes	Disc
1.	1	Mayola[b]	–	–		–	–	–
	2	Port Loko	+.64	+.48		+.20	–	+.18
	3	Pond Inlet[b]	–	–		–	–	–
	4	Frobisher Bay	–.06	+.01		–.17	+.07	+.16
	5	Santa Teresa	–.08/+.21	+.12/+.17		+.27/+.07	+.16/+.10	+.39/+.38
	6	Yarrabah	–.09/+.29	–.21/+.36		+.11/+.33	+.11/+.14	+.08/_.26
	7	Telefomin	+.21/+.06	+.13/+.07		+.17/+.13	+.20/+.12	0/0
	8	Hanuabada	+.42/+.42	+.37/+.31		+.23/+.36	+.31/+.26	+.28/+.15
	9	Inverkeilor	+.15	+.20		+.08	+.13	+.17
	10	Edinburgh	+.27	+.22		+.30	+.23	+.25

TABLE 7.4 (Continued)

Study	Sample No.	Name	KOHS	EFT	PRFT	MAT	Shapes	Disc
2.	11	Wemindji	+.09/+.12			+.29/+.18		
	12	Fort George	+.28/+.06			+.29/+.14		
	13	Hartley Bay	+.29/+.05			+.20/+.02		
	14	Port Simpson	−.06/+.47			−.02/+.16		
	15	Tachie	+.02/+.08			+.22/+.14		
	16	Fort St James	−.19/−.04			−.17/+.06		
	17	Westport	+.17/+.02		+.17/−.09	+.22/+.04		
3.	18	Aroland	+.30/+.26	—	+.02/−.05	+.38/+.24		
	19	Longlac	−.24/−.14		+.03/+.03	+.16/+.29		
	20	Sioux Lookout	+.22/+.13		+.44/+.14	+.31/+.32		
	21	Sioux Lookout (Eurocanadian)	−.16/−.22		−.01/−.03	−.09/−.19		
		Mean Correlations[c]	+.14	+.20	+.08	+.19	+.18	+.20

Note: See Tables 7.2 and 7.3 for significance levels.
a. Where two correlations are given, the first is for "Mother" and the second for "Father"; where one only, it is for "Parents".
b. In Mayola and Pond Inlet there is no variance on socialization rating.
c. After applying Fisher's transformation.

TABLE 7.5
TASK INTERCORRELATIONS WITH YEARS OF WESTERN EDUCATION

Study	No.	Name	KOHS	EFT	PRFT	MAT	Shapes	Disc
1.	1	Mayola[a]	—	—	—	—	—	—
	2	Port Loko	.57	.62	—	.57	—	.24
	3	Pond Inlet[a]	—	—	—	—	—	—
	4.	Frobisher Bay	.49	.37	—	.52	.45	.18
	5	Santa Teresa	.36	.61	—	.53	.33	.18
	6	Yarrabah	.20	.39	—	.48	.36	.17
	7	Telefomin[a]	—	—	—	—	—	—
	8	Hanuabada	.52	.43	—	.66	.29	.13
	9	Inverkeilor	.53	.38	—	.47	.40	.04
	10	Edinburgh	.51	.43	—	.47	.44	.10
2.	11	Wemindji	.35	—	—	.56	—	—
	12	Fort George	.53	—	—	.66	—	—
	13	Hartley Bay	.55	—	—	.47	—	—
	14	Port Simpson	.47	—	—	.24	—	—
	15	Tachie	.32	—	—	.42	—	—
	16	Fort St James	.40	—	—	.42	—	—
	17	Westport	.08	—	-.07	.23	—	—
3.	18	Aroland	.59	—	.18	.55	—	—
	19	Longlac	.22	—	.21	-.09	—	—
	20	Sioux Lookout	.21	—	-.19	.14	—	—
	21	Sioux Lookout (Eurocanadian)	.36	—	.11	.29	—	—
		Mean Correlation[b]	+.43	+.49	+.07	+.45	+.40	+.18

Note: See Tables 7.2 and 7.3 for significance levels
a. Insufficient variance for Mayola, Pond Inlet and Telefomin.
b. After applying Fisher's transformation.

TABLE 7.6
ANALYSES OF VARIANCE FOR THE THREE STUDIES: F-RATIOS FOR SIX TASKS

Level		KOHS Blocks	Embedded Figures	Ravens Matrices	Morrisby Shapes	Discrimination	Rod and Frame
Study 1							
Ecocultural	F=	159.1	200.4	199.6	136.2	7.43	—
	p	.001	.001	.001	.001	.001	—
Acculturational	F=	57.3	64.2	63.5	47.9	3.81	—
	p	.001	.001	.001	.001	.001	—
Study 2							
Ecocultural	F=	3.9	—	17.3	—	—	—
	p	.05	—	.001	—	—	—
Acculturational	F=	4.4	—	1.5	—	—	—
	p	.05	—	NS	—	—	—
Study 3							
Acculturational	F=	0.83	—	1.71	—	—	0.31
	p	NS	—	NS	—	—	NS

Task

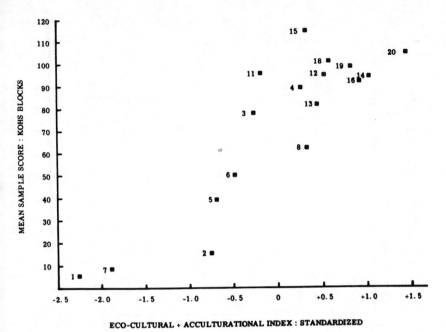

FIGURE 7.1 Mean Sample Score on KOHS Blocks as a Function of Sample Position on the Ecocultural + Acculturational Index

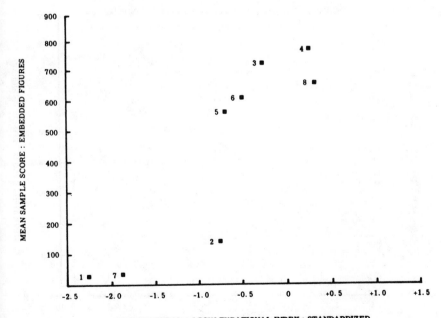

FIGURE 7.2 Mean Sample Score on Embedded Figures as a Function of Sample Position on the Ecocultural + Acculturational Index

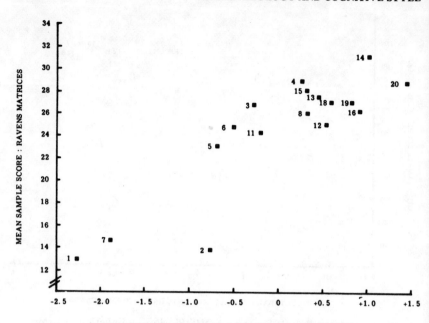

FIGURE 7.3   Mean Sample Score on Ravens Matrices as a Function of
Sample Position on the Ecocultural + Acculturational Index

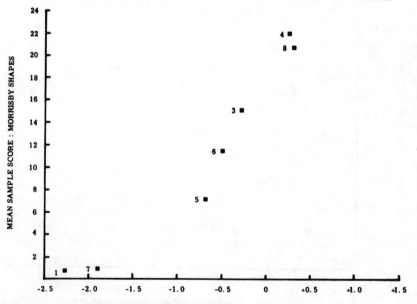

FIGURE 7.4   Mean Sample Score on Morrisby Shapes as a Function of
Sample Position on the Ecocultural + Acculturational Index

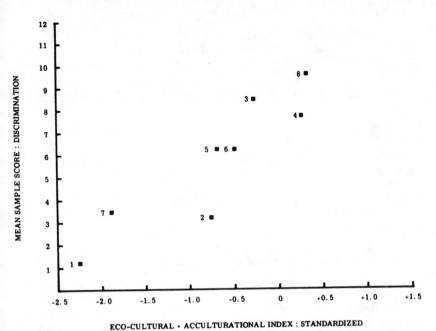

ECO-CULTURAL + ACCULTURATIONAL INDEX : STANDARDIZED

FIGURE 7.5   Mean Sample Score on Discrimination as a Function of Sample Position on the Ecocultural + Acculturational Index

TABLE 7.7
SAMPLE-LEVEL CORRELATIONS BETWEEN INDICES AND FIVE TASKS

Index	Tasks				
	KOHS	EFT	Matrices	Shapes	Discrimination
Simple					
Ecocultural	.73	.88	.74	.74	.77
Acculturational	.65	.38	.63	.48	.51
Combined					
EC + AC	.77	.94	.76	.83	.91
Multiple	.92	.97	.92	.89	.93
Number of Samples	17	8	17	8	8

Note: All correlations are positive for n=17, r > .40, p < .05 and for n=8, r > .60, p < .05.

TABLE 7.8
INDIVIDUAL-LEVEL CORRELATIONS
BETWEEN INDICES AND FIVE TASKS

	Task				
	KOHS	EFT	Matrices	Shapes	Discrimination
Simple					
Ecocultural	.65	.84	.56	.76	.36
Acculturational	.47	.32	.50	.27	.16
Education	−.28	.22	−.10	.16	−.05
Combined					
EC + AC	.67	.79	.66	.71	.40
Multiple	.72	.87	.70	.79	.43
Number of Individuals	793	364	814	358	247

Note: All correlations are positive except those indicated, and all are significant
(p <.05) except Education by Discrimination.

are significant in only two of five cases (Kohs Blocks and Raven Matrices). Multiple correlations are all substantial, and with their use it is possible to account for eighty percent and more of the variance across these samples.

At the level of individual scores, Table 7.8 provides a set of correlation coefficients for each of the five tasks. At this individual level, the magnitude of coefficients is generally lower, but in all cases both the ecocultural and acculturational indices are significant. And when their multiple correlation is computed, between fifty and seventy-five percent of the variance is accounted for except in the case of the Discrimination task. In addition to correlations with the two indices, Table 7.8 also provides the simple correlation with individual experience of western education; in all cases it is lower in magnitude and is negative for three of five tasks. However, it must be recalled here that, within samples, education generally correlates significantly and positively with these tasks (Table 7.5). The appearance of these lower, and even negative, coefficients in this analysis indicates the overriding role of ecocultural variables across samples when they are pooled across cultures.

With these data before us, we may now turn to a consideration of their relation to the hypotheses.

DISCUSSION

The data which have just been presented are complex and require a good deal of examination. Specifically how they relate to the hypotheses and some further relationships (for example, their age and sex patterning) will be considered here; more general relationships with other data, and with the model, will be considered in Chapters 8 and 9.

Our hypotheses were outlined at two levels (sample and individual), and for the sample-level hypotheses, there are two (ANOVA and correlational) modes of evaluation. First, the analyses of variance within each of the studies has provided fairly consistent support for the hypotheses dealing with differentiation task performance (S:EC-1; S:AC-1) as a function of ecocultural and acculturational influences. For Kohs Blocks and EFT in Study 1, and for Kohs Blocks in Study 2, both factors were significant. However, in Study 3 no significant effect was found for acculturation.

A similar, but less consistent, picture emerged for the other tasks, with the Matrices varying by ecocultural level in Studies 1 and 2, and by acculturation level in Study 1 (but not in 2 or 3). And for the shapes and the Discrimination task, both ecocultural and acculturation factors were significant in Study 1. Over both differentiation and realted tasks, then, the ecocultural factor was significant in all cases, while acculturation was significant in six of ten cases.

In the graphical presentation of the distribution of sample means (Figures 7.1 to 7.5), there is a clear relationship in each case between the standardized ecocultural plus acculturation index and the standardized sample mean. (These graphs point up quite clearly both the relative sampling emphasis upon hunting and gathering groups, and the scarcity of samples in the low-middle range of the overall dimension. Given the emphases present in the literature upon agricultural samples [mainly in Africa], this first bias is not problematic; on many of these tasks, samples have yielded mean scores in the range indicated here by Mayola, Port Loko, and Telefomin [see, for example, Dawson, 1967; MacArthur, 1973, and Witkin and Berry, 1975]. The second bias [few samples in the low-middle range of the dimension] is also minimally problematic. Moderately acculturated agricultural samples [for example, with lower educational levels than in Port Loko] are now fairly well-studied [see, for example, the above references] and they, too, provide evidence for similar performance on some of these tasks.) These relationships appear to approach linearity in the case of Kohs Blocks, EFT, and Discrimination, while there is an indication of a leveling at mid-range for the Matrices, and some acceleration at mid-range for the Shapes. For the Matrices, this may represent a "ceiling effect," since the maximum score possible was thirty-six. And for the Shapes, the scoring procedure which deducted points for wrong answers may have contributed to the shape of the curve in the lower ranges of the dimension.

In our correlational analyses (Table 7.7) we find general support for both hypotheses (S:EC-1 and S:AC-1), although the ecocultural index emerged as more substantial and consistent than the acculturational index. As we noted, when their multiple effect is analyzed, the proportion of the variance across samples which may be accounted for ranges between eighty percent and ninety-four percent. By any standard, these levels of relationship are substantial and indicate the power of these two independent variables in the determination of a sample's position in the range of cognitive development.

While these sample-level analyses are supportive of the hypotheses, it is important (for both methodological and pragmatic reasons) to ask whether individual-level prediction can also be attained. In Table 7.8, the simple and multiple correlations between the indices and all individuals across samples were reported. Although lower in magnitude than the sample-level coefficients, there remains a significant and substantial set of intercorrelations. It is apparent that the power of these two independent variables is not confined to the prediction of mean sample performance, but may be usefully employed in the analysis of individual differences as well. It is important to note, however, that this analysis has retained the two indices as sample, rather than individual, characteristics; that is, there is still some element of aggregation in these coefficients. Nevertheless, the cognitive measures are taken individual by individual, and with the use of these indices, individual prediction is clearly possible.

One interesting contrast in correlations is between the within-sample relationship and the across-sample relationship with education (I:Ed-1). In Table 7.5, mean correlations ranged from +.07 to +.49, while in Table 7.8, correlations ranged on either side of the zero point. The most obvious interpretation is that individual education becomes masked by ecocultural experience when the latter is varied. However, when it is held constant (as in the intrasample correlations in Table 7.5), the effect of education can be observed. If we accept as valid these intrasample relationships with education, an interpretive task remains: What does education do to performance? We will be returning to this question in Chapter 10.

Our final hypothesis concerns the influence of socialization upon performance on these tasks. Implicit in the above sample analyses has been a socialization component, since the sample compliance-assertion ratings constituted a major element in the ecocultural index. At the individual level, Table 7.4 provided a complex set of relatively low-level correlations. Although many reach statistical significance, on the whole they do not account for much of the variance. A number of possibilities exist for explaining this minimal relationship. First, it could be the case that the socialization link to differentiation noted by Witkin et al. (1962) and Dyk and Witkin (1965) does not hold up cross-culturally. However, given the substantial relationships found in the group-level analyses with the ecocultural index, this is unlikely to be the case. Indeed in separate analyses at the sample level employing the socialization variables (both the compliance-assertion ratings and the self-ratings), correlations ranged between +.59 and +.77 for the former and +.71 and +.87 for the latter. Clearly socialization is not irrelevant to the distribution of mean sample scores. It is possible, then, to argue that socialization appears to be an important variable, but one which has not been assessed adequately at the individual level in this study. Recalling our earlier comments regarding the error inherent in respondent ratings of parents, especially when they are retrospective, perhaps it is not surprising to find such a low overall set of relationships.

Of the seven hypotheses examined in this chapter all have received significant support. Cognitive style has been shown to vary systematically with ecological variation and with acculturation, while the role of adaptive cultural features has also been implicated. Perhaps most importantly, the basic patterning of the data has been shown to stem from the ecological setting in which individuals develop; acculturation brings with it some inevitable modifications, but they appear to be no more than "variations on a theme." This is, of course, what would be expected from the notion of "style" which Witkin et al. (1962) have introduced. For if a "style" dissappears in the face of new circumstances, it is scarcely a personal style, but nothing more than a fleeting behaviour under the influence of external circumstances. This question of the source of basic patterning will be considered again in Chapter 9 where we will attempt to allocate relative contributions to these patterns of behavioural variations through multiple regression analysis.

Of course correlation cannot by itself demonstrate causation; inferences based upon both theoretical and empirical arguments must be brought to bear on the observed relationships. While we will be considering this question fully in Chapter 9, it is important to recall here that these relationships were expected on the basis of both cultural and psychological theory, and that the proposed mechanisms which connect ecological to cultural to behavioural elements were deliberately built into the model and the hypotheses. Alternative or rival hypotheses (including chance) may eventually be held to account for these observed relationships, but at this point the links appear to be strong.

To complete this discussion, three topics of general interest deserve to be considered: relationships among the cognitive tasks, sex differences in performance on the tasks, and developmental trends.

Task Interrelationships

With respect to task interrelationships, correlations were reported sample by sample in Tables 7.2 and 7.3. These may be supplemented (in Table 7.9) by two further analyses: One is at the sample level in which the seventeen sample means are employed; the other is at the individual level in which all

TABLE 7.9
SAMPLE AND INDIVIDUAL-LEVEL CORRELATIONS
AMONG TASKS[a]

	Tasks				
Tasks	*KOHS* $n=17$	*EFT* $n=8$	*Matrices* $n=17$	*Shapes* $n=8$	*Discrimination* $n=8$
KOHS n=793		.95	.89	.94	.89
EFT n=364	.89		.96	.91	.92
Matrices n=814	.74	.87		.94	.93
Shapes n=358	.52	.59	.62		.91
Discrimination n=247	.42	.37	.42	.39	

Note: All correlatons are positive and significant (p < .05)
a   Sample-level correlations are above the diagonal; individual-level correlations are below the diagonal.

individuals scores are employed. Sample-level coefficients appear above the diagonal, and individual level coefficients appear below it.

It is clear that all correlations are substantial. However they do range in magnitude in a fairly systematic way. The two differentiation tasks (Kohs and EFT) are most strongly related to each other (.89 and .95). From that starting point, at both levels of analysis, there is a mutually consistent lowering of coefficients through the Matrices to the Shapes to Discrimination. This effect is most apparent at the individual level. In this pattern lies some support not only for a "style" interpretation, but also for the hierarchical model outlined in Chapter 3. That is, the differentiation . . . core (kohs and EFT being conceptually a part of the differentiation . . . structure correlates the most strongly, while Discrimination, not involving any disembedding, correlates the least strongly. And the spatial (Shapes) and inferential (Matrices) tasks correlates the least strongly. And the spatial (Shapes) and inferential (Matrices) tasks correlate at an intermediate level consistent with their analytical and restructuring requirements. Without claiming that this evaluation of the correlation matrix constitutes a validation of the hierarchical conceptualization, it is important to note that the pattern of correlation is consistent with such a formulation. To actually test such a hierarchial scheme, what is required in future research is for large batteries of tests to be employed with large samples (both intraculturally and crossculturally), and for factor analysis to be undertaken. Only then might the formulation receive the check which is required for a formal validation.

Sex Differences

Another issue which may be considered is the presence or absence of sex differences in these six test results. In the intracultural literature, there has been a fairly consistent finding of males scoring higher than females on differentiation tasks. The cross-cultural approach presents an excellent opportunity for the assessment of the universality of such a phenomenon; and the ecocultural perspective provides a value-free framework within which to operate.

It is clear from our earlier discussion of socialization family practices and social pressures toward conformity that these vary with ecological press; there is also evidence that this variation is not constant in its impact upon boys and girls growing up in these various ecocultural settings (Barry et al., 1957). In general, there is an overall greater emphasis on nurturance and responsibility for girls, and on achievement and self-reliance for boys, in the samples included in their study. Further, in pastoral and agricultural societies, responsibility and obedience were emphasized for both boys and girls, while in hunting societies achievement was emphasized for both. Thus it is likely that sex differences might not be present in hunting societies, especially if in other social practices (in addition to socialization) sex equality is also apparent. Our discussion in Chapter 5 of Eskimo and Cree social life suggests that such equality is present; indeed there is an Eskimo proverb that "a man is only as good a hunter as his wife is a seamstress," implying equal role valuation and respect.

The patterning of sex differences in the six tasks is presented in Table 7.10; note that in these point biserial correlations, a positive sign indicates a higher male score, while a negative sign indicates a higher female score. It is clear that many coefficients at the "loose" end are negative, while at the "tight" end they are positive. A statistical check on the significance of this relationship for the two differentiation tasks can be made by correlating the ecocultural index of the seventeen samples with the positivity of the task-by-sex correlation.

These statistics (+.81 and +.76, respectively, for Kohs Blocks and EFT) indicate substantial support for this hypothesis. And for the three other tasks (Matrices, Shapes, and Discrimination) positive correlations are also found (+.36, +.37, and +.84, respectively) between ecocultural position and the degree of sex differences in the sample. These findings indicate that sex differences are not constant across the samples, but vary according to the ecocultural setting of the group. While true for all tasks, this patterning is most clear for the two differentiation tasks, and for Discrimination. Although on the average males tend to score higher on these tasks (32 of 51 coefficients are positive), which is consistent with the usual findings in western samples,

TABLE 7.10
PERCEPTUAL TASK BISERIAL CORRELATIONS WITH SEX[a]

Study	Sample		Variables					
	No.	Name	KOHS	EFT	PRFT	MAT	Shapes	Disc
1.	1	Mayola[b]	+35	+30		+26	–	+11
	2	Port Loko[b]	+21	+45		+05	–	+40
	3	Pond Inlet	-06	-08		+06	-07	-13
	4	Frobisher Bay	+11	-01		+08	+02	-28
	5	Santa Teresa	+16	+04		-28	-13	-20
	6	Yarrabah	+13	+34		+31	+26	+04
	7	Telefomin	+30	+41		+25	+31	+61
	8	Hanuabada	-03	-14		-28	-09	+06
	9	Inverkeilor	+04	+04		+03	+11	+26
	10	Edinburgh	+28	+33		+23	+16	+18
2.	11	Wemindji[c]	-51			+08		
	12	Fort George[c]	-47			+09		
	13	Hartley Bay	+19			+15		
	14	Port Simpson	+23			+05		
	15	Tachie	0			+26		
	16	Fort St James	+09			+22		
	17	Westport	-16		-08	-09		
3.	18	Aroland	-17		-31	-10		
	19	Longlac	-04		+01	-13		
	20	Sioux Lookout	+16		-09	+10		
	21	Sioux Lookout (Eurocanadian)	-11		+26	-12		

Note　a. Female is coded 1, male 2.
　　　b. Insufficient variance for Shapes in Mayola and Port Loko.
　　　c. In Wemindji and Fort George all female participants were tested by one (female) investigator; the high negative correlations between Kohs and sex may in part be an experimenter effect.

this cross-cultural patterning indicates that it is a variable relationship, one which is adaptive to the economic and stratification variables from which the ecocultural index is constructed.

Age Differences

The developmental course of differentiation and other perceptual tasks has been of interest intraculturally; the issue of the cross-cultural course, whether it is similar or different, has been an open question. In western settings, performance on differentiation tasks tends to peak around twenty-five and then decline slowly. The same trend appears in these samples, except that sharper dropping off is characteristic of the older groups in some of the samples. However, this phenomenon may be due largely to variation in acculturation level across ages. In most samples there is a negative correlation between age and education, and when this is partialled from the age by task correlation, significance is generally reduced.

Chapter 8

ACCULTURATION AND DIFFERENTIATION

Our model has anticipated two kinds of behavioural change as a function of acculturation. The first has been termed "behavioural shifts" where the general expectation is that behaviour in acculturating samples will shift away from their "traditional" levels in the direction of behaviour which is characteristic of the community providing the acculturative influences. The second has been termed "acculturative stress"; included here are those behaviours which are novel and problematic reactions and which are often associated in the literature with the turmoil of social change. We have seen, in the previous chapter, that shifts in level of psychological differentiation tend to be in the direction of the larger society in which a sample is located; this finding confirms the general expectation about shifts in behaviour derived from our model. It also demonstrates the malleability of behaviour in the face of new influences which are independent of the ecologically adaptive process which nurtured the original behavioural development.

However, many field observations suggest that behaviour is not infinitely malleable during acculturation, that a point will be reached where societal and personal systems will break down under the stress of change, and problematic behaviour will emerge (e.g., Hallowell, 1951; Chance and Foster, 1962; Fried, 1964; Vallee, 1968; Spradley and Phillips, 1972). From a practical point of view, although it is important to understand the changes which occur in the levels of differentiated and other behaviours in acculturating communities, it may be even more important to comprehend the disruptive behaviours which will emerge and perhaps interfere with these behaviours. However, our model anticipates that these two classes of behaviour will be related, in at least two ways, so that in the study of the psychological effects of acculturation, both should be included.

[171]

At the level of individual functioning, a relationship is expected on the basis of the central meaning of psychological differentiation: that a person is able to disembed item from context, self from environment, and has available a set of internal referents. Although acculturative influences may be pervasive in a community, affecting both daily life and social institutions, it is predicted that each individual in the community will experience these pressures to a different extent, depending on his level of psychological differentiation. That is, those individuals who are highly differentiated will be able to maintain the self in the face of change and will thereby suffer less stress, while those who are less differentiated will be more embedded in the cultural changes and will thereby suffer greater stress. If the notion of a personal "style" has any meaning, its test will come precisely during the process of external change; if a behavioural cluster is truly characteristic of an individual, and not solely an instantaneous function of his environment, then we should expect to find a persistence of the style during change (as we have already noted in the two previous chapters) *and* a relationship between this style and the experience of the change. On this basis, then, our clear expectation is that, in all samples, individual differences in differentiated behaviour will be negatively related to manifestations of acculturative stress.

This expectation of a negative relationship between differentiation and acculturative stress has at least two other plausible bases. The first is simply that the experience of stress will impair performance on differentiation tasks, or in more extreme cases that de-differentiation will actually occur when the organism is under sufficient pressure. This possibility will be considered later when the pattern of our data has been presented. Another source for expecting a negative relationship is in the very nature of adaptation. In Chapter 2, we considered briefly three varieties of adaptation: *adjustment, reaction,* and *withdrawal.* As we have seen in the last chapter, in most cases there is a shift in the characteristic level of differentiated behaviour as a function of acculturation; behaviour usually adjusts to the new situation. However, this is not a complete phenomenon; correlations are less than unity across samples with acculturation, and the more acculturated sample usually approaches, but does not reach the new norm. So we may conclude that adjustment does not always occur (nor does it occur in all persons), that attempts at reaction or withdrawal may also be present in our samples. If this is so, given the nature of acculturating settings, these two alternative modes of adaptation are likely to be unsuccessful; the new authority structure usually does not permit reaction and withdrawal may be economically difficult. Thus we may conclude that some individuals adjust by way of shifting their level of differentiation, and others do not and experience acculturative stress; this dual pattern of adaptation would, of course, result in a negative correlation between differentiation and stress measures. This possibility will also be considered once again after our data have been displayed.

At the group level, on the basis of these arguments, our expectation might be that the higher the typical sample performance on tasks of perceptual differentiation, then the lower will be the average experience of acculturative stress. However simple and elegant such an expectation, there are features of acculturating communities which raise some serious questions for it, and suggest some alternative expectations. One may ask: What are the most pervasive features of the acculturating influences (urbanization, education, and wage employment); how do they relate to features of societies which are ranged along the ecocultural dimension; and how do they relate to differentiated behaviours?

Perhaps the most pervasive features of these acculturative infleunces is the social and political pressures they carry; social and political stratification are inherent in the nature of Western society, especially in the colonial atmosphere which pervades areas undergoing acculturation. In the process of urbanization, higher population densities are experienced, rules become more numerous, and authorities exert powerful controls; these all lead to greater social and political influence and normative restriction. During education, quite apart from *what* is taught, the process involves rules of attendence, seating, responsiveness to authority, and formal examination. And for wage employment, more rules of attendence, performance, and general conduct are imposed. Thus the dominant change may be described as an increase in social control exercised by neighbors and authorities over the day-to-day behaviour of the individual.

A second feature of these acculturative influences is the emphasis which is placed on good educational and job performance. Insofar as perceptual differentiation may be associated with educational achievement and the carrying out of technical operations, one might expect that high perceptual differentiation would be congruent with the acculturative demands. However, it is usually the case in such communities that educational and occupational opportunities are minimal (see, e.g., Bigart, 1972; Robbins, 1973). Thus, although one might expect perceptual differentiation to be congruent with the needs of an industrializing community, and hence valued by it, there is no indication that such valuing is extant; on the contrary, unskilled roles are usually assigned to those completing education and seeking wage employment.

What is apparent, then, is that the acculturative influences primarily bring to bear a heavy emphasis upon acceptance of social control and authority. A reasonable hypothesis, therefore, is that those communities where such norms are well developed in the traditional life of the people (that is "tight") will be far better prepared for these pressures than those which were traditionally "loose" in their social organization. Thus, we expect that acculturative stress will appear with higher frequency in traditionally migratory and "loose" communities which are undergoing acculturation, while stress will be lower for those who were traditionally sedentary and "tight."

However, this expectation raises an important problem: How is it possible for nomadic samples (which as we have seen typically exhibit higher levels of perceptual differentiation) to also exhibit higher levels of acculturative stress, given our earlier expectation that at the individual level of analysis, differentiated behaviour should be negatively related to stress? Any possible answer to this difficulty can be considered only after a detailed examination of our empirical relationships. We thus turn to such an examination, beginning with an outline of the variables and measures subsumed under the term "acculturative stress."

CONCEPTS AND SCALES

Many concepts and measures have been proposed as suitable for the assessment of the psychological disturbance which often accompanies acculturation (Coelho, 1972). And just as many concepts and measures have been proposed to describe the nature of the sociocultural changes which precipitate it (Triandis, 1973). For the purposes of the present study the specification of this latter variable has already been made in Chapter 6, where the index of acculturation was derived from the three variables of mean sample education, the availability of wage employment, and the degree of urbanization. This purely descriptive index has been developed in an attempt to avoid the more culturally and politically loaded terms such as "Westernization" and "modernization." Similarly, the specification of the psychological variable is made in terms of general psychological stress rather than in the more value-loaded terms such as "culture shock," "mental health," or "personal adjustment." Thus a relatively neutral variable has been proposed (Berry, 1971a) to reflect the nature of both antecedent and dependent variable components of the phenomenon-acculturative stress. As we noted in the presentation of the model, there are three variables subsumed under the general title of acculturative stress: psychosomatic stress, feelings of marginality, and attitudes toward modes of relating to the society bearing the acculturative influences.

Psychosomatic Stress

The notion of *stress* has become very popular in the last decade, particularly in psychological studies, but also in anthropology (e.g., Appley and Trumbull, 1967; Naroll, 1959; Spradley and Phillips, 1972). Most uses of the term may be traced to the original work of Selye (1956) who argued that, at the physiological level, the *General Adaptation Syndrome* is a common reaction of organisms to stressors in the environment. This syndrome is comprised of three states. The first (alarm reaction) includes an initial *shock phase* (in which resistance is lowered) and a *counter shock phase* (in which defensive mechanism become active). The second stage is one of resistance, leading in most cases to organismic adaptation to the stressor. And finally, if the stressor continues and/or the resistance is unable to maintain adaptation, the third state, of exhaustion begins, during which adaptive responses cease. Thus, in response to an environmental situation which requires some adjustment by the organism (the stressor), the body enters a general adaptation syndrome (a state of stress), and as a result, exhibits certain behaviour, called stress responses.

For many researchers (Chance, 1965; Cawte et al., 1968; Langner, 1962); these stress responses are clearly exhibited in somatic responses or symptoms; and when the stressors are sociocultural and psychological, the responses are referred to as psychosomatic. Following this research tradition, our most direct measure of acculturative stress is a checklist of psychosomatic symptoms. Of the many which are available, the one selected as the most suitable was the twenty-item version of Cawte et al., (1968) which had been developed for cross-cultural use from the longer Cornell Medical Index of Brodman et al. (1952). These twenty items were selected on the basis of clinical judgment and factor analyses for stable components, using data from Aboriginal populations in Australia. The items are divided into six categories: seven items are labelled "somatic," one "exhaustion," two "other," six "anxiety," two "paranoid irritability"; these items are provided in Table 8.1.

Participants were asked to indicate their answers with a simple "yes" or "no." In most cases, these answers were given with little hesitation, and in those cases where qualifications were requested or offered, a repetition of the instructions usually resulted in the answer being given in these terms. Scoring is based upon assigning a one to "yes" and zero to "no"; thus a maximum score of twenty and a minimum of zero was possible. No attempt was made to validate the responses, for it is an assumption of the test that the real existence and the imagined existence of these symptoms are both significant psychologically and are important in the same sense.

In all settings, the checklist was administered in the preferred language of the participant. For the Amerindian translations, a procedure of back translation (Brislin, 1970) was employed, until forward and back versions were identical. And for all items, since they deal with basic human difficulties, few problems were experienced in making equivalent forms; perhaps this translation ease is due to the prior selection of these items for cross-cultural relevance and stability by Cawte and his asociates.

TABLE 8.1
PSYCHOSOMATIC STRESS CHECKLIST

Item Number	CMI Number	A: Somatic
1.	7	Do you have pains in the heart or chest?
2.	11	Do you usually belch a lot after eating?
3.	13	Do you constantly suffer from bad constipation?
4.	14	Do your muscles and joints constantly feel stiff?
5.	16	Is your skin very sensitive or tender?
6.	19	Do you suffer badly from frequent severe headaches?
7.	20	Do you often have spells of severe dizziness?
		B. Exhaustion
8.	32	Do you usually get up tired and exhausted in the morning?
		C: Other
9.	35	Do you wear yourself out worrying about your health?
10.	39	Do you usually have great difficulty in falling asleep or staying asleep?
		D: Anxiety
11.	44	Do strange people or places make you afraid?
12.	46	Do you wish you always had someone at your side to advise you?
		E: Depression
13.	47	Do you usually feel unhappy and depressed?
14.	49	Do you often wish you were dead and away from it all?
		D: Anxiety (continued)
15.	50	Does worrying continually get you down?
16.	54	Are you extremely shy or sensitive?
		F: Paranoid Irritability
17.	59	Does it make you angry to have anyone tell you what to do?
18.	60	Do people often annoy or irritate you?
		D: Anxiety (continued)
19.	61	Do you often shake or tremble?
20.	65	Do you often break out in a cold sweat?

Source: From Cawte et al. (1968).

Marginality

Our second measure within the concept of acculturative stress is a scale of *marginality*. This concept itself has been a major one in the history of scientific attempts to understand the nature of acculturation. Originated by Park (1928) and Stonequist (1937), the theory of marginality was an attempt to comprehend the psychological and social condition of persons caught between two cultural systems; being "poised in psychological uncertainty" between two worlds, neither one fully accepting, was argued to be the condition of the marginal man. The theoretical and empirical history of the concept has been difficult; as a theory, it was severely criticized for its limited generality (Antonovsky, 1956), and empirically it was minimally examined. With the publication of a major monograph by Dickie-Clarke in 1966, and an earlier report by Mann (1958), the study of marginality became a focal one; and with the recent volume of studies edited by Gist and Dworkin (1972) it has attained the status of a valid research question once again.

A major distinction has been drawn (Dickie-Clarke, 1966) between the "marginal situation" and the "marginal personality" (or "psychological marginality"). The former is a sociocultural variable; it is a set of conditions characteristic of culture contact between two (or more) groups, one dominant over the other, where a new culture (or "subculture") emerges which is marginal to both the contributing cultural systems. The latter is a set of feelings or traits thought by Park and Stonequist to be characteristic of individuals caught in the marginal situation; these included aggression, suspicion, and ambivalence. Whether these characteristics are associated with the marginal situation is an empirical question; some support for this expectation has indeed been found by Kerckhoff and McCormick (1955), Mann (1958, 1973), and Berry (1970).

A convenient measure of psychological marginality has been developed by Mann (1958), in part from the earlier scale of Kerckhoff and McCormick (1955). It consists of fourteen items (called the "Revised M Scale"), and was employed by Mann with a sample of coloureds in South Africa who are marginal to both the African and European segments of the population. With that sample, Mann was able to identify three factors which he termed "insecurity feelings," "self-pity," and "sensitivity." This scale is provided in Table 8.2.

Scoring the scale is based upon a one being assigned to an answer which is in agreement with the statement, and a zero to non-agreement. It was intended originally to elicit answers in terms of strong agreement and strong disagreement as well, but these were very rare in the response style of these samples. Thus a simple dichotomized scoring is used, identical to that employed for the stress checklist. A maximum score of fourteen and a minimum of zero are thus possible.

TABLE 8.2
MARGINALITY SCALE

1.	Successful people do their best to prevent others from being successful too.
2.	I feel that nobody really understands me.
3.	I am so restless that I cannot sit in a chair for very long.
4.	People seem to change from day to day in the way they treat me.
5.	Life is a strain for me.
6.	I suddenly dislike something that I liked very much before.
7.	If others hadn't prevented me, I would be far better off than I am now.
8.	I feel that I don't belong anywhere.
9.	I wish I could be as happy as others.
10.	I let myself go when I am angry.
11.	I am more nervous than most people.
12.	I feel that I am somehow apart from the people around me.
13.	I regret the decisions I have made.
14.	The world is a dangerous place full of evil men and women.

Source: From Mann (1958).

Relational Attitudes

One of the features of the marginal situation, as it has been described, is the dual nature of the experience; ambivalence in attitudes is said to be a major problem for the marginal man. Although one may examine many different areas of attitude content, the one issue which emerges in informal discussion and in pilot research is "How shall we relate to the two societies between which we live?" In the psychological laboratory, there is strong evidence for the discomforts of attitudinal inconsistency (e.g., Triandis, 1971) and in field situations Dawson (1975) has repeatedly shown that individuals may be caught between "traditional" and "modern" life styles and experience substantial conflicts.

But in many settings, serious conflict may not be experienced if some sociopolitical compromises are possible between these two poles; in such settings conflict and ambivalence may not be experienced. In an early study of this issue (Sommerlad and Berry, 1970), the question was posed to Australian Aboriginal populations in terms of ways in which they would like to relate to the dominant Australian society. The choices were conceptualized as favouring "assimilation," "integration," or "rejection," with scales of nine, nine, and six items respectively being developed for their assessment. As noted in Table 8.3, no necessary oppositions were built into the items, so that the conflict would not necessarily attend the responses.

Each item in Table 8.3 is coded as an assimilation, integration, or rejection item. These designations are derived from a conceptual framework which raises two questions and provides two dichotomous answers to them. The first is whether traditional culture is valued and should be retained, or whether it is not valuable and should be given up; the second is whether positive relations with the larger society should be sought, or whether the larger society should be kept as distant as possible. The four possible answers

TABLE 8.3
ATTITUDES TOWARDS MODES OF GROUP RELATIONS

Item Number	Sub Scale	
1.	R	The Indians should be completely self-sufficient so they do not need to co-operate with the whites in any way.
2.	I	It is better if an Indian marries with one of his people rather than with a white.
3.	A	Any Indian who is successful should try to forget that he is of Indian descent.
4.	R	It is better for the Indians to stay on their reserves than to come into the city where they encounter difficulties.
5.	R	The Indians should only co-operate with the whites when they have something to gain.
6.	I	Having a National Indians Organization is not really a good idea since it makes the Indians different from other Canadians.
7.	R	There are no aspects of the whites' culture that might be beneficial to the Indians.
8.	A	The Indians should co-operate as little as possible with the whites.
9.	A	The only real way an Indian can become successful is by dissociating himself from other Indians.
10.	A	Any Indian living within the white community should try and behave in the same way as those around him.
11.	I	The Indians should do all they can to ensure the survival of their people.
12.	A	Although it is alright for Indian parents to maintain their cultural differences within the white community, they should encourage their children to be just like other Canadians
13.	A	The social activities of the Indians should be restricted to the Indians themselves.
14.	A	If a number of Indians are working on the same job, they should be put in the same section so they are together.
15.	I	Encouraging the Indians to stay as a group is only hindering their acceptance into the community.
16.	I	Most of the Indians living in the city today are not really interested in knowing anything about the life or culture or their ancestors.
17.	R	The Indians should lead their own way of life, independently of the rest of society.
18.	I	So little remains today of the Indian culture that it is not really worth saving.

TABLE 8.3 (Continued)

Item Number	Sub Scale	
19.	I	Focusing attention on the Indians' traditional way of life is only preventing them from making any progress in society.
20.	I	The Indians should seek their friends among other Indians.
21.	A	The Indians should act as a separate community in every way within society.
22.	I	Indian children should be encouraged to choose other Indians as their playmates.
23.	A	If an Indian sets up his own business, he should try and employ Indians to work for him.
24.	R	The fact that Canada has only developed since the arrival of the whites clearly shows that the Indians must follow the example of the whites if they themselves are to make any progress.

to these two questions are indicated in Table 8.4 and labelled as assimilation, integration, rejection, and deculturation.

For items in the "assimilation" subscale, the notions of giving up traditional culture and moving into the larger society are phrased in various ways, while for items in the "integration" subscale, the notions of both retaining traditional culture and pulling together with the larger society are expressed. And for items in the rejection subscale, the notions of cultural retention away from the larger society are included. The fourth combination (deculturation) is not given expression in the scales, since both common sense and pilot work indicated that such an outcome was not to be chosen by anyone; however, some features of the concept of marginality are related to feelings in this combination.

When these questions are posed to Amerindian peoples, individual scores on the three subscales may be obtained, using a five-point Likert scale (strongly agree, agree, uncertain, disagree, strongly disagree). In the case of these attitudes, extreme responses were fairly frequent, and so a 5, 4, 3, 2, 1 scoring was retained. When these questions are posed to Euro-Canadian samples, the phrasing is in terms of their attitudes toward how Amerindian peoples *should* be relating to the larger society. In this case, then, the rejection (self-segregation) which was implied when Amerindians respond may be interpreted as a conventional segregation attitude on the part of the Euro-Canadian samples. For the nine-item subscales (assimilation and integration) the maximum possible score is forty five, the minimum nine, and the mid-point twenty seven; and for the six-item rejection (segregation) subscale the maximum is thirty, the minimum six, and the mid-point eighteen. However, in reporting the results for these scales, deviations above or below the mid-point are used.

TABLE 8.4
TWO MAJOR QUESTIONS
CONFRONTING ACCULTURATING COMMUNITIES

		Is traditional culture of value and to be retained?	
		Yes	No
Are positive relations with the larger society to be sought?	Yes	Integration	Assimilation
	No	Rejection (Segregation)	(Deculturation)

RESULTS

Sample means for the constituents of acculturative stress are provided in Table 8.5. Since these variables were introduced after the completion of Study 1, only the samples in Studies 2 and 3 are included.

Within each of the three scales, item-to-total correlations are generally substantial. For stress, they range from +.23 to +.57, with a mean of +.44; for marginality, they range from +.35 to +.68, with a mean of +.51. Within the three attitude scales, item-to-total correlations are within similar ranges, with mean correlations of +.39, +.35, and +.53 for assimilation, integration, and rejection, respectively. And among the three attitude scales, total-to-total correlations are generally as expected (from the a priori analysis in Table 8.4), with assimilation and rejection correlating negatively (-.19), assimilation and integration also correlating negatively (-.28), and integration and rejection correlating positively (+.09).

We may ask how these various scales relate to one another, and whether, empirically, there is sufficient clustering to warrant the more general notion of "acculturative stress." Relationships among these variables are presented in Table 8.6, for each of the Amerindian samples, and (for comparison purposes) for the two Euro-Canadian samples.

It is clear that, for our two primary variables, there is a solid grouping of responses; however, for our relational attitude variables, a more complex pattern of lower correlations is apparent.

As the major variable of acculturation, we consider the relationships of formal education and the acculturative stress variables to be of importance; these coefficients are presented in Table 8.7.

It is clear that consistent negative relations exist in the Amerindian samples between educational level and feelings of stress and marginality. And an equally clear picture emerges for correlations with relational attitudes; assimilation and integration are accepted with increasing education, while the opposite is the case with rejection.

For our sample-level hypotheses (S:EC-2; S:AC-2), both analyses of variance within studies and correlational analyses across studies may be employed

TABLE 8.5
SAMPLE MEANS: ACCULTURATIVE STRESS SCALES

Study	Sample		Variables				Relational Attitudes		
			Stress		Marginality		Assimilation	Integration	Rejection
	No.	Name	Mean	Sd	Mean	Sd	Mean	Mean	Mean
2.	11	Wemindji	6.43	4.1	6.30	3.4	−2.70	+4.28	+2.13
	12	Fort George	7.03	4.2	5.20	3.0	−1.72	+3.23	+1.07
	13	Hartley Bay	4.07	3.3	3.25	2.6	+1.88	+2.55	−2.49
	14	Port Simpson	5.08	3.9	2.88	2.3	+0.91	+2.38	−0.98
	15	Tachie	5.71	4.2	3.86	3.2	+0.02	+3.30	−0.70
	16	Fort St. James	5.20	3.5	4.30	3.2	+0.80	+3.38	−0.57
	17	Westport	1.79	2.3	1.89	2.3	+3.50	+0.98	−2.86
3.	18	Aroland	3.94	2.3	3.29	2.3	+0.50	+1.76	+1.08
	19	Longlac	6.00	4.5	5.73	3.4	+0.92	+1.33	+1.58
	20	Sioux Lookout	5.07	3.3	3.77	2.8	+0.97	+2.20	−1.53
	21	Sioux Lookout (Eurocan)	2.95	2.7	1.83	1.9	+2.35	+1.20	−4.15

TABLE 8.6
ACCULTURATIVE STRESS VARIABLES: INTERCORRELATIONS

Study	No.	Name	Stress x Marginality	Assim	Stress x Integ	Rej	Assim	Marginality x Integ	Rej
2	11	Wemindji	+.71	−.08	−.05	+.26	−.15	−.09	+.36
	12	Fort George	+.76	−.52	−.03	+.05	−.18	−.07	+.31
	13	Hartley Bay	+.66	+.14	−.29	+.06	−.01	−.17	+.06
	14	Port Simpson	+.51	+.05	−.15	+.23	−.05	−.22	+.01
	15	Tachie	+.69	−.06	−.33	+.46	−.03	−.21	+.45
	16	Fort St. James	+.64	−.36	−.02	+.43	−.02	−.22	+.28
	17	Westport	+.69	+.28	0	−.24	+.31	−.02	−.30
3	18	Aroland	+.58	−.08	−.27	+.09	−.02	−.29	+.34
	19	Longlac	+.61	−.19	−.19	+.09	−.03	−.35	+.23
	20	Sioux Lookout	+.76	−.08	−.15	+.26	−.04	−.27	+.31
	21	Sioux Lookout (Eurocanadian)	+.66	−.02	+.07	+.15	+.18	+.08	−.07
		Mean	+.71	−.18	−.19	+.23	−.07	−.24	+.29

Note: Mean correlation is calculated across 9 Amerindian samples only; Fisher's transformation employed.

TABLE 8.7
ACCULTURATIVE STRESS VARIABLES INTERCORRELATIONS WITH EDUCATION

Study	Sample		Variables				
	No.	Name	Educ x Stress	Educ x Marginality	Educ x Assim	Educ x Integ	Educ x Rejection
2.	11	Wemindji	−.29	−.36	+.33	+.06	−.32
	12	Fort George	−.43	−.61	+.55	+.07	−.54
	13	Hartley Bay	−.27	−.37	+.16	+.15	−.38
	14	Port Simpson	−.18	−.17	+.02	+.03	−.25
	15	Tachie	−.04	−.04	+.24	+.22	−.19
	16	Fort St James	−.34	−.24	+.30	+.21	−.20
	17	Westport	−.13	+.08	−.13	+.15	−.13
3.	18	Aroland	−.16	+.21	+.18	+.10	−.14
	19	Longlac	−.21	−.11	+.27	+.15	−.30
	20	Sioux Lookout	+.04	+.01	+.10	+.17	−.03
	211	Sioux Lookout (Eurocanadian)	−.05	+.01	−.13	+.13	−.04
	Mean		−.24	−.21	+.28	+.14	−.27

Note: Mean correlation across 9 Amerindian samples only; Fisher's transformation employed.

TABLE 8.8
ANALYSES OF VARIANCE FOR THE TWO STUDIES:
F-RATIOS FOR FIVE SCALES

Level	Scale				
	Stress	Marginality	Assimilation	Integration	Rejection
Study 2					
Ecocultural F=	4.6	24.4	430.1	177.6	38.8
p <	.01	.001	.001	.001	.001
Accultura-tional F=	0.4	1.2	0.5	0.9	0.3
p <	NS	NS	NS	NS	NS
Study 3					
Accultura-tional F=	6.1	14.3	1.9	0.7	22.8
p <	.001	.001	NS	NS	.001

in their evaluation. When the six samples in Study 2 are considered as three ecocultural settings by two levels of acculturation, analysis of variance yields a significant F-ratio on all scales for ecocultural but not for acculturational level. These F-ratios are summarized in Table 8.8.

In the same table, data are provided for Study 3, showing significant variation by acculturation for three of the five scales; in this study, no effect of ecocultural placement could be examined.

Considering further the sample-level hypotheses, Table 8.9 provides correlations between the two indices and the five scales, and the multiple correlation when both indices are taken into account. Note that no hypothesis was advanced for the EC + AC index, since the expected relationship with each single index was in opposing directions. Indeed, as Table 8.9 indicates, each pair of coefficients does relate in opposite directions, and they do relate substantially, with only three of ten coefficients failing to reach significance. When the multiple correlation is considered, between twenty-five percent and eighty percent of the variance across samples can be accounted for.

At the individual level (I:EC-2, I:AC-2), Table 8.10 provides coefficients between each individual's scale score and the index of the community in which he resides. In addition, the simple coefficient for education is indicated, and the multiple correlation (for the ecocultural and acculturational variables) is provided. At this individual level, coefficients with the two indices are all substantial and in the expected direction. However, correlations with level of education are generally lower but consistent with the sign of the coefficient for the acculturational index. It is of interest to compare these coefficients with education with those mean coefficients in Table 8.7; the results of the two analyses are substantially in agreement. The multiple correlations can account for twenty-five percent to fifty percent of the

TABLE 8.9
SAMPLE-LEVEL CORRELATIONS BETWEEN
INDICES AND FIVE MEASURES

Index	Measures				
	Stress	Marginality	Assimilation	Integration	Rejection
Simple Ecocultural	+.44	+.70	−.69	+.25	+.80
Acculturational	−.44	−.76	+.80	−.64	−.79
Multiple	.51	.84	.86	.66	.90
Number of Samples	9	9	9	9	9

Note: For n = 9, r ⩾ .58, p <.05

variance; this is somewhat less than was the case for the sample-level analyses, but nevertheless it is clearly a high level of individual prediction.

A final hypothesis (I:Int-1) concerns the interaction between acculturative stress and cognitive scores. In Table 8.11, correlation coefficients are provided for within-sample relationships. Across the nine Amerindian samples, mean correlations range from −.19 to −.57, all supporting the predicted negative relationship between these two sets of variables.

TABLE 8.10
INDIVIUDAL-LEVEL CORRELATIONS BETWEEN
INDICES AND FIVE MEASURES

Index	Measures				
	Stress	Marginality	Assimilation	Integration	Rejection
Simple Ecocultural	+.45	+.43	−.59	+.50	+.31
Acculturational	−.41	−.46	+.66	+.29	−.39
Education	−.19	−.23	+.28	+.19	−.17
Multiple	.69	.67	.71	.56	.49
Number of Individuals	433	423	453	453	453

Note: All correlations are significant (p < .05)

TABLE 8.11
ACCULTURATIVE STRESS AND COGNITIVE TASK SCORES: CORRELATIONS IN AMERINDIAN SAMPLES

Study	Sample		Correlations Among Variables					
			Stress x			Marginality x		
	No.	Name	KOHS	Matrices	PRFT	KOHS	Matrices	PRFT
2	11	Wemindji	-.28	-.47	—	-.30	-.32	—
	12	Fort George	-.03	-.01	—	-.54	-.56	—
	13	Hartley Bay	-.09	-.36	—	-.15	-.24	—
	14	Port Simpson	+.09	-.09	—	+.10	-.06	—
	15	Tachie	-.26	-.30	—	-.08	-.17	—
	16	Fort St James	-.20	-.27	—	-.01	-.36	—
	17	Westport	+.12	+.23	-.04	-.05	+.10	+.10
3	18	Aroland	-.39	-.28	-.57	+.11	+.04	-.08
	19	Longlac	-.64	-.39	-.43	-.28	-.06	-.22
	20	Sioux Lookout	-.32	-.44	-.54	-.28	-.22	-.36
	21	Sioux Lookout (Eurocanadian)	-.29	-.11	-.11	-.20	+.14	-.24
		Mean	-.29	-.35	-.57	-.19	-.25	-.26

Note: Means correlations across 9 Amerindian samples only; Fishers transformation employed.

DISCUSSION

In our last chapter the question of "shifts" in behaviour with acculturation was considered. And in general we found that most of the behaviours examined did indeed move away from levels which were characteristic of the more traditional samples, and in many cases, the "shifts" were in the direction of the norms found in the culture which was providing the acculturative influences. But as we noted, these shifts were essentially "variations on a theme"—they were relatively minor changes in what was basically an adaptation to ecocultural factors. This conclusion though, should not lead to the judgement that acculturation is an unimportant factor in the lives of many traditional peoples. For, as we have attempted to show in this chapter, the second kind of behavioural change, that of acculturative stress, is a basic phenomenon in its own right and is related to these other background and behavioural variables in systematic ways.

At the group level, across samples, we proposed (S:EC-2) that those cultural groups at the "loose" end of the ecocultural dimension would experience the greatest acculturative stress. The basis for this expectation was that stress would be induced by inconsistencies and dissimilarities in social structure and authority patterns which exist between the traditional samples and those bringing the acculturative pressures; the greater inconsistency exists for hunting, migratory, and low stratified ("loose") societies, and hence we expected greater stress to appear there.

In both ANOVA and correlational assessments (Tables 8.8 and 8.9) general support emerged for this hypothesis. All five F-ratios were significant by ecocultural level, and three of five correlations with the ecocultural index reached significance. Such a pattern of relationships with ecological and cultural factors is taken as an indication that stress may indeed be induced by a discrepancy between sociocultural systems. The cultural and psychological preparation for dealing with urbanization and authority which varies across the ecocultural dimension appears to be a likely factor in the distribution of acculturative stress. Of course other interpretations are possible, and other mediating factors may be suggested; one which is readily apparent is that these variations in acculturative stress may reflect more the levels of "traditional stress" to be found in hunting-based societies, rather than any feature of the acculturative situation. Whatever the interpretation, the empirical variation of acculturative stress with ecocultural position is difficult to deny. However, there are two reasons for considering its variation to lie primarily in factors associated with acculturation. One is the parallel between these results and those in the literature on stress levels among immigrants, and the other is the fairly systematic correlations between the stress phenomena and level of acculturation.

The general relationship between the experience of acculturative stress and ecocultural factors may be the counterpart of an emerging finding in the study of migrant adaptation to their new countries. In this area of research, it is a common finding (see, e.g., Fried, 1964; Krupinski, 1967) that individuals who change their cultural milieu through migration experience higher rates of mental breakdown and psychosomatic symptoms than the host population. Inconsistencies between the cultures of the migrant and the host country are thought to be responsible for this general phenomenon. Little work has been done trying to relate the relative cultural dissimilarity to stress, although this could be done easily though the analysis and rating of cultural variables (similar to the present use of traditional cultural archives). However, some recent work by Murphy (1965, 1969) has demonstrated that higher rates of breakdown are not always the case; in culturally plural host countries, where the migrant can find a culturally similar community, the usual findings do not apply. It is apparent that the variable of cultural inconsistency or dissimilarity may be approached not only by considering source and host cultural elements, but also by examining the organization and diversity of culture within the host country. When this is done, a result emerges which is similar to that found in the study of Amerindian response to acculturation: The greater the cultural dissimilarity, then the greater the psychological stress.

Our other hypothesis at the group level was that the experience of acculturative stress would be related to the amount of acculturative pressures borne by the sample (S:AC-2). In Study 2, there was no variation by acculturation on any of the five scales, employing ANOVA. However in Study 3, significant variation appeared for stress, marginality, and rejection; for them the highest scores were in the transitional sample (Longlac) and the least in the traditional one (Aroland).

With correlational analyses (Table 8.9) the pattern becomes a little more clear: Four of the scales correlate significantly, and all are negative (with the exception, of course, of assimilation). Thus, although not as strong a pattern of relationship as with ecocultural position, the level of acculturation is systematically related to the mean sample level of stress. For this reason (as well as for its parallel to the findings with migrants), it appears that the phenomenon of acculturative stress exists in part as a function of acculturation.

At the individual level of analysis, the hypotheses (I:EC-2, I:AC-2, and I:ED-2) predicted that individual scores on the five scales would be related to ecocultural position and to acculturation. In Table 8.10 correlations with the two indices were all significant, and in the direction anticipated by the hypotheses. This pattern of results supports the one emerging from the sample-level analysis. In terms of the magnitude of the coefficients, the individual correlations are generally lower, but the multiple correlations are still able to account for between and twenty-five and fifty percent of the variance.

Of particular interest is the somewhat lower level of correlation between the five scales and experience of Western education in Table 8.10 when compared with Table 8.7. One possible reason for this is that, as in the case of the cognitive style variables in Chapter 7, the ecocultural position of an individual may override education when all individuals are pooled across ecocultural systems. Another possible reason is that there may be a curvilinear relationship between education in particular (and acculturation level more generally) and the experience of acculturative stress. There is some evidence (see Berry, in press, for a review) that the course of psychological problems often studied in relation to acculturation may rise with initial contact, reach a crisis, and thereafter subside. Indeed, such a pattern is apparent in Study 3, where the mid-level sample in terms of acculturation (Longlac) exhibited higher stress scores than both the more traditional and more acculturated samples.

The final hypothesis (I:INT-1) was concerned with relationships between cognitive and acculturative stress variables. In Table 8.11, the hypothesis was examined employing three cognitive style and two stress measures within samples. Although not supported in every case, the overall pattern and the mean correlations are fairly clear: There tends to be a negative relationship between individual measures of cognitive style and acculturative stress.

The operative factors, however, cannot easily be specified. Our hypothesis was based originally upon a conceptual analysis of what it means to be differentiated—to be independent of environmental events, to keep self separate from context and to have internal self-referents available. But two other plausible explanations were mentioned in the introductory section of this chapter. The first of these considers the possibility that stress comes first, independently of differentiation, but interferes with (and depresses) performance on differentiation tasks; and the third relates to the nature of the adaptive process itself—if differentiation is adaptive (adjustive) in acculturating settings (but has not been well developed), then reactive (stress) behaviour is the only alternative.

The first of these is not difficult to discount, at least on the basis of intracultural literature. First, there is considerable evidence to show that there is marked stability of differentiation, even over time periods where stress has been experienced (e.g., Kraidman, 1959; Witkin et al., 1967). Second, there is evidence to indicate that a "stress interference" interpretation is not likely, at least among those with higher levels of differentiation, for those who are differentiated have often shown better adaptation to stress (e.g., Lapidus, 1968; Markus et al., 1970). Both sets of studies indicate that differentiation, in a sense, is a "prior" characteristic; it remains stable in the face of stress and indeed helps in its control. And, of course, our own data in Chapter 7 show that levels of differentiation are essentially patterned by ecocultural factors, while acculturation plays a variation on a theme: If a behaviour is indeed a "style," it must exhibit this characteristic stability. The second alternative interpretation has evidence both for and against it. There may very well be something tautological about the inverse relationship between differentiation and stress; that is, logically if one cannot adapt (i.e., adjust one's differentiation score upward) then one must react (i.e., exhibit higher stress levels). This, in fact, is indicated by the inverse relationship found between rejection attitudes and the differentiation tasks. On the other hand, differentiation task scores went up in the more acculturated pair of the two samples from a single cultural group, and there is no sign of enlarged standard deviations in the acculturated samples, both of which might have indicated that some individuals adapted their performance, while others could or did not. We may conclude then that we are observing a real psychological phenomenon, rather than a tautological one, that acculturative stress and differentiation are systematically related behaviours, and that this relationship is a function of the basic nature of differentiation.

SCALE INTERRELATIONSHIPS

As in the case of the cognitive style variables, it is useful to consider to what extent the five acculturative stress variables actually relate to one another. In Table 8.6 evidence was presented for a substantial degree of covariation between stress and marginality within samples (mean r = +.71). Lower levels were observed between these two variables and the three relational attitudes. Further data are presented in Table 8.12, where sample-level correlations appear above the diagonal, and individual-level coefficients appear below it. At the sample level of analysis, there is substantial intercorrelation, supporting the use of the general concept of acculturative stress. A less substantial set of relationships appears at the individual level of analysis, but it is still one which supports the use of an overall concept. Clearly, stress and marginality are mutually highly related; so too are the three relational attitudes among themselves. In all three analyses there is a consistent positive covariation of stress, marginality, and the attitude of rejection; there is also a consistent negative covariation between stress, marginality and rejection on the one hand, and the attitude of assimilation. Integration and assimilation attitudes are also consistently negatively related, but for integration an inconsistent pattern is evident; at the sample level of analysis relationships are positive with stress and marginality, while at the individual level, relationships are weak but negative. Overall, then, there is a clear and consistent pattern of relationships among four of the five variables; this suggests that we are dealing with a psychological cluster which warrants the use of a single term to cover the concept. Within this cluster, those who exhibit high stress also experience

TABLE 8.12
SAMPLE AND INDIVIDUAL-LEVEL CORRELATIONS
AMONG ACCULTURATIVE STRESS SCALES

Scale	Scale				
	Stress *n=9*	Marginality *n=9*	Assimilation *n=9*	Integration *n=9*	Rejection *n=9*
Stress n= n=433		+.80	−.84	+.75	+.54
Marginality n=423	+.58		−.91	+.85	+.72
Assimilation n=453	−.24	−.27		−.72	−.87
Integration n=453	−.17	−.22	−.45		+.45
Rejection n=453	+.28	+.26	−.24	+.31	

Notes: Sample-level correlations are above the diagonal; individual-level correlations
are below the diagonal.
All correlations are significant (p $<$.05)

a high degree of marginality and hold an attitude of rejection toward the larger society. Conversely those who are low in stress are low in marginality and tend to have an attitude of assimilation toward the larger society.

Sex Differences

As in the case of the cognitive style variables, the question of sex differences often arises in the distribution of psychosomatic stress. A good deal of evidence exists, in the general literature, which shows females tending to have higher responses on psychosomatic symptom checklists (e.g., Dorhenwend and Dorhenwend, 1969). And in the cross-cultural literature, similar sex differences have been apparent (e.g., Chance, 1965; Cawte et al., 1968). In these Amerindian samples, point biserial correlations between sex and stress and marginality are −.13 and −.02, both indicative of slight but nonsignificant overall higher scores for female respondents. However in Table 8.13 there are variations from sample to sample in this coefficient, one which is similar to those found in the case of the cognitive variables. Employing the same correlational strategy here as we did in Chapter 7, we find a correlation of −.91 between the sex-by-scale coefficient and the ecocultural index for stress, and −.52 for marginality. That is, the "tighter," more stratified the society, the more likely it is that, within samples, females will be more

TABLE 8.13
SEX DIFFERENCES IN STRESS AND MARGINALITY
POINT BISERIAL CORRELATIONS BY SAMPLE

	Sample	Stress x Sex	Marginality x Sex
11	Wemindji	−.01	+.07
12	Fort George	+.08	+.09
13	Hartley Bay	−.22	+.02
14	Port Simpson	−.30	−.08
15	Tachie	−.16	−.08
16	Fort St James	−.33	−.16
18	Aroland	−.13	−.17
19	Longlac	−.01	−.09
20	Sioux Lookout	−.11	−.07

Female coded 1; Male coded 2

stressed than males. Conversely, the "looser" the society, the more likely it is that males will be more stressed; but it must be remembered that the overall pattern is for females to have higher stress levels generally. For marginality, the pattern is less strong: The overall sex difference is zero across the nine samples, there is less deviation above or below the zero point sample by sample, and the correlation between positivity of the coefficient and ecocultural index is only −.52. Nevertheless, it conforms to the same general pattern which we noted for stress; this should not be surprising given the high correlation between the two variables within each of the samples.

We find once again, then, that it is not possible to claim any simple relationship between sex of respondent and a psychological variable across cultures. The degree of sociocultural "tightness" of a society must be taken into account, and, when it is, a striking consistency appears not only for cognitive style, but also for acculturative stress.

Age Differences

Another demographic factor which has often been associated with stress intraculturally is the age of respondent. In general, as individuals grow older, there is an increase in the somatic difficulties which are experienced, perhaps quite apart from any problems associated with social change. Across cultures, where often aging is physically a more difficult process (in the absence of adequate medical care), correlations might be expected to be fairly substantial between stress variables and age. In our nine Amerindian samples, this is generally the case; Table 8.14 provides these correlations.

TABLE 8.14
STRESS AND MARGINALITY WHOLE AND PARTIAL CORRELATIONS WITH AGE AND EDUCATION

Sample	Stress				Marginality			
	Age		Education		Age		Education	
	whole	*partial*	*whole*	*partial*	*whole*	*partial*	*whole*	*partial*
11 Wemindji	+.37	+.25	-.29	-.07	+.35	+.17	-.36	-.19
12 Fort George	+.33	+.01	-.43	-.30	+.48	+.02	-.61	-.43
13 Hartley Bay	-.06	-.24	-.27	-.28	-.13	-.40	-.37	-.52
14 Port Simpson	-.03	-.16	-.18	-.29	-.26	-.43	-.17	-.40
15 Tachie	-.08	-.15	-.04	-.12	-.14	-.23	-.04	-.18
16 Fort St James	+.20	0	-.34	-.28	+.11	-.05	-.24	-.28
18 Aroland	+.29	+.26	-.16	+.06	-.17	+.05	+.21	+.12
19 Longlac	+.12	+.03	-.21	-.22	-.16	-.24	-.11	-.20
20 Siouc Lookout	+.14	+.13	+.04	+.01	.+.06	+.05	+.01	0
Mean	+.17	+.01	-.24	-.19	+.01	-.14	-.22	-.27

Note: Mean correlations calculated with Fisher's transformation.

However, cross-culturally it is not possible simply to examine age and stress correlations, because education and age are often so highly correlated themselves; and since education (as an indicator of acculturation) has already been implicated in the etiology of these stress scores, it is important to examine relations with both of them similtaneously. Table 8.14 also provides partial correlations for age, and again for education, with the other factor partialled out.

These analyses essentially confirm our original finding of a negative relationship between stress variables and education: Mean whole correlations were -.24 and -.22 with stress and marginality, respectively, and our mean partial correlations are now -.19 and -.27, respectively, with education. Thus, in general, age has not made much difference to the strength of the overall relationship between the stress variables and education; the two samples where there is a fairly large change are Wemindji and Aroland, both relatively low in mean education.

However, these analyses do show that age is not as significant a coefficient overall in the samples, either in their whole or partial form; for stress the correlations drop from +.17 to +.10, and for marginality they decline from +.01 to -.14 when education is partialled out.

TWO ACCULTURATIVE STRESS PARADOXES

In our discussion of sample- and individual-level hypotheses, we noted an apparant paradox in relations between stress variables and the ecocultural placement. Essentially we predicted (and found) that those who are differentiated within a group will exhibit less acculturative stress, while those groups which are toward the "loose" end of the ecocultural dimension would experience stress more. Given that in Chapter 7 we found the "loose" samples to have higher levels of differentiation, there is an apparent inconsistency in the patterning of our findings. The resolution of this problem may be found in examining the level of analysis which we have employed. On the one hand, the ecocultural analysis is at the level of the group—one index number for each group; the same is true for the level of differentiation and acculturative stress, at least when we wish to examine their relationship to ecocultural level. On the other hand, differentiation exists in our data at the individual level. There is a range of individual scores within the group, and this is true also for acculturative stress variables. These levels and relationships are indicated schematically in Figure 8.1.

That the mid-point of the perceptual differentiation variables (at each of the three hypothetical levels) is predictable from the ecocultural index, or in turn is predictive of the mid-point on the acculturative stress variables, is not logically inconsistent with the inverse correlations across the distributions

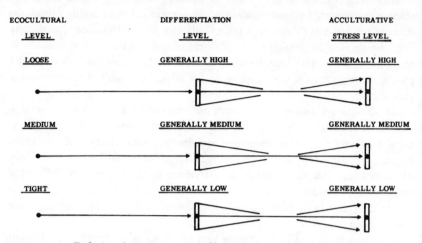

FIGURE 8.1   Relationships Between Differentiation and Acculturative Stress

within groups between these two sets of variables. What is intriguing (but not inconsistent) is how these inverse relationships within group distributions remain fairly constant across the larger distribution between groups. A possible answer is that since each sociocultural group establishes its own sets of cultural and behavioural norms (a basic element in the definition of culture), discontinuities will be culturally defined, rather than psychologically defined. That is, high or low differentiation will be viewed by members of a culture group in relation to the distribution of differentiation within that group; the "fact" that it is really high, medium, or low in some worldwide distribution (as viewed by an omniscient psychologist) is irrelevant to the experience of stress by individuals within that culture. This interpretation is consistent with the repeated finding of negative coefficients in samples, regardless of their location on some etic dimension, whether it be ecocultural placement or position on the total differentiation or stress dimensions.

A second question may be posed: How is it that acculturative stress responses tend to diminish as experience of acculturation increases? We have noted that, theoretically, acculturative stress is conceived of as stress induced by acculturation; but we have also noted that, empirically, both individual and group scores on stress variables are negatively correlated with estimates of acculturation. At the individual level, the question may be resolved fairly easily: as acculturative influences persist, individuals become more similar to the culture bearing the influences, and stress behaviours diminish. At the group level, the question involves more steps. The initial clue to providing an answer lies in the patterning of stress variables within cultures in the present study and in the general literature. In our Amerindian samples, there is some evidence of a curvilinear relationship between stress variables and acculturation. It is apparent in the three Ojibway samples, where the relatively traditional sample (Aroland) exhibits a low mean on stress and marginality; both measures are much higher as the transitional sample (Longlac) but decline again as the more acculturated group (Sioux Lookout). Since only *pairs* of samples are available for the other Amerindian cultures, this pattern cannot be tested. However, there is now a large literature (see Berry, in press, for a review) suggesting that such a curvilinear course is a general one for many psychological variables associated with social change. In marginality and identity studies of migrants, such "crises" of transition are common; a less stressful state both precedes and follows a mid-period of turmoil.

If this general pattern is operating in Amerindian communities (and the Ojibway pattern suggests that it is) then the acculturation level of the samples included in a particular study will determine whether positive or negative relationships between stress and acculturation variables should be expected. In the samples included in this study, none was at a period of initial culture contact, while some (for example, Sioux Lookout and Port Simpson) were highly acculturated. Thus an overall negative relationship is plausible, although there is some sample-by-sample evidence (e.g., Wemindji to Fort George and Aroland to Longlac) for acculturative stress increases in the lower range of acculturation.

We have now examined the patterning of differentiation as a function of ecological, cultural, and acculturational factors, and the patterning of acculturative stress as a function of these background variables and differentiation variables. We have also, within each behavioural domain, tested some hypotheses which stemmed from our model. What remains is to examine these findings in relation to the model itself and to ask whether there are better ways to fit our variables together. And finally we will want to enquire about the meaning and uses of these findings. We turn now to a consideration of the patterning of differentiation (in Chapter 9) and a search for some implications (in Chapter 10).

Chapter 9

THE PATTERNING OF DIFFERENTIATION

Over the past two chapters, we have presented the results of our studies; essentially we have described the nature of our findings and have done this primarily in the context of our hypotheses. Much more may be said, however, about the way these data cohere, the way they relate to the model, and the way they could be used to modify the model for the future study of differentiation. In this chapter, we provide an over view of the findings from the last two chapters, and we will be attempting to examine these data from three further but related points of view. First, we will consider the question of how the behavioural data cohere across the three studies and across the two chapters; how do they relate among themselves, to the theory of psychological differentiation, and to other data in the literature? Second, although we have examined the data in relation to our hypotheses (which stemmed from the model), we need to consider how these data relate to the model itself; are the behavioural data consistent with it, and are the other components (ecological, cultural, and acculturational) systematically related as we had expected? And third, we want to reverse the whole approach (which essentially has been one of hypotheses-testing) and consider all the data anew; we want to enquire about the best possible way to fit these materials together. We will not shed all of our theories and assumptions, however, but will turn back only as far as the ecocultural complex of relationships, which are now well established in anthropology and are independent of our particular study. Rather, our new examination will consider, by way of multiple regression analysis, the most suitable relationships and weights needed to understand and predict the patterning of differentiation which has emerged in this study.

OVERVIEW OF FINDINGS

Toward the end of Chapter 6, we presented a number of hypotheses which were derived from the model. Some were proposed at the sample level; that is, they were phrased as predictions about the characteristic behavioural development of a group as a function of the group's position on an independent variable. And some were proposed at the individual level; that is, they were phrased as predictions about individual differences as a function of the independent variables. In Table 9.1, an overview of the main findings is given.

Although in one sense Table 9.1 covers a lot of internal complexities, in another sense it covers a lot of ground. These internal complexities—which are hidden—will be considered in the next section of this chapter. But for the time being our purpose is to provide a general overview of the lay of the land. Essentially, we have found support for each of our hypotheses at both the sample and individual levels. And no hypothesis was left entirely without support. Because of the multiple assessments required for each hypothesis, a few indications of qualified support (and even a single test without support) are tolerable in the overall set of relationships.

This pattern of support constitutes a powerful indicator that there is systematic covariation between the set of independent variables and the differentiated and acculturative stress behaviours. Cultural groups (and individuals) which are hunting and gathering in subsistence pattern, nomadic in settlement pattern, and loose in sociopolitical stratification emerge as clearly different in cognitive style from those which are agricultural, sedentary, and tight. And within this range of ecological and cultural adaptations, those which occupy intermediate positions ecoculturally also exhibit intermediate behavioural adaptations. Similarly for acculturative stress, the position of the cultural group (and individual) on the same ecocultural dimension emerges as a substantial indicator of these behaviours and experiences. Taken at the level of a general overview, it is difficult to avoid the conclusion that the hypothesized relationships have been confirmed; however, a number of more focused evaluations are necessary before such a statement may be made with confidence.

COHERENCE OF THE BEHAVIOURAL DATA

Our task here is to dig deeper into the workings of the overall findings in order to discover their internal structure and coherence. Of particular interest is a pair of topics currently being debated in the cross-cultural arena ("performance versus process" and "cognitive structure"), a consideration of the structure of intertest relationships, and an examination of the age and sex patterning of the behavioural data.

TABLE 9.1
OVERVIEW OF THE MAIN FINDINGS AND EVALUATION OF THE HYPOTHESES

Level	Independent Variable	Behavioural Domain				
		Perceptual-Cognitive			Acculturative Stress	
		KOHS	EFT	Ravens	Stress	Marginality
Sample	Ecocultural	+	+	+	(+)	+
	Acculturation	+	0	+	(+)	+
	Ecocultural + Acculturation	+	+	+		
Individual	Ecocultural	+	+	+	+	+
	Socialization	(+)	(+)	(+)		
	Acculturation	+	+	+	+	+
	Education	(+)	+	(+)	+	+
	Interaction				+	+

Note: A + sign indicates a finding in support of the hypothesis at the .05 level of confidence; a (+) indicates qualified support; and a 0 indicates no support. A blank indicates that no hypothesis was advanced (see Table 6.10).

A distinction has been made in the cross-cultural literature (Cole and Bruner, 1971; Cole and Scribner, 1974) between the *performance* of a task and the *competence* or *process* which may underly such performance. Of course, in any observational, testing, or experimental situation, the psychologist is only able to monitor an individual's performance; to deal with either the underlying competence or process which may be associated with a performance, one must employ inferential techniques. It is generally agreed (e.g., Berry and Dasen, 1974; Cole and Scribner, 1974) that cross-cultural differences are not likely to be great in either cognitive competence or cognitive process—that the variation which may be observed in the cross-cultural literature is primarily a performance variation.

In the present studies, it is considered that the underlying cognitive processes are not variable (some evidence to support this view will be presented in the following section). The cross-cultural variations in cognitive style are performance differences; to argue thus is not to devalue the importance of studying such variation. For many reasons (both scientific and applied) it is a matter of great import to comprehend the distribution of cognitive style as a function of its ecological, cultural, and acculturational settings.

How to achieve this understanding of systematic relationships is also an important issue, and two general strategies have been proposed. In one, the method is to experimentally vary the conditions or setting of a performance within a culture until the background variables responsible are teased out; this is the approach of "experimental anthropology" or "ethnographic cognition" employed by Cole and his colleagues (1971, 1975). In the other, the method is to examine performance differences across a number of cultural settings (which have been selected for characteristics related theoretically to the behaviours of interest) and to identify the background variables by statistical procedures; this is the approach taken in the present series of studies. In both approaches, the goal is to comprehend the systematic covariation across cultures of behavioural (performance) and contextual (background cultural and ecological) variables. But in both, there appears to be little chance for unambiguous access to the competence and process levels.

Another issue of current interest is the structure of cognition cross-culturally. It is argued (e.g., by Cronbach, 1972; Irvine and Sanders, 1972; MacArthur, 1975; Poortinga, 1975) that before comparisons of cognitive performance may be made across cultures, a similarity of cognitive structure should be present. (The term "structure" here refers to correlational or factorial structure in a battery of psychological tests. It should not be confused with the notion of structure in differentiation theory as it was outlined in Chapter 3. In one sense, cognitive "structures" should be similar before comparisons are allowable; but in terms of differentiation theory, experience is more "structured" in those who are more differentiated.) If such similarity is not present, it is argued, then comparisons of nonidentical behaviours are unacceptable. A number of suggestions have been made regarding the demonstration of such construct equivalence: One is to examine the pattern of test score intercorrelation in each cultural sample, and another is to engage in factor analysis of the correlation matrix.

Evidence is now accumulating for a fairly common structure of cognition across cultures. The factor analytic approach to analyzing test scores has yielded a few studies (e.g., DeFries et al., 1974; Wilson et al., 1975) showing near identity of cognitive factors in two groups (Japanese and Caucasians) living in Hawaii. A similar (but not identical) structure emerged for a sample in Korea (Park, Johnson, DeFries, Vandenberg, McClearn, Wilson, Ashton, Rashad and Mi, in press). When larger cultural sweeps are made, however, somewhat different factor structures have emerged, but still sufficiently similar for proponents of this approach to make cross-cultural comparisons (e.g., MacArthur, 1975). Clearly the issue is far from settled; cognitive structures eventually may or may not prove to be similar across cultural groups, but on the basis of the present evidence two points need to be made. First, there appears to be a trend toward finding greater similarity of structure across cultural groups which are not greatly culturally different, and conversely finding less similarity of structure across greater cultural sweeps. Second, it must be recognized that all of these studies have employed tests which are "imposed etics" (Berry 1969a); thus the similarity in structure may be a function of the performances which these tests seek to measure. Other ("emic") behaviours, which may not be assessed by these test batteries, could if included in future studies, radically alter the factors which have been observed.

As we noted previously, the data collected in the present studies cannot be subjected to factor analyses; there are too few tests and too few individuals in each sample to make such analyses valid. However, the method of inspecting the intercorrelation matrices (Poortinga, 1975) sample by sample yields some indication that no group is radically different from the others (Tables 7.2 and 7.3) or from the overall intercorrelations across all samples and all individuals (Table 7.9). We may thus infer some degree of communality in the cognitive style construct and permit its comparative use across the samples in this study.

These same correlational data also provide some evidence for the hypothetical structure of psychological differentiation and its relationships to other tasks advanced by Witkin et al. (1971) and presented hierarchically in Chapter 3. Those tasks which are conceptually part of psychological differentiation (EFT and Kohs Blocks) are the most strongly related to each other both within samples and across samples, and at both the individual and sample level of analyses. And those tasks which are not part of psychological differentiation, but which conceptually involve some analysis and structuring (Matrices and Shapes), tend to correlate at a lower level. Finally, the Discrimination task, which conceptually does not involve analysis or structuring, intercorrelates at a lower level than the other tasks.

The stability of this pattern may be judged by examining the intercorrelation pattern sample by sample. There appears to be minimal variation in the intercorrelation pattern which can be associated either with ecocultural and acculturation variables, or with the mean sample level of differentiation; test-sophisticated Western urban dwellers, unacculturated hunters, and equally unacculturated agriculturalists do not differ in the degree of this behavioural coherence. One might have expected that the lower mean performance could have introduced such a relationship; however, this appears not to have been the case. On the contrary, even in the lowest differentiated samples, variance was present. This presence of individual differences is what such a theoretical position requires; in fact as we noted in Chapter 3, it was the presence of individual differences in perceptual functioning which led Witkin et al. (1954, 1962) to the study of psychological differentiation in the first place.

This consistency in the perceptual domain is supported by other workers: Among hunters, both Weitz (1971) and MacArthur (e.g., 1973) have generally found such among Kohs Blocks, EFT, and PRFT, while with agriculturalists, Dawson (1967), Wober (1966, 1967) and Okonji (1969) have also found it. Other kinds of samples, which we have not been concerned with here, have further indicated consistencies in this domain (see Witkin and Berry, 1975). It is possible to conclude, therefore, that those tasks which have been designed to assess differentiation (and which on factor-analytic studies have previously loaded on such a factor) do have a relatively high degree of coherence right across the panorama of cultural variation.

Such a hierarchical formulation, if eventually supported by large-scale studies employing factor-analytic techniques, provides a plausible structure for task relationships, one which avoids many of the arguments which now surround the "uniqueness" of cognitive style, field independence, analytical ability, spatial ability, and general intelligence (Cronbach, 1970: 282, 332; Vernon, 1972). It is likely that tests of cognitive style will rarely exhibit completely unique variance; the search for such uniqueness, therefore, is probably futile. What appears to be the more profitable venture is to seek a comprehension of the patterning of test performance and shifts in such patterning, across a variety of ecological, cultural, and acculturational settings. This is not to say that discriminant validity is unimportant. It is simply to say that its absence in a single study in a single culture is insufficient to dismiss one particular concept and accept an alternative.

The age-patterning of the behavioural data is an important aspect of the theory of psychological differentiation. As we noted in Chapter 3, the basic postulate of the theory is that differentiation in general will develop from infancy to adulthood. Numerous studies intraculturally have demonstrated increases in performance on differentiation tasks over that age range and have also demonstrated relative individual stability over the same period (e.g., Witkin et al., 1967). Problems of working with young children cross-culturally led to the decision, in the present study, not to sample below the age of ten in Study 1, and to sample only from the adult population in Studies 2 and 3. However, from the lower age ranges it is possible to extract data which relate to this basic developmental postulate of differentiation theory. In Study 1, some samples (e.g., the Eskimo and Hanuabada) exhibited marked increase in performance from age ten to around age twenty-five; thereafter, there was a decline in older age to levels which were approximately equal to the youngest performance. In other samples (e.g., the Temne and Telefolmin), curves were generally more flat, with only a small peak of performance in the young adult age range. For some samples, then, clear developmental increases were apparent, while for others, the trend was smaller; but for all, the characteristic rise from childhood to young adulthood was generally present. In Studies 2 and 3, a small rise is also apparent from the first few years of young adulthood, followed by a decline in later years. Thus, there is evidence of a drop in performance in most of our samples, which is consistent with trends noted intraculturally (Witkin et al., 1962). These patterns are similar to those found by Jahoda (1970b), where older (over twenty-five years) West African persons were more field-dependent than younger persons. And they are consistent with reports of later decline for Eskimo and Central African persons on EFT by MacArthur (1971). Other data with different kinds of samples (see Witkin and Berry, 1975) tend to support this cross-cultural pattern of a developmental rise to young adulthood, followed by a decline in later years; however, it may be the case that decline begins somewhat earlier in subsistence-level samples than for those in Western settings, or simply that older persons in these samples have been less exposed to acculturative influences, and hence obtain lower scores.

Sex differences, although not a necessary part of differentiation theory, have often been found intraculturally, the predominant relationship being that of greater field independence for females. The question of the unversality of this difference is of great importance, for only in the cross-cultural arena can cultural and biological factors be contrasted: If the difference persists, then it is due either to a cultural universal or to some biological factor; but if the difference varies, it cannot be due to some cultural or biological universal.

As we have seen in Chapters 7 and 8, there are variable relationships between sex and scores on cognitive style (and acculturative stress) variables; sometimes males obtain higher scores and sometimes females score higher. The relationship, however, is not a random one, for there appears to be a regular patterning in the differences. On the five cognitive variables, although there was an overall tendency for males to obtain higher scores, there was a clear relationship between the presence of sex differences and the ecocultural position of the sample: In the "tighter," more stratified samples males tended to score relatively higher, while in the "looser," less stratified samples, sex differences disappeared or were reversed.

This result was first reported by Berry (1966) and immediately confirmed by MacArthur (1967). Since then, results generally consistent with our description have appeared in the literature (see Witkin and Berry, 1975). Originally an interpretation was offered in terms of role dependency: "In societies, where women assume a dependent role, they will have more field-dependent perceptual characteristics than men, but in societies where women are allowed independence, sex differences will disappear" (Berry, 1966: 228). It is thus not simply a matter of role *differences* but a role *valuation;* men and women (and boys and girls) may carry out quite separate functions in their society (as indeed they do in our hunting and agricultural samples), but if the society is tightly controlling some members (usually women and children) and stratifying the roles (allocating differential prestige and value to them), then sex differences on differentiation tasks tend to appear. Of course there may be some "special learning" available for males in hunting societies, but this is often balanced by equivalent training in crafts for females; so this does not appear to be a crucial factor. What does appear, fairly consistently, is that those who are maintained in dependent positions, with little value attached to their roles, will attain lower levels of psychological differentiation.

A similar patterning and interpretation are apparent in the data on acculturative stress. In many studies with Western samples, females have exhibited higher scores on stress checklists. The data in the present study show an overall tendency for higher female scores, but there is wide variation across samples: In the "tighter" samples, females did exhibit greater stress and marginality, while in the "looser" samples, the sex differences disappeared or were reversed. Once again an interpretation in terms of the differing relative position of males and females in these samples is the most plausible.

EVALUATING THE MODEL

In this chapter we have been concerned with an evaluative overview of the results of the studies. In the first section, we were concerned with the question of support for our hypotheses; if none had been found, then further discussion would not have been fruitful. Our second section was concerned with internal analyses of the behavioural data; it was an attempt to dig into the complexities which the first overview section necessarily hid from view. In this third section we return to a more global perspective on our data and ask as we did in the first section for our hypotheses, how the data relate to the model which we proposed in Chapter 4.

We have already briefly examined in Chapter 6 the way in which our ecological and cultural elements cohere, and in turn how the acculturation index relates to them (Tables 6.6 and 6.8). We have also, in Chapters 7 and 8, referred to the predictive power from these indices to our various behavioural measures. Does this set of relationships provide support for the model as we outlined it in Chapter 4; that is, are the lines of correlation, and their strength, sufficient to conclude that the model has any predictive validity?

Our first observation is that the model, as presented in Chapter 4, is more complex than the data which we have available; the hypothesized "feedback" relationships cannot be evaluated at the present time. To ignore these return influences in our initial presentation (for example, from contact culture to acculturative influences, or from traditional behaviour to ecology) would be to blind ourselves to reality; however to actually measure them has been beyond the scope of the present investigation. To pursue these two examples further, how can one assess the impact of non-attendance at school on the educational policy of the government, or the effect of hunting on available resources, in a way which is usable in a behaviourally oriented model? At the present level of the art, the answer is that we cannot. So the evaluation of the model must be limited to employing the data which we have collected, and we must leave unexamined those aspects for which we have no data; that is, the evaluation must necessarily be an incomplete one.

Among the background variables themselves, we have found substantial interrelationships. To say this is not to claim that they have been newly discovered in this study (for the School of Cultural Ecology has already demonstrated such a complex set of relationships for a wide variety of cultures); it is to claim, however, that the samples which have been selected for this study adhere to the parameters of a more general model of ecological-cultural relationships. If these background patterns had not been found, two conclusions would have followed: first, that our sampling of worldwide cultural variation had been faulty (and not, as we have noted, that these background relationships are nonexistent); and second, given this faulty sampling, that our prediction to behavioural variables would not have been worthwhile. However, we have found considerable anticipated clustering among our ecological, cultural, and socialization variables; this permits us to claim some generality for the study as a whole, and makes useful the prediction to the behavioural levels of the model.

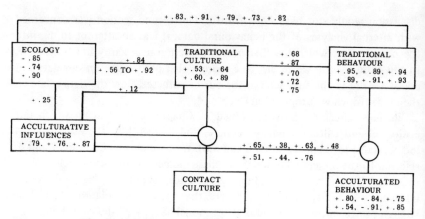

FIGURE 9.1   The Overall Model with Illustrations of Correlations Across the
Seventeen Samples

To illustrate this coherence, Figure 9.1 provides a version of the model
which leaves out the feedback relationships. Coefficients are included within
and between components to indicate the strength of relationships. They are
extracted from Tables 6.6 and 6.8 for the nonbehavioural variables, from
Tables 7.9 and 8.12 for the behavioural variables, and from Tables 7.7 and
8.9 for the links between them. The specific referents for each coefficient can
be identified by inspecting these earlier tables. Note that these are simple
correlations, not multiple, where much higher levels of prediction were noted
in the earlier chapters (Tables 7.7 and 8.9).

From Figure 9.1, it is clear that substantial, simple prediction is possible
from our background indices to levels of behaviour to be found in samples
gleaned cross-culturally. And remembering that when multiple correlations
are used with these predictors, our coefficients rise to between +.89 and +.97
for the five cognitive variables at the sample level, and to between .43 and
.87, at the individual level, the evidence is that our modelled lines of
influence and their strengths are capable of powerful prediction. Similarly for
the acculturative stress variables, multiple coefficients range between .51 and
.90 at the sample level, and .49 and .71 at the individual level. With this
evidence, it would be difficult not to conclude that the model has been
substantially supported.

MULTIPLE REGRESSION ANALYSES

Despite this fairly high level of prediction, it is always possible to improve
our understanding of a set of relationships by engaging in multiple regression
analysis. This second approach to the evaluation of the model, then, takes the
data and seeks the statistical relationships among them which best predict the

behavioural variation. This procedure allows the maximal predictive relationship to emerge from the data. But perhaps more importantly, it permits some insight into the relative predictive capability of each independent variable.

Although it is possible to consider each of the constituent elements of the indices as independent variables, the fairly high level of covariation among them (Table 6.6) suggested that the regression analyses be carried out with only the two aggregated indices—the ecocultural and the acculturational. And in keeping with the phrasing of the hypotheses, the analyses were conducted at both the sample and individual level. Table 9.2 provides the beta weights for both levels of analysis.

A fairly clear pattern emerges from Table 9.2. For the five cognitive measures (Kohs, EFT, Matrices, Shapes, and Discrimination) there is a consistently heavier weight given to the ecocultural index at both the sample and individual levels of analysis. But for the five acculturative stress variables, there is a greater weight upon the acculturation index at both levels of analysis. In no case was a beta weight nonsignificant. That is, both independent variables contribute to the distribution of these ten behaviours, but the ecocultural variables appeared as the more important in the distribution of cognitive style, while the acculturation variables emerged as more important for the patterning of acculturative stress. This pattern of results supports the basic structuring of the model into two "input-streams," the ecocultural and the acculturational. And, of course, they correspond to the two generally accepted sources of cultural change and development—adaptation and diffusion.

Because these beta coefficients indicate the *independent* contribution of each cluster of independent variables, this regression analysis provides a clearer examination of the relationships in the model than was possible by the use of simple correlation. However, inspection of Tables 7.7, 7.8, 8.9, and 8.10 reveals that the same relative emphases were apparent even in the simple coefficients. Over all the analyses, then, the conclusions emerge that there is a basic ecocultural patterning of cognitive style, one which is influenced to a lesser degree by acculturation, and that there is a basic acculturational patterning of acculturative stress, but one which is influenced also by the traditional ecological and cultural setting of the group.

In Chapter 6 it was argued that to some extent these patterns of relationship might be affected by the selection of two samples from each culture. This non-independence of cases (Galton's Problem) was solved in this study by assigning the relatively traditional sample of a culture to one subsample and the relatively acculturated sample to the other subsample. We may note here that the beta weights for the ecological index do not vary substantially in the subsamples from the overall values reported in Table 9.2. For example, on Kohs Blocks at the sample level, the weight is .508 in the eight relatively

TABLE 9.2
SAMPLE-AND INDIVIDUAL-LEVEL BETA WEIGHTS FOR
ECOCULTURAL AND ACCULTURATIONAL INDICES AND TEN BEHAVIOURAL MEASURES

Index	KOHS	EFT	Matrices	Shapes	Discrimination	Stress	Marginality	Assimilation	Integration	Rejection
Sample Level										
n =	17	8	17	8	8	9	9	9	9	9
Ecocultural	0.657	0.887	0.671	0.743	0.778	0.286	0.400	−0.364	0.131	0.527
Acculturational	0.562	0.385	0.544	0.482	0.515	−0.294	−0.554	0.611	−0.716	−0.543
Individual Level										
n =	793	364	814	358	247	433	423	453	453	453
Ecocultural	0.560	0.813	0.502	0.422	0.384	0.241	0.318	−0.277	0.296	0.189
Acculturational	0.354	0.208	0.398	0.219	0.205	−0.416	−0.404	0.507	0.324	−0.207

traditional samples, and .855 in the eight relatively acculturated samples, compared to .657 overall. The corresponding weights at the individual level are .539, .589, and .560. A similar stability occurs for all cognitive variables. However, for the acculturative stress variables, there is a trend for the acculturation index to obtain even heavier beta weights among the more acculturated samples; this is a comprehensible phenomenon since, as we have seen, the stress behaviours are more strongly affected by acculturative influences. Over all, though, there is fair stability in the beta weights across subsamples; to a large degree the dual questions of Galton's Problem and subsample reliability have been answered by this regression strategy.

In concluding this chapter, it is important to note that the approaches to the data by way of the hypotheses, the internal analyses, the model evaluation, and regression analyses have all provided support for the importance of the cluster of independent variables which were selected for use in these studies. Although we began with a number of conceptually distinct independent variables, ranging from socialization to subsistence pattern to the experience of Western education, there emerged a clustering among them sufficient to extract just two independent variables: the ecocultural and the acculturational indices. Prior to this series of studies, only one of the independent variables—socialization—had been implicated in the development of cognitive style. From this starting point, a number of variables of theoretical importance were added until the total set became implicated. And at that point the process of clustering became important.

Ironically, the one variable of importance in most intracultural studies did not emerge here as a major element in the patterning of individual differences, most likely because of the crude measurement of individual socialization. However at the cultural level, socialization emerged as a highly relevant variable, along with a new set of cultural elements which covary with it. These estimates of sociocultural stratification, in turn, appeared to have a significant ecological base. Thus, just as socialization may be viewed as having a broader cultural setting in stratification and authority systems, so too may this set of cultural elements be viewed as having a broader ecological base, at least among subsistence-level societies. In considering a psychological construct cross-culturally, a widening set of independent variables has emerged, one which appears to control a large portion of the variation at both group- and individual-difference levels of analysis.

Of course other independent variables may be proposed to account for the observed behavioural variation. These may be more important in studying cognitive style in other kinds of societies, or in samples which do not fit the parameters of the present research model. But, with one exception, it is difficult to conceive of other variables, which have some a priori theoretical status, which might have been included in the present research. This one exception is that of biological variables; however, given the great practical difficulty in assessing such variables in fieldwork, and the great theoretical difficulty of attempting to relate them to behavioural differences, such a possible alternative must be acknowledged, but be left unexamined here. Alternative explanations or theoretical interpretations of the meaning of the obtained relationships are also plausible; we will turn to these in Chapter 10.

Chapter 10

IMPLICATIONS AND APPLICATIONS

In this final chapter our intention is to stand back a little and examine some of the issues which have been raised from time to time during our earlier detailed consideration of specific tests and variables and their inter-relationships. Although many issues will receive some attention during this examination, they all essentially fall into five fairly discrete topics. The first of these is the implication of our study for the theory of psychological differentiation: how did it fare as an imposed etic—should we keep it as is, modify it, or discard it during future cross-cultural research? Second, we will consider two alternative theoretical interpretations for our results—"general intelligence" and "adaptability." Third, we will examine some general impli-cations of our findings for the study of individual and group differences, in relation to both the "adaptive value" of differentiation which is relevant during traditional life and the "imported value" relevant during acculturation. Fourth, some implications of the study for for future cross-cultural research on psychological differentiation will be considered. Finally, we will attempt to show how these and similar studies may be applied to the solution of problems and questions which are now arising in non-Western countries; are there relationships between "development"—psychological and national—and are there useful insights to be gained from these materials for issues of education and mental health during the process of social change?

THEORY OF PSYCHOLOGICAL DIFFERENTIATION

As we pointed out in Chapter 6, a theory may be employed cross-culturally for a number of reasons. If our interest lies primarily in the theory, then we may simply wish to check the extent to which the theory is supported in these newer behaviour settings: Does it still make sense, hold up, find support in these faraway places? A second reason may be that we wish to use the theory as a guide for exploring behaviours as they occur in other cultural settings. In this case, our interest is not primarily in the theory, but in the behaviours to be found in these other settings. However, because no observations are free of theoretical bias or other imported assumptions, the researcher may as well make them explicit so that the result is not a false description of local behaviour. A third reason is that the researcher may wish to consider the original theory in the light of the behaviours which he has discovered in these new cultural settings; is it possible to integrate the theory and the behaviour in a way which yields a more universal theoretical understanding? These three approaches to the cross-cultural use of theory correspond to the imposed etic, emic, and derived etic strategies (Berry, 1969a), and to the three goals of cross-cultural research for transporting and testing, exploring a new variation, and comparing and integrating of concepts (Berry and Dasen, 1974: 14). What can be said of psychological differentiation from these three points of view?

First, we may conclude that some of the basic elements of the theory have stood up remarkably well in these novel behaviour settings. The origins in social factors, both intraculturally and cross-culturally, have been confirmed for all behaviours which were examined; in some cases this support was stronger than in others, but in no case was there a disconfirming pattern in the data. Where the age range was suitable, developmental rises in performance were also generally in support of the ontogenetic element of the theory. And from the point of view of internal coherence of behaviour, there was support for the theory in terms of congitive style and in its relationship to stress. Finally, as the notion of "style" requires, we have found evidence, at the group level, for behavioural persistence during the process of environmental change.

It is difficult to escape the conclusion, therefore, that the theory of psychological differentiation has been well supported by these cross-cultural studies. This should come as no surprise, since two of its basic elements (ontogenetic development and socialization origins) are pan-human and universal to the species. Such a conclusion and interpretation is supported on balance by other studies of the theory (Witkin and Berry, 1975). But, of course, such a conclusion may be made with respect to other theoretical systems (for example, the Piagetian, by Dasen, 1972). This is to say that although psychological differentiation is generally supported cross-culturally, it is not uniquely supported; other systems have already received such support, and still others may receive such in the future. Thus no exclusive claims can or will be made for the value of the psychological differentiation approach to cross-cultural research. Considerably more thought (about the points of convergence and divergence among theories) and considerably more empirical work (in a wider variety of cultural settings) are needed before such a comparative evaluation can even begin.

From the perspective of our second reason for cross-cultural use of theory, we may also conclude some usefulness for the psychological differentiation approach. The behaviours which have been reported in the ethnographic literature for hunters and for agriculturalists appeared ready-made for a study guided by this theory. Quite independently of a knowledge of Witkin's work, anthropologists have been describing cultures and behaviours of hunters and agriculturalists in terms which suggest an uncanny correspondence. Although the tasks which are employed to assess psychological differentiation are often remote from the participants' experience, the kinds of behaviours which they exemplify are often reported by ethnographic observers. This is to say that the "theory fits the natural behaviour"; during the course of the present work, very little discomfort was experienced in continually viewing behaviour and culture in terms of this theory.

However this would not imply a perfect fit, for it is clearly the case that these novel behaviour settings have turned up some new exemplars of differentiated behaviour and some new cultural antecedents of differentiation. In the case of the former, it may be possible to incorporate them into a psychological test battery.

Other behaviours, such as hunting and navigating activity, emotional controls, interpersonal and social distance, and more may all be candidates for future inclusion. And for the latter, the socialization antecedents of differentiation may now be considered as only one independent variable; the general conformity pressures associated with family type and social stratification may provide an even more powerful cultural surround; and these cultural features in turn may now be veiwed as part of an even larger ecological context, where direct perceptual and other learning from economic roles and demographic factors provides even further antecedents to the development of individual and group differences in psychological differentiation. Thus, although the theory "fitted" the natural behaviour and the culture, the latter provided new information about potential constituent behaviours and antecedent variables which were largely unanticipated before the theory went across cultures.

Finally, our third reason points us toward a new integration of findings and original theory. The direction of such an integration is suggested by our discussion of the newly discovered elements. On the one hand, it may be possible to develop the theory, and tests used to assess differentiated behaviour, employing concepts and behaviours which have emerged in these studies. These might include notions of the "individualism" and "atomism" found in many hunting societies and of "cooperation" found in agricultural ones. And, as we have already noted, tasks based more naturally upon navigation, tracking, and harvesting activities, and upon social and emotional situations might all be developed in future research. On the other hand, the implicating of general societal pressures, and of an ecological context in this cross-cultural work, might direct attention intraculturally to antecedents which have previously been overlooked. Most obviously social class, caste, and regional differences may be better comprehended within such an expanded framework, or use of the "adaptive" approach might be of value in considering the origins of problematic behaviours within and between ethnic groups. The value of the cross-cultural enterprise can only be fully realized when such returns from the field are taken up and explored in the original sociocultural system in which the theory was developed.

ALTERNATIVE THEORETICAL INTERPRETATIONS

It has been argued persuasively (Brislin et al., 1973) that the interpretation of cross-cultural differences is fraught with difficulty because so many rival plausible alternative explanations are possible. In this section, the two major alternatives to differentiation theory will be examined: "general intelligence" and "adaptibility."

Perhaps the cross-cultural issue which generates the most debate is that of the usefulness of the concept of general intelligence in the interpretation of cognitive variation. A specific issue in this general debate (that of the genetic or racial basis of cognitive variation) will not be considered here, for the simple reason that genetic data are unavailable for the samples in this study. It is possible, though, that the following discussion of the concept (and the later discussion of "adaptive value") may reduce the intensity of the racial debate.

A long history of monographs which employ the notion of intelligence (e.g., Porteus, 1937; Weyl and Possony, 1963; Vernon, 1969; Feldman, 1974) testifies to the importance of the concept for many workers in the area. The debate may be separated into two components—the conceptual and the psychometric; the first is concerned with theoretical and functional analyses and arguments, while the latter is primarily concerned with patterns of relationships found among test scores. The former examines the nature, relevance, and purpose of the concept, while the latter takes these for granted and proceeds to statistical analysis. In essence, the conceptual approach questions the usefulness of the concept cross-culturally on theoretical grounds, while the psychometric approach treats it as an empirical question.

Among those approaching the issue from a theoretical perspective, Berry (1972a), Klein et al. (1973), Wober (1974), and Price-Williams (1975) raise the question of varieties, styles, and culturally relative "emic" notions of intelligence. If it is "clever" to do different things in different cultures, how is it possible to impose a Western notion of general intelligence upon groups of people living in widely varying cultural systems? A position of "radical cultural relativism" has been taken (Berry 1972a), which suggests that functional and conceptual equivalence should be established prior to test development or use; it is inappropriate to rely upon construct equivalence on the basis of post hoc psychometric analyses.

Among those approaching the issue from a psychometric point of view, Irvine (1966, 1970) Vernon (1969, 1972) and MacArthur (1973, 1975) largely base their arguments upon item and score correlations and the factor structures which emerge from them. On this basis, it is sometimes argued that "general intelligence" is the most elegant way to conceive of the emergent factor structure (e.g., Vernon, 1972).

Clearly these contrasting positions are not to be solved easily. With those of one position arguing for the theoretical and logical absurdity of applying "intelligence" tests cross-culturally, and those of the other position doing it any way, little rapprochement is possible. The future resolution probably lies in the development of numerous tasks which represent emic notions and are conceptually equivalent to "intelligence." These may then be applied in appropriate cultural settings and psychometric analyses performed. Only then is there likely to emerge a generally acceptable construct of intelligence, one which is relatively free of gross cultural bias. Until then, the more conservative strategy of looking at what people do, in ways which are conceptually and functionally related to their ecological and cultural settings, appears to be more reasonable. Of course, any approach to behaviour cross-culturally which has been guided by any theory may be criticized from the same perspective. It is for this reason that the theory of psychological differentiation was examined for its pan-cultural base in socialization and authority systems, and tasks were examined for their functional relevance to subsistence-level life styles. And because such examination yielded a fairly clear matching among theory, ecology, culture, and behaviour, the concept of psychological differentiation is preferred to that of "general intelligence."

Another theoretical interpretation of behavioural variation cross-culturally has been advanced by Biesheuvel (1972). His notion of "adaptability" avoids most of the biases and problems of "general intelligence," primarily because it is founded on a pan-cultural problem—that of the need for human organisms to adapt to their surroundings and to adjust to changes in them. This notion is essentially an ecological one, focusing as it does on the relationships between organisms and their environments. As such, it resembles the approach taken in these studies and parallels our two sets of dependent variables: The ecological adaptation of cognitive style and the response to change in the form of acculturation.

More specifically, the notion of "adaptability" refers to the "potentiality to meet educational, vocational and social demands" (1972: 50). Biesheuvel, who also dismisses the cross-cultural usefulness of the notion of "general intelligence" has argued that the notion of adaptability has considerable advantage over the older conceptualization: It need not be biased toward Western culture, it is not an abstract concept but is easily defined operationally, and it is holistic, not limited only to cognitive functioning.

Because there are so many overlapping features between Biesheuvel's use of "adaptability" and the entire design and execution of the present series of studies, it is not an easy task to distinguish clearly between the two approaches. Indeed, Biesheuvel (1972: 57) has noted that the field-dependence concept is "relevant to adaptability toward new cultural demands; tests which measure it should be useful in predicting to what extent cognitive capacity will be effectively utilized in meeting educational and vocational demands." This prediction, as we have seen in Chapter 8, is borne out both by the "shifts" in differentiation to meet acculturative demands and by the systematic relationships obtained between individual levels of psychological differentiation and measures of acculturative stress.

This expected relationship between "adaptability" and acculturation led Biesheuvel (1972: 59) to consider the possibility that a "general adaptability" might be termed "acculturability" or the "capacity to meet cultural change." Clearly, then, it may prove possible to translate the approach and results of the present study into "adaptability" terms. But it is less clear what the advantages would be, since the notion as presented by Biesheuvel is less elaborated theoretically and has limited explicit empirical examination. Conversely, the present ecological approach, employing a fairly well-developed theoretical system and a coherent set of empirical tests, seems to match the arguments in favour of "adaptability" and surpasses that concept in terms of theoretical and empirical fullness. However, no opposition is envisaged between the approaches; perhaps the choice will be determined by the interests and goals of a particular research enterprise.

THE ADAPTIVE VALUE OF PSYCHOLOGICAL DIFFERENTIATION

A basic point of view throughout this report has been that behaviour is adaptive to culture, and culture in turn is adaptive to its ecological setting. And at various points in the presentation we have stressed that no general values can emerge within this framework; the value of each adaptation is necessarily relative to its adaptive problem in its own adaptive setting. Thus the question of whether being differentiated is good or bad can receive no general response; in this general form it is absurd, just as absurd as asking the question: "Is it better to be an amoeba than a gorilla?" Nevertheless, the question of value has attended not only the cross-cultural use of the notion of differentiation, but it has plagued many other concepts, including that of intelligence. In this section we will expand on this discussion of adaptive value, and apply the strategy to the concept of psychological differentiation (and to one specific aspect of it—sex differences).

Our first question in following this approach is to ask, "What are the adaptive requirements; what kinds of ecological demands (Berry, 1966) are placed upon individuals who develop in a particular ecological context?" An answer to this question amounts to a statement of the adaptive problem. This task of analysis was attempted in the introductory sections to Chapters 7 and 8, where cognitive styles which may be considered useful in various ecological settings were outlined. In general, we provided an answer (in terms of the theory of psychological differentiation) which suggested that one kind of cognitive style would be required in one setting (the hunting and gathering) but not in another setting (the agricultural). In terms of our value question, then, high differentiation would be "better" in hunting and gathering societies, and low differentiation would be "better" in agricultural societies; and indeed this is generally what has been found in these studies.

When applied to the question of sex differences in differentiation or "intelligence," ecological analysis provides an equally value-free resolution. Males and females carry out the same or differing roles depending on the sociocultural or ecological context of the group. Those carrying out some roles are "better" if more differentiated, and some "better" if less differentiated. Again what is at stake is not the applicability of the notion of differentiation, but the valuation (the rewards allocated to roles) by the social group. And again no universal value is likely to be applicable, given the nature of extant cultural differences; it is ethnocentric to argue otherwise.

Returning to the intracultural value of differentiation, Witkin et al. (1971) have pointed out that in one sense being more differentiated might be considered to be "better" than being less differentiated. This valuation rests on the argument that a more differentiated individual "has available to him more diversified resources for coping than the less differentiated person" (1971: 12). But as the authors point out, the mere availability of more kinds of behaviour is not predictive of how or whether these behaviours will be used in adapting. Thus even in this ontogenetic sense, greater differentiation does not necessarily imply greater adaptive ability.

Finally, in this section, we must consider the question of value during acculturation. It may very well be the case that within an ecocultural system, value judgements can only be relative to the adaptive problem; but as group contact increases in frequency and intensity, life requirements stem no longer only from the traditional adaptive setting, but now there is an "imported value." This distinction exists in the cross-cultural literature on the use of psychological tests (e.g., Ord, 1972; Drenth, 1975): In the search for persons capable of profiting from western education or wage employment, it is acceptable to use tests and norms which are relative to the requirements of the school or the factory. In broader terms, the society bringing the acculturative influences may devalue or undervalue the traditional "adaptive value" of certain behaviours and substitute an "imported value" for them. And being in a relatively less powerful social position, those undergoing acculturation may have no recourse; for them it is a whole new value system. In these cases, one should be free to make such arguments, but the ethical, social, and political implications of them should also be acknowledged. One should not mistake the switching of values for the universality of one's own.

Despite these reservations, it may still be the case that greater differentiation is associated with greater adaptability during acculturation. Indeed our own data indicate that, independently of tests and cultural groups, differentiation is negatively related to acculturative stress. Perhaps in this limited sense of having "more diversified resources for coping," some value may be legitimately attached to psychological differentiation.

FUTURE DIRECTIONS IN CROSS-CULTURAL STUDIES OF PSYCHOLOGICAL DIFFERENTIATION

At least three directions for future research are readily apparent. One is toward the cross-cultural assessment of more of the behavioural domains subsumed by the theory of psychological differentiation. Another is toward the inclusion of other antecedent variables now known intraculturally to be predictive of cognitive style. And the third is to extend the sampling of cultures beyond the present ecological framework, both to more acculturated and urbanized settings and to other samples representing distinctive ecological and cultural adaptations.

A theory as broad as that of psychological differentiation encompasses more than perceptual and cognitive behaviour. As outlined in Chapter 3, the theory extends to other behaviours, and within the notion of cognitive style a number of features of social functioning may be attended to. In recent years, such social behaviours have become well-studied intraculturally (Witkin et al., in press), and their exploration cross-culturally is a topic of great interest.

We noted in Chapter 7 that some attempts have been made already to study social behaviours and emotional controls cross-culturally (Berry, 1967; Berry, 1974a; Berry and Annis, 1974a), but theoretical and measurement problems made their interpretation in terms of differentiation theory very tenuous. Although tests of "independence" of the Asch (1956) type were conducted in all seventeen samples in this study, it proved impossible to demonstrate systematic relationships (at the individual differences level) between performance on that test and any of the cognitive style tests. Despite this problem, the patterning of the sample means paralleled the patterning of cognitive style in relation to the ecocultural and acculturational indices (see Berry, 1967, 1974a). In fact the correlation between the ecocultural plus acculturational index and sample mean on the independence task is +.70. This sample-level patterning indicates that "independence" is very much more evident in hunting and gathering samples and less evident in agricultural samples. Clearly there is a phenomenon present to be investigated, but just as clearly better access to the behaviour is required if the individual differences are to be systematically related to those of cognitive style.

Even less successful were attempts (Berry and Annis, 1974a) to measure other aspects of social behaviour ("social reserve"), and some features of emotional control. Not only did these variables not display coherence with cognitive style variables at the individual difference level, but they attained only marginally interesting patternings across ecocultural settings. Future cross-cultural studies of psychological differentiation could profitably move in the direction of both these social and affective domains.

A second direction in which such studies might move is toward the inclusion of antecedent variables now being implicated intraculturally, but largely ignored cross-culturally. One of these variables is the possible X-chromosome linkage with field dependence (Goodenough et al., 1974). Given recent attempts (e.g., Beals and Kelso, 1975) to demonstrate a covariation of genetic markers and cultural forms, it may be that some element of genetic adaptation, in addition to cultural adaptation, occurs in the face of ecological pressures. Indeed, it is likely that biological and cultural adaptation are parallel processes (Hallowell, 1963), and are therefore confounded (Cavalli-Sforza and Feldman, 1973: 43); the ecological pressures which direct cultural adaptation may simultaneously direct genetic selection.

Another biological variable has been proposed by Dawson (1966, 1967, 1972); differential levels of protein intake may affect the sex hormone balance (testosterone/estrogen), which in turn appears, in his studies, to be related to differential levels of field independence. Those with low protein levels (in the extreme case, those with kwashiorkor) tend to have lower androgen levels and lower levels of psychological differentiation. In terms of the ecocultural model, hunters whose adaptation requires a field-independent cognitive style tend to obtain high levels of protein; in contrast, agriculturalists, whose adaptation does not require field independence, tend to obtain lower levels of protein (and, on a worldwide basis, tend to suffer more kwashiorkor). If the hormonal link to cognitive style is confirmed, then it may be viewed as yet another functional adaptation between ecological setting and behavioural development.

In addition to the protein-to-hormone links proposed by Dawson, there exists a relatively well-established relationship among nutrition, general growth, and psychological functioning (see, e.g., Cravioto et al., 1966). Recently Klein et al. (1972) have demonstrated correlations between physical growth and performance on a number of psychological tasks; the most substantial relationships existed in the area of perceptual functioning, which was assessed in part by an embedded figures test. It is clear from such studies that future work should attempt to include estimates of general nutritional status and of protein intake in particular.

Third, some attention should be paid to sampling from settings not represented in the present series of studies (e.g., to pastoral societies) and to extending the ecocultural analyses to the limits of the present model. Indeed, there would be benefit to an extension beyond its parameters, in order to probe its limits. One set of studies (Jones, 1972, 1973) has shown that the model does not hold up when fishing samples which are not at subsistence-level are compared to urban samples in Labrador and Newfoundland. On the other hand, numerous studies (see Witkin and Berry, 1975, for a review) have shown that when the parameters are observed, varying levels of support are forthcoming, even from data collected within other theoretical systems (e.g., Dasen, 1974, 1975, within the Piagetian framework).

In the following section on applications, there is a discussion of the limits of the model when highly acculturated and urbanized samples are included within the framework. In this section, we look in the opposite direction, at extensions toward less complex social systems. In Chapter 3 the two factors of cultural system "differentiation" and "integration" (Lomax and Berkowitz, 1972) were outlined. It was pointed out that over the large middle range of cultural adaptations, these two factors tended to move in parallel. However, prior to this central range (among Australian and African gatherers) cultural "integration" was high in relation to cultural "differentiation." But after this central range cultural "integration" was low in relation to cultural "differentiation" (among near Eastern and European agricultural peoples).

Over the course of the present studies, there has emerged a fairly powerful covariation of psychological differentiation and the ecocultural dimension. But because all (but one) of the samples in the study were taken from the central range of the Lomax and Berkowitz cultural "differentiation and integration" scale, it is not possible to unambiguously specify which of the two sociocultural variables is most likely to be operating. It thus becomes essential to sample from groups among African and Australian gathering peoples and from more urbanized agriculturalists around the Mediterranean. If samples from the former range exhibit high psychological differentiation and samples from the latter range exhibit low psychological differentiation, then the "cultural differentiation" factor is implicated. However, if samples from the former range exhibit relatively low psychological differentiation, and samples from the latter exhibit relatively high psychological differentiation, then the "cultural integration" factor will be implicated.

There are two sets of information which suggest what the likely outcome will be. The first is that the cognitive style of the Arunta (who are Australian gatherers) in the present study was not as field-independent as their position on the ecocultural dimension would predict (see Table 7.1, and Figures 7.1 to 7.5 for sample number 5). It may be that although low on the Lomax "cultural differentiation" scale and in a similar position on the ecocultural dimension, their relatively higher position on the "cultural integration" scale limited somewhat the development of a more field-independent cognitive style. A second source of information is that among many highly urbanized samples (for example, the Scottish farmers and city people in Berry, 1966) field independence appears to be relatively high, despite their high position on the Lomax and Berkowitz "cultural differentiation" scale. Once again, it may be that their relatively lower position on the "cultural integration" scale has contributed to this more field-independent cognitive style. Overall, then, it appears that it is the "integration" element ("tightness") rather than the "differentiation" element which may eventually account for the variation in cognitive style which has been observed in the present study.

Some of the points raised in this section on future directions for research are being incorporated into a comparative study of psychological differentiation in Pygmy and Bantu samples in the Central African Republic. (This study, co-directed by H. A. Witkin and J. W. Berry, involves the following individuals in various aspects of the research: Robert Annis, Luca Cavalli-Sforza, Jan Deregowski, Gustav Jahoda, Jan van de Koppel, Jacques van Meel, Claude Sénéchal and Mary Stewart-van Leeuwen.) First, the Pygmy are clear examples of African gatherers, whose sociocultural "differentiation" is low, but whose "integration" is relatively high on the Lomax and Berkowitz (1972) scale. Although there is an expectation of a field-independent cognitive style among the Pygmy (in relation to the neighbouring agricultural Bantu peoples), it will be possible to examine closely the interplay of the integration or "tightness" features of the societies in relation to their differentiation features. Furthermore, two of the failures of the present study will receive major attention in the Pygmy-Bantu study. Individual socialization, measured by both observation and interview, will be a primary focus of the research. And studies of psychological differentiation in the social domain will again be attempted. Another unresolved question, that of "sensotypes" (Wober, 1966) will also be researched. It is important to check the generality across cultures of the Western observation that psychological differentiation manifests itself across sense modalities.

Left unattended to by this study are the lack of research with pastoral peoples and the dearth of studies of non-African agriculturalists. Although one New Guinea agricultural sample (Telefomin) and one sedentary Amerin-

dian sample (Tsimshian) were included in the present study, there is a clear
need for research attending to Amerindian and South East Asian agriculturalists. In their absence, the cultures sampled (although providing a quasi-
manipulation of the independent variables) provide a notably unrepresentative
base from which to make large-scale generalizations.

SOME POTENTIAL APPLICATIONS

In a number of recent publications (e.g., Jahoda, 1973; Sinha, 1973; Berry
and Lonner, 1975) the question of the relevance of psychology to those
countries often called "developing" has been raised. A two-part answer has
generally been suggested: Psychology has not been of much use in the past,
but the potential for the application of psychology cross-culturally is really
very high. At this point it is appropriate to ask, specifically for our own
studies, of what possible use can this material be to those countries and
peoples who have suffered western intrusion?

The context in which such a question is posed is largely one characterized
by fairly rapid sociocultural change and conflicts between traditional cultures
and emerging goals. This description is an appropriate one for all the samples
which were included in these studies and is probably an apt characterization
for over eighty percent of the world's population. Such a situation is often
referred to as one of "development," and a large literature of books and
journals has grown up around the problem. A concise overview of these
developmental problems from a number of perspectives has been published in
the *International Social Science Journal* (1972). However, because the term
"development" has a special meaning already in psychology, it may be more
appropriate to refer to the area of concern as "social change."

It is precisely in the study of social change where the findings reported
here have their greatest potential use. As we have noted previously, our major
independent variables (ecocultural and acculturation) essentially parallel the
two major sources of cultural variation (adaptation and diffusion); and it is
these two elements which are directly involved in the problems of social
change. Thus we may phrase the problems involved in social change in terms
of the patterning of traditional culture and behaviour, the nature of the
acculturative influences, and the transition and conflict between the two.
Elements of each have been considered in the model and have been assessed
during fieldwork; we may thus be in a position to contribute our findings to a
further understanding of social change and its behavioural correlates.

Our discussion will focus first on the question of development itself, and
then we will consider two specific policy areas—education and mental health.
But first we must consider the question of the limits of our present model;

for if further social change takes us beyond the original parameters of our model, then our predictive ability and validity will both be zero.

As we noted in the discussion of the ecology component of our model (Chapter 4), the ecological and cultural analyses can only be relevant to those peoples who are living at subsistence level. However, since many peoples have only recently begun the shift away from such an economic base, the model was applied to these kinds of communities as well. When communities are well removed from subsistence level—that is, where behavioural and cultural adaptations to the ecological setting are no longer apparent—we fully expect to have reached the limits of our model. In these cases, diffusion from other (probably western, industrialized) cultures will be far more involved with the nature of cultural and behavioural variation. We must consider, then, at what point in the process of social change the ecocultural perspective ceases to have predictive validity, and all variation can be understood from the perspective of acculturation. This, of course, is not an easy question to answer. Our own data suggest, though, that this point is not reached quickly (say, within a single generation). There is considerable evidence for behavioural and cultural persistence well into the period of rapid social change. The data of others (for example, those of Dawson, 1967, with mine employees and MacArthur, 1975, with samples from his International Biological Programme Studies) tend to confirm this relative persistence of behaviour. In the area of cultural persistence, workers in the Arctic (such as Honigmann and Honigmann, 1965) in Asia (e.g., Guthrie, 1970) and in Africa (e.g., Little, 1974) also find evidence for persistence well into a period of social change. We may conclude, then, that behavioural and cultural persistence is present, and perhaps for very long periods; acculturative influences do not quickly supersede ecocultural adaptation.

The long-term trend, though, may be highly unpredictable. We not only have to contend with what we have assumed to be a fairly linear "acculturation takeover," but there is now some evidence for non-linearity or even discontinuity in the process of social change. Evidence for this comes both from archival studies, such as Blumberg and Winch (1973), who show a curvilinear relationship between familial and societal complexity, and from survey studies, such as those of Kavolis (1970) and Suzman (1974) who consider the nature of "post-modern man." In both cases, there is the suggestion that neat linear change is not the case, that simple predictions based on our present understanding of acculturative influences would be unwise. Thus the safest course is to remain at the near subsistence level in our focus and to extend our gaze only to the short term.

Development, as a concept in the social sciences, has often been used in the popular sense of simply becoming bigger, wealthier, and, at the extreme, more like the western world. The ethnocentric usage has been dismissed by many in the past few years; for example in anthropology Belshaw (1972: 83; italics added) considers that " 'development' represents an increase in the capacities of a society to organize *for its own objectives,* and to carry out its programmes more effectively. The essential element here is organization." The concern for a group's own objectives largely eliminates the ethnocentrism inherent in the concept's popular usage. In the same way, Berry (1971b) pointed out that for psychology, "the term 'development' implies a progressive change . . . continuously directed toward a certain end condition" (Drever, 1952). That is, a person who is in state A now develops toward state B; for us to have 'development' then. . . . we need to know and describe quite precisely what state A is; we need to be able to specify our goal, state B; and "we need to know how to get from state A to state B, coping with problems along the way" (Berry, 1971b: 153). Development, then, in its value-free usage, implies both in anthropology and psychology a progressive movement between two conditions, the second of which is more highly valued.

Taking this definition and our own findings together and applying them to issues of education and mental health during social change, we discover some fairly clear implications. First, if education is to serve the 'development' of an individual, group, or nation, it must start with the present state of affairs and work toward some valued future state. Imposed educational systems that make incorrect assumptions about the initial behaviour and culture or choose non-valued states as the eventual goal cannot possibly contribute to 'development.' Within this proposed framework, an accurate description of a wide variety of traditional behaviour is required, a clear statement of individual and cultural goals must be articulated, and a programme of moving between the two must be worked out. If these elements are absent, then education as development is not taking place.

Results from our cross-cultural studies can help us with two of these elements, and perhaps provide some indications of the third. We have presented a model and supportive data which show that culture and behaviour vary considerably across ecological settings. The behaviours considered are, of course, far from a complete sampling of the behavioural repertoire, but it is a beginning to the behavioural mapping required for our first element. Specifically, we have seen that cognitive styles are highly variable in their development, and highly predictable from a knowledge of ecocultural (and to a lesser extent acculturational) factors. These specific data combined with the general model suggest that there is a good probability of finding high differentiation in other hunting and gathering societies and lower levels in agricultural ones. A firm basis thus exists for expecting certain kinds of behaviours to be characteristic of certain kinds of cultural groups, and this contributes to our understanding of certain kinds of the likely starting points in various ecocultural settings.

An articulation of cultural and individual goals toward which to move is a more difficult research task. Often in the past, psychologists, anthropologists, and educators have simply assumed that these goals would be much like the state of affairs found in technological societies. However, the current difficulties being experienced by such societies, combined with more tolerant and pluralistic (Berry, 1974b) ideas of ethnic and cultural group life styles, both suggest that this assumption will be dropped by policy makers, just as it was earlier discarded by ethnic and cultural groups themselves.

Whatever goals are set, it should be apparent that the old assumptions about "cultural deprivation" cannot survive a framework in which education is viewed as development. Groups, armed with information about their own characteristic patterns of skills, may opt for any number of goals. If they choose to build upon the strengths they already possess, for example on analytical and spatial abilities in hunting and gathering societies or upon social sensitivity in agricultural ones, then such "reinforcing education" is development; and if they choose to strengthen those skills which are not high in relation to other groups, then such "compensatory education" is also development.

Our third element is that of moving from one state to another while coping with problems to be encountered along the way. As in our model, we may consider two kinds of problems to be encountered: behavioural shifts and acculturative stress. In our second element, we argued that developmental education could take place by reinforcing traditional strengths or by compensating for traditional weakness in the skill pattern; both involve shifting traditional behaviours to new levels. How to do this, of course, is a matter of educational technology; but our studies do indicate some individual- and group-level variables which may be related to the behaviours of concern. For example, on the basis of our data, if levels of differentiation were considered in need of raising, programmes concerned with changing socialization techniques and authority systems might be considered, along with some direct training similar to the perceptual learning hunters experience in their particular ecology. This may or may not be easy to accomplish, and necessarily requires detailed research in each cultural setting before implementation; but the point is that on the basis of our research, behavioural variations and their sociocultural and ecological covariates have been pinpointed as a basis for such applied educational work.

In our earlier discussions of acculturative stress, we considered that the behavioural shifts required (either informally by the acculturative pressures, or now formally through deliberate educational programmes) may be too great for the adaptive ability of an individual or group, and stress might be exhibited. The implication of this point of view is that those working with programmes of social change, be they general (for example, economic) or specifically educational, should be wary of requiring too great a behavioural shift. Stress reactions may negate any benefits intended to flow from economic or educational change. But as we have seen, this generalization must take into account both group- and individual-level characteristics. That is, programmes of social change should not be totally incongruent with traditional cultural characteristics, and programmes of education should not be inconsistent with traditional behaviour and skills. However, since this problem is attended to at the group level, individual programmes should take into account levels of psychological differentiation. These levels both must be considered, since their interplay is a very complex antecedent of mental health during the process of social change.

These brief discussions illustrate the potential applicability of this psychological research across cultures. Whether such applications are indeed made depends as much on governments as on psychological science. In the past, a combination of ignorance and irrelevance has characterized much of psychology; hopefully the further pursuit of psychology cross-culturally, and a consideration of its potential return to the people who suffer our studies, will contribute to the development both of psychology and of the peoples experiencing change.

REFERENCES

ABBIE, A.A. (1969) The Original Australians. New York: American Elsevier.
ABERLE, D.F., COHEN, A.K., DAVIS, A.K., LEVY, M.J., and SUTTON, F.X. (1950) "The Functional prerequisites of a society." Ethics 60: 100-111.
ANNIS, R.C. and FROST, B. (1973) "Human visual ecology and orientation anisotropies in acuity." Science 182: 729-731.
ANTONOVSKY, A. (1956) "Toward a refinement of the marginal man concept." Social Forces 35: 57-62.
APPLEY, M.H. and TRUMBULL, R. (eds) (1967) Psychological Stress. New York: Appleton-Century-Crofts.
ASCH, S.E. (1956) "Studies in independence and conformity 1: A minority of one against a unanimous majority." Psychological Monographs 70, no. 416.

BARAN, S. (1971) "Development and validation of a TAT-type projective test for use among Bantu-speaking people." Special Report PERS 138. Johannesburg: National Institute for Personnel Research.
BARBEAU, M. (1940) "Old Fort Simpson." Beaver (Sept): 20-23.
BARKER, R.G. (1963) "On the nature of the environment." Journal of Social Issues 19: 17-38.
BARKER, R.G. (1965) "Explorations in ecological psychology." American Psychologist 20: 1-14.
BARKER, R.G. (1969) Ecological Psychology. Stanford: Stanford University Press.
BARRY, H. (1969) "Cross-cultural research with matched pairs of societies." Journal of Social Psychology 79: 25-34.
BARRY, H., BACON, M., and CHILD, I. (1957) "A cross-cultural survey of some sex differences in socialization." Journal of Abnormal and Social Psychology 55: 327-332.
BARRY, H., CHILD, I., and BACON, M. (1959) "Relation of child training to subsistence economy." American Anthropologist 61: 51-63.
BARRY, H. and PAXSON, L.M. (1971) "Infancy and early childhood: Cross-cultural codes 2." Ethnology 10: 466-508.
BEALS, K.L. and KELSO, A.J. (1975) "Genetic variation and cultural evolution." American Anthropologist 77: 566-579.
BELSHAW, C. (1957) The Great Village. London: Routledge & Kegan Paul.
BELSHAW, C.S. (1972) "The contribution of anthropology to development." International Social Science Journal 24: 80-94.
BERNDT, R.M. and BERNDT, C.H. (1964) The World of the First Australians. Sydney: Angus & Robertson.
BERRY, J.W. (1966) "Temne and Eskimo perceptual skills." International Journal of Psychology 1: 207-229.

BERRY, J.W. (1967) "Independence and conformity in subsistence-level societies." Journal of Personality and Social Psychology 7: 415-418.

BERRY, J.W. (1968) "Ecology perceptual development and the Müller-Lyer illusion." British Journal of Psychology 59: 205-210.

BERRY, J.W. (1969a) "On cross-cultural comparability." International Journal of Psychology 4: 119-128.

BERRY, J.W. (1969b) "Ecology and socialization as factors in figural assimilation and the resolution of binocular rivalry." International Journal of Psychology 4: 271-280.

BERRY, J.W. (1970) "Marginality, stress and ethnic identification in an acculturated aboriginal community." Journal of Cross-Cultural Psychology 1: 239-252.

BERRY, J.W. (1971a) "Ecological and cultural factors in spatial perceptual development." Canadian Journal of Behavioural Science 3: 324-336.

BERRY, J.W. (1971b) "Psychological research in the North." Anthropologica 13: 143-157.

BERRY, J.W. (1971c) "Müller-Lyer illusion: Culture, ecology, or race?" International Journal of Psychology 6: 193-197.

BERRY, J.W. (1972) "Radical cultural relativism and the concept of intelligence," pp. 77-88 in L.J. Cronbach and P.J.D. Drenth (eds.) Mental Tests and Cultural Adaptation. The Hague: Mouton.

BERRY, J.W. (1974a) "Differentiation across cultures: Cognitive style and affective style," in J.L.M. Dawson and W.J. Lonner (eds.) Readings in Cross-Cultural Psychology. Hong Kong: University of Hong Kong Press.

BERRY, J.W. (1974b) "Psychological aspects of cultural pluralism: Unity and identity reconsidered." Topics in Culture Learning 2: 17-22.

BERRY, J.W. (1975a) "An ecological approach to cross-cultural psychology." Nederlands Tijdschrift voor de Psychologie 30: 51-84.

BERRY, J.W. (1975b) "Ecology, cultural adaptation and psychological differentiation: traditional patterning and acculturative stress," pp. 207-228 in R. Brislin, S. Bochner, and W.J. Lonner (eds.) Cross-Cultural Perspectives on Learning. New York: Halsted Press (a Sage Publications book).

BERRY, J.W. (forthcoming) "Social and cultural change," in H.C. Triandis, R. Brislin, and J. Draguns (eds.) Handbook of Cross-Cultural Psychology, vol. 4. Boston: Allyn & Bacon.

BERRY, J.W. and ANNIS, R.C. (1974a) "Ecology, culture and psychological differentiation." International Journal of Psychology 9: 173-193.

BERRY, J.W. and ANNIS, R.C. (1974b) "Acculturative stress: The role of ecology, culture and differentiation." Journal of Cross-Cultural Psychology 5: 382-406.

BERRY, J.W. and DASEN, P.R. (eds.) (1974) Culture and Cognition. London: Methuen.

BERRY, J.W. and LONNER, W.J. (eds.) (1975) Applied Cross-Cultural Psychology. Amsterdam: Swets & Zeitlinger.

BICCHIERI, M.G. (ed.) (1972) Hunters and Gatherers Today. New York: Holt, Rinehart & Winston.

BIERI, J. (1961) "Complexity-simplicity as a personality variable in cognitive behaviour," pp. 355-379 in D.W. Fiske and S.R. Maddi (eds.) Functions of Varied Experience. Homewood, Ill.: Dorsey.

BIERI, J. (1966) "Cognitive complexity and personality development," pp. 13-37 in O.J. Harvey (ed.) Experience, Structure and Adaptability. New York: Springer.

BIESHEUVEL, S. (1972) "Adaptability: Its measurements and determinants," pp. 47-62 in L.J. Cronbach and P. Drenth (eds.) Mental Tests and Cultural Adaptation. The Hague: Mouton.

BIGART, R.J. (1972) "Indian culture and industrialization." American Anthropologist 74: 1180-1188.

BLUMBERG, R.L. and WINCH, R. (1973) "Societal complexity and familial complexity: Evidence for the curvilinear hypothesis." American Journal of Sociology 77: 898-920.

BOAS, F. (1895) The Social Organization and Secret Societies of the Kwakiutl Indians. Washington: National Museum.

BOAS, F. (1911) The Mind of Primitive Man. New York: Macmillan.

BOWDEN, E. (1969) "An index of sociocultural development applicable to precivilized societies." American Antropologist 71: 454-461.

BOWDEN, E. (1972) "Standardization of an index of sociocultural development for precivilized societies." American Anthropologist 74: 1122-1132.

BRANDT, R.M. (1972) Studying Behaviour in Natural Settings. New York: Holt, Rinehart & Winston.

BRISLIN, R. (1970) "Back translation for cross-cultural research." Journal of Cross-Cultural Psychology 1: 185-216.

BRISLIN, R., LONNER, W.J., and THORNDIKE, R. (1973) Cross-Cultural Research Methods. New York: John Wiley.

BRODMAN, K., ERDMANN, A.J., LORGE, I., GERSHENSON, C.P., and WOLFF, H.G. (1952) "The Cornell Medical Index health questionnaire III. The evaluation of emotional disturbances." Journal of Clinical Psychology 8: 119.

BROWN, R. (1965) Social Psychology. New York: Free Press.

BRUNSWIK, E. (1957) "Scope and aspects of the cognitive problem," pp. 5-31 in A. Gruber (ed.) Cognition: The Colorado Symposium. Cambridge, Mass.: Harvard University Press.

BUTT, A. (1950) "The social organization of the Eastern and Central Eskimos." B. Litt. thesis, Oxford University.

CAMPBELL, D.T. (1970) "Natural selection as an epistemological model," pp. 51-85, in R. Naroll and R. Cohen (eds.) Handbook of Method in Cultural Anthropology. New York: Natural History Press.

CAMPBELL, D.T. and FISKE, D.W. (1959) "Convergent and discrimminant validation by the multitrait-multimethod matrix." Psychological Bulletin 56: 81-105.

CAMPBELL, D.T. and STANLEY, J.C. (1966) Experimental and Quasi-Experimental Designs for Research. Chicago: Rand McNally.

CARNEIRO, R.L. (1970) "Scale analyses, evolutionary sequences and the rating of cultures," pp. 834-871 in R. Naroll and R. Cohen (eds.) Handbook of Method in Cultural Anthropology. New York: Natural History Press.

CAVALLI-SFORZA, L. and FELDMAN, M.W. (1973) "Models for cultural inheritance: 1. Group mean and within group variation." Theoretical Population Biology 4: 42-55.

CAWTE, J., BIANCHI, G.N., and KILOH, L.G. (1968) "Personal discomfort in Australian Aborigines." Australian and New Zealand Journal of Psychiatry 2: 69-79.

CHANCE, N.A. (1965) "Acculturation, self-identification and personal adjustment." American Anthropologist 67: 372-393.

CHANCE, N. and FOSTER, D. (1962) "Symptom formation and patterns of psychopathology in rapidly changing Alaskan Eskimo society." Anthropological Papers of the University of Alaska 11: 32-42

COELHO, G.V. (ed.) (1972) Mental Health and Social Change: An Annotated Bibliography prepared for the National Institute of Mental Health. Washington, D.C.: Government Printing Office.

COHEN, R. (1970) "Generalizations in ethnology," pp. 31-50 in R. Naroll and R. Cohen (eds.) Handbook of Method in Cultural Anthropology. Garden City: Natural History Press.

COHEN, Y. (ed.) (1968) (1971) Man in Adaptation. Chicago: Aldine.

COLE, M. (1975) "An ethnographic psychology of cognition," pp. 157-175 in R. Brislin, S. Bochner, and W.J. Lonner (eds.) Cross-Cultural Perspectives on Learning. New York: Halsted Press (a Sage Publications book).

COLE, M. and BRUNER, J. (1971) "Cultural differences and inferences about psychological processes." American Psychologist 26: 867-876.

COLE, M., GAY, J., GLICK, J., and SHARP, D. (1971) The Cultural Context of Learning and Thinking. New York: Basic Books.

COLE, M. and SCRIBNER, S. (1974) Culture and Thought. New York: John Wiley.

COOMBS, C.H., DAWES, R.M. and TVERSKY, A. (1970) Mathematical Psychology: An Elementary Introduction. Englewood Cliffs, N.J.: Prentice-Hall.

CRAIG, B. (1967) "The houseboards of the Telefomin subdistrict, New Guinea." Man 11: 260-273.

CRAVIOTO, J., DELICARDIE, E.R., and BIRCH, H.G. (1966) "Nutrition, growth and neurointegrative development: an experimental and ecologic study." Paediatrics 38: 319-372.

CRONBACH, L.J. (1970) Essentials of Psychological Testing. New York: Harper & Row.

CRONBACH, L.J. (1972) "Judging how well a test measures: New concepts, new analyses," pp. 413-426 in L.J. Cronbach and P.J.D. Drenth (eds.) Mental Tests and Cultural Adaptation. The Hague: Mouton.

DAMAS, D. (ed.) (1969) Ecological Essays. National Museums of Canada Bulletin No. 230, Anthropological Series No. 86.

DASEN, P.R. (1972) "Cross-cultural Piagetian research: A summary." Journal of Cross-Cultural Psychology 3: 23-39.

DASEN, P.R. (1974) "The influence of ecology, culture and European contact on cognitive development in Australian Aborigines," pp. 381-408 in J.W. Berry and P.R. Dasen (eds.) Culture and Cognition. London: Methuen.

DASEN, P.R. (1975) "Concrete operational development in three cultures." Journal of Cross-Cultural Psychology 6: 156-172.

DAWSON, J.L.M. (1966) "Kwashiorkor, gynaecomastia and feminization processes." Journal of Tropical Medicine and Hygiene 69: 175-179.

DAWSON, J.L.M. (1967) "Cultural and physiological influences upon spatial perceptual processes in West Africa." Parts 1 and 2. International Journal of Psychology 2: 115-128, 171-185.

DAWSON, J.L.M. (1969) "Theoretical and research bases of bio-social psychology." University of Hong Kong Gazette 16: 1-10.

DAWSON, J.L.M. (1971) "Theory and research in cross-cultural psychology." Bulletin of the British Psychological Society 24: 291-306.

DAWSON, J.L.M. (1972) "Effects of sex hormones on cognitive style in rats and men." Behaviour Genetics 2: 21-42.

DAWSON, J.L.M. (1973) "Effects of ecology and subjective culture on individual traditional-modern attitude change, achievement motivation, and potential for economic development in the Japanese and Eskimo societies." International Journal of Psychology 8: 215-225.

DAWSON, J.L.M. (1975) "Theory and measurement in the study of individual modernity in Asia," in J.W. Berry and W.J. Lonner (eds.) Applied Cross-cultural Psychology. Amsterdam: Swets & Zeitlinger.

DE FRIES, J.C., VANDENBERG, S.G., McCLEARN, G.E., KUSE, A.R., WILSON, J.R., ASHTON, G.C., and JOHNSON, R.C. (1974) "Near identity of cognitive structure in two ethnic groups." Science 183: 338-339.

DeVOS, G. (1968) "Achievement and innovation in culture and personality," pp. 348-370 in E. Norbeck, D. Price-Williams, and W. McCord (eds.) The Study of Personality: An Interdisciplinary Appraisal. New York: Holt, Rinehart & Winston.

DICKIE-CLARKE, A.F. (1966) The Marginal Situation. London: Routledge & Kegan Paul.

DOOB, L.W. (1972) Patterning of Time. New Haven: Yale University Press.

DOHRENWEND, B.P., and DOHRENWEND, B.S. (1969) Social Status and Psychological Disorder: A Causal Inquiry. New York: John Wiley.

DRENTH, P.J.D. (1975) "Psychological tests for developing countries: rationale and objectives." Nederlands Tijdschrift voor de Psychologie 30: 5-22.

DREVER, J. (1952) A Dictionary of Psychology. London: Penguin.

DRIVER, H. (1961) Indians of North America. Chicago: University of Chicago Press.

DRIVER, H. and MASSEY, W.C. (1957) "Comparative studies of North American Indians." Transactions of the American Philosophical Society 47, part 2.

DRUCKER, P. (1955) Indians of the Northwest Coast. New York: American Museum of Natural History.

DUNNING, R.W. (1960) "Differentiation of status in subsistence level societies." Transactions of the Royal Society of Canada 54: 25-32.

DYK, R. (1969) "An exploratory study of mother-child interaction in infancy as related to the development of differentiation." Journal of Child Psychiatry 8: 657-691.

DYK, R. and WITKIN, H.A. (1965) "Family experiences related to the development of differentiation in children." Child Development 36: 21-55.

EAGLE, M., GOLDBERGER, L., and BREITMAN, M. (1969) "Field dependence and memory for social versus neutral, and relevant versus irrelevant incidental stimuli." Perceptual and Motor Skills 29: 903-910.

EDGERTON, R.B. (1971) The Individual in Cultural Adaptation. Berkeley: University of California Press.

EDGERTON, R.B. (1974) "Cross-cultural psychology and psychological anthropology: one paradigm or two." Reviews in Anthropology 1: 52-65.

EMBER, M. (1963) "The relationship between economic and political development in nonindustrialized societies." Ethnology 2: 228-248.

FELDMAN, C.F. (1974) The Development of Adaptive Intelligence. San Francisco: Jossey-Bass.

FELDMAN, D.A. (1975) "The history of the relationship between environment and culture in ethnological thought: An overview." Journal of the History of the Behavioural Sciences 11: 67-81.

FISHER, A.D. (1967) "The Cree of Canada: Some ecological and evolutionary considerations." Western Canadian Journal of Anthropology 1: 7-19.

FORDE, D. (1934) Habitat, Economy and Society. London: Metheun.

FORRESTER, J.W. (1971a) World Dynamics. Cambridge, Mass.: Wright Allen.

FORRESTER, J.W. (1971b) "Counter intuitive behavior of social systems." Technology Review 73: 53-68.

FREEMAN, L.C. and WINCH, R.F. (1957) "Societal complexity: An empirical test of a typology of societies." American Journal of Sociology 62: 461-466.

FRENCH, D. (1963) "The relationship of anthropology to studies in perception and cognition," pp. 388-428 in S. Koch (ed.) Psychology: A Study of a science, Vol. 6. New York: McGraw-Hill.

FRIED, M. (1964) "Effects of social change on mental health." American Journal of Orthopsychiatry 34: 3-28.

FRIJDA, N. and JAHODA, G. (1966) "On the scope and methods of cross-cultural research." International Journal of Psychology 1: 109-127.

FYFE, C. (1962) History of Sierra Leone. London: Oxford University Press.

GIFFEN, N.M. (1930) The Roles of Men and Women in Eskimo Culture. Chicago: University of Chicago Press.

GIST, N.P. and DWORKIN, A.G. (eds.) (1972) The Blending of Races: Marginality and Identity in World Perspective. New York: John Wiley.

GLADWIN, T. (1970) East Is a Big Bird. Cambridge, Mass.: Belknap.

GOODENOUGH, D.R. (in press) "Field dependence," in H. London and J. Exner (eds.) Dimensions of Personality, New York: Wiley.

GOODENOUGH, D.R., GANDINI, E., OLKIN, I., PIZZAMIGLIO, L., THAYER, D. and WITKIN, H.A. (in press) "A study of x-chromosome linkage with field dependence and spatial visualization." Unpublished Manuscript, Educational Testing Service.

GOODENOUGH, D.R. and KARP, S.A. (1961) "Field dependence and intellectual functioning." Journal of Abnormal and Social Psychology 63: 241-246.

GORDON, B. (1953) "An experimental study of dependence-independence in a social and laboratory setting." Ph.D dissertation, University of Southern California.

GOTTSCHALDT, K. (1926) "Uber den Einfluss der Erfahrung auf die Wahrnehmung von Figuren, 1." Psychologische Forschung 8: 261-317.

GREEN, L. (1973) "Effects of field independence, physical proximity and evaluative feedback on affective reactors and compliance in a dyadic interaction." Ph.D dissertation, Yale University.

GRIBBLE, J.B. (1920) Forty Years Among the Aborigines. Sydney: Church Missionary Society.

GUETZKOW, H., KOTLER, P. and SCHULTZ, R. (eds.) (1972) Simulation in Social and Administrative Science. Englewood Cliffs, N.J.: Prentice-Hall.

GUTHRIE, G.M. (1970) The Psychology of Modernization in the Rural Philippines. Quezon City: Ateneo de Manila University Press.

HALLOWELL, A.F. (1946) "Some psychological characteristics of Northeastern Indians," pp. 195-225 in F. Johnson (ed.) Man in Northeastern North America, Peabody Foundation for Archaeology 3.

HALLOWELL, A.F. (1951) "Values, acculturation and mental health." American Journal of Orthopsychiatry 20: 732-743.

HALLOWELL, A.F. (1963) "Personality, culture and society in behavioural evolution," pp. 429-509 in S. Koch (ed.) Psychology: A Study of a Science, Vol. 6. New York: McGraw-Hill.

HAMMOND, K.R. (ed.) (1966) The Psychology of Egon Brunswik. New York: Holt, Rinehart & Winston.

HARVEY, O.J. (1966) "Ends, means and adaptability," pp. 3-12 in O.J. Harvey (ed.) Experience, Structure and Adaptability. New York: Springer.

HARVEY, O.J., HUNT, D.E., and SCHRODER, A. (1961) Conceptual Systems and Personality Organization. New York: John Wiley.

HAWTHORN, H.B. BELSHAW, C.S., and JAMIESON, J.M. (1960) The Indians of British Columbia. Toronto: University of Toronto Press.

HOLLEY, M. (1972) "Field dependence, sophistication of body concept and social distance selection." Ph.D. dissertation, New York University.

HONIGMANN, J. (1968) "Interpersonal relations in atomistic societies." Human Organization 27: 220-229.

HONIGMANN, J. (1969) "Psychological anthropology," in Biennial Review of Anthropology.

HONIGMANN, J. and HONIGMANN, I. (1965) Eskimo Townsmen. Ottawa: Canadian Research Centre for Anthropology.

HORNEY, K. (1955), in R. Munroe Schools of Psychoanalytic Thought. New York: Holt.

HOUSTON, B.K. (1969) "Field independence and performance in distraction." Journal of Psychology 72: 65-69.

HRDLICKA, A. (1941) "The Eskimo child." Smithstonian Institute Reports 3673: 557-562.

HUNTINGTON, E. (1915) Civilization and Climate. New Haven: Yale University Press.

HUNTINGTON, E. (1945) Mainsprings of Civilization. New York: John Wiley.

IRVINE, S.H. (1966) "Towards a rationale for testing attainments and abilities in Africa." British Journal of Educational Psychology 36: 24-32.

IRVINE, S.H. (1969a) "Factor analysis of African abilities and attainments: constructs across cultures." Psychological Bulletin 71: 20-32.

IRVINE, S.H. (1969b) "Figural tests of reasoning in Africa: studies in the use of Ravens Matrices across cultures." International Journal of Psychology 4: 217-228.

IRVINE, S.H. (1970) "Affect and construct: A cross-cultural check on theories of intelligence." Journal of Social Psychology 80: 23-30.

IRVINE, S.H. and SANDERS, J.T. (1972) "Logic, Language and method in construct identification across cultures," pp. 425-446 in L.J. Cronbach and P.J.D. Drenth (eds.) Mental Tests and Cultural Adaptation. The Hague: Mouton.

JACKSON, D.N. (1956) "A short form of Witkin's Embedded Figures Test." Journal of Abnormal and Social Psychology 53: 254-255.

JACOBS, P. (1968) "Information in error: A reanalysis of matrices responses." Unpublished.

JAHODA, G. (1970a) "A cross-cultural perspective in psychology." Advancement of Science 27: 1-14.

JAHODA, G. (1970b) "Supernatural beliefs and changing cognitive structures among Ghanaian university students." Journal of Cross-cultural Psychology 1: 115-130.

JAHODA, G. (1973) "Psychology and the developing countries: Do they need each other?" International Social Science Journal 25: 461-474.

JOHNSON, R.C., THOMSON, C.W., and FRINCKE, O. (1960) "Word values, word frequency and visual duration thresholds." Psychological Review 67: 332-342.

JONES, P. (1972) "Physical environment, cultural influences and the development of spatial perceptual ability." Abstract Guide of the Twentieth International Congress of Psychology, Tokyo.

JONES, P. (1973) "Intra-cultural differences in spatial-perceptual abilities." Paper presented at Canadian Psychological Association Annual Meeting, Victoria, B.C.

JUSTICE, M. (1969) "Field dependency, intimacy of topic and interperson distance." Ph.D. dissertation, University of Florida.

KARDINER, A. (1945) Psychological Frontiers of Society. New York: Columbia University Press.

KARP, S.A. (1966) "Field dependence and aging." Research Reports of the Sinai Hospital of Baltimore 1: 1-9.

KAVOLIS, V. (1970) "Post-modern man: Psychocultural responses to social trends." Social Problems.

KELLY, G.A. (1955) The Psychology of Personal Constructs. New York: Norton.

KERCKHOFF, A.C. and McCORMICK, T.C. (1955) "Marginal status and marginal personality." Social Forces 34: 48-55.

KLEIN, R.E., FREEMAN, H.E., KAGAN, J., YARBROUGH, C., and HABICHT, J.P. (1972) "Is big smart? The relation of growth to cognition." Journal of Health and Social Behavior 13: 219-225.

KLEIN, R.E., FREEMAN, H.E., and MILLETT, R. (1973) "Psychological test performance and indigenous conceptions of intelligence." Journal of Psychology 84: 219-222.

KONSTADT, N. and FORMAN, E. (1965) "Field dependence and external directedness." Journal of Personality and Social Psychology 1: 490-493.

KOHS, S.C. (1923) Manual for Kohs Blocks-Design Tests. Chicago: Stoelting.

KOOIJMAN, S. (1962) "Material aspects of the Star Mountains culture." Nova Guinea 2: 15-44.

KRAIDMAN, E. (1959) "Developmental analysis of conceptual and perceptual functioning under stress and non-stress conditions." Ph.D. dissertation, Clark University.

KRECH, D., CRUTCHFIELD, R., and BALLACHEY, E. (1963) Individual in Society. New York: McGraw-Hill.

KROEBER, A. (1939) Cultural and Natural Areas of North America. University of California Publications in American Archaeology and Ethnology: 38.

KROEBER, A. and KLUCKHOHN, C. (1952) Culture—A Critical Review of Concepts and Defenitions. Cambridge, Mass.: Peabody Museum.

KROPINSKI, J. (1967) "Sociological aspects of mental ill-health in migrants." Social Science and Medicine 1: 267-281.

LANGNER, T.S. (1962) "A twenty-two item screening scale of psychiatric symptoms indicating impairment." Journal of Health and Human Behaviour 3: 269-276.

LAPIDUS, L.B. (1968) "The relation between cognitive control and reactions to stress: A study of mastery in the anticipatory phase of child birth." Ph.D. dissertation, New York University.

LAUGHLIN, W.S. (1968) "Hunting: An integrating biobehavior system and its evolutionary importance," pp. 304-320 in R.B. Lee and I. Devore (eds.) Man the Hunter. Chicago: Aldine.

LEE, R.B. (1968) "What do hunters do for a living, or how to make out on scarce resources," pp. 30-48 in R.B. Lee and I. Devore (eds.) Man the Hunter. Chicago: Aldine.

LEE, R.B. and DEVORE, I. (1968) "Problems in the study of hunters and gatherers," pp. 3-12 in R.B. Lee and I. Devore (eds.) Man the Hunter. Chicago: Aldine.

LEEPER, R.W. (1966) "A critical consideration of Egon Brunswik's probalistic functionalism," pp. 405-454 in K.R. Hammond (ed.) The Psychology of Egon Brunswik. New York: Holt, Rinehart & Winston.

LEWIN, K. (1935) A Dynamic Theory of Personality. New York: McGraw-Hill.

LEWIN, K. (1936) Principles of Topological Psychology. New York: McGraw-Hill.

LEWIN, K. (1951) Field Theory in Social Science. New York: Harper.

LEWIS, C. (1970) Indian Families of the Northwest Coast: The Impact of Change. Chicago: University of Chicago Press.

LIJPHART, A. (1971) "Comparative politics and the comparative method." American Political Science Review 65: 682-693.

LITTLE, K. (1974) Urbanization as a Social Process. London: Routledge & Kegan Paul.

LOMAX, A. and BERKOWITZ, N. (1972) "The evolutionary taxonomy of culture." Science 177: 228-239.

LONG, J. (1970) Aboriginal Settlements. Canberra: Australian National University Press.

MacARTHUR, R.S. (1967) "Sex differences in field dependence for the Eskimo: Replication of Berry's finding." International Journal of Psychology 2: 139-140.

MacARTHUR, R.S. (1970) "Cognition and psychosocial influences for Eastern Eskimos and Nsenga Africans: Some preliminaries." Paper presented at the Memorial University of Newfoundland Symposium on Cross-cultural Research, St. Johns.

MacARTHUR, R.S. (1971) "Mental abilities and psychosocial environments: Igloolik Eskimos." Paper presented at Mid-project Review, International Biological Programme, Igloolik Projeck, Toronto.

MacARTHUR, R.S. (1973) "Some ability patterns: Central Eskimos and Nsenga Africans." International Journal of Psychology 8: 239-247.

MacARTHUR, R.S. (1975) "Differential ability patterns: Inuit Nsenga and Canadian whites," in J.W. Berry and W.J. Lonner (eds.) Applied Cross-cultural Psychology. Amsterdam: Swets & Zeitlinger.

MANN, J. (1958) "Group relations and the marginal man." Human Relations 11: 77-92.

MANN, J. (1973) "Status: The marginal reaction—mixed bloods and Jews," Watson, pp. 213-223 in P. Watson (ed.) Psychology and Race. London: Penguin.

MARKUS, E.J., BLENKER, M., BLOOM, M. and DOWNS, T. (1970) "Relocation stress and the aged." Interdisciplinary Topics in Gerontology 7: 60-71.

MARX, M.A. and HILLIX, W.A. (1963) Systems and Theories in Psychology. New York: McGraw-Hill.

McCULLOCH, M. (1950) People of the Sierra Leone Protectorate. London: International African Institute.

McELWAIN, D.W., KEARNEY, G.E., and ORD, I.G. (1970) The Queensland Test. Melbourne: Australian Council for Educational Research.

McFALL, R.M., and SCHENKEN, D. (1970) "Experimenter expectancy effects, need for achievement and field dependence." Journal of Experimental Research in Personality 4: 122-128.

McFEAT, T. (ed.) (1965) Indians of the North Pacific Coast. Toronto: McClelland & Stewart.

McNETT, C.W. (1970) "A settlement pattern scale of cultural complexity," pp. 872-886 in R. Naroll and R. Cohen (eds.) A Handbook of Method in Cultural Anthropology. New York: Natural History Press.

MEADOWS, D.H., MEADOWS, D.L., RANDERS, J., and BEHRENS, N. (1972) The Limits to Growth. New York: Universe.

MEGGARS, B.J. (1954) "Environmental limitations on the development of culture." American Anthropologist 56: 801-824.

MEGGITT, M.J. (1962) Desert People. Chicago: University of Chicago Press.

MESSICK, S. and FRENCH, J.W. (1975) "Dimensions of cognitive closure." Multivariate Behavioral Research: 3-16.

MINTURN, L. and LAMBERT, W.W. (1964) Mothers of Six Cultures: Antecedants of Child Rearing. New York: John Wiley.

MINTURN-TRIANDIS, L., and LAMBERT, W.W. (1961) "Pancultural factor analysis of reported socialization practices." Journal of Abnormal and Social Psychology 62: 631-639.

MORRISBY, J.R. (1955) Manual for the Shapes Test. London: National Foundations for Educational Research.

MURDOCK, G.P. (1957) "World ethnographic sample." American Anthropologist 59: 664-687.

MURDOCK, G.P. (1967) "Ethnographic Atlas: A summary." Ethnology 6: 109-236.

MURDOCK, G.P. (1969) "Correlations of exploitive patterns," pp. 129-146 in D. Damas (ed.) Ecological Essays. National Museum of Canada Bulletin No. 230, Anthropological Series No. 86.

MURDOCK, G.P. and MORROW, D.O. (1970) "Subsistence economy and supportive practices: Cross-cultural codes 1." Ethnology 9: 302-330.

MURDOCK, G.P. and PROVOST, C. (1973) "Measurement of cultural complexity." Ethnology 12: 379-392.

MURPHY, H.M.B. (1965) "Migration and the major mental disorders: A reappraisal," pp. 5-29 in M.B. Kantor (ed.) Mobility and Mental Health. Springfield: Charles C. Thomas.

MURPHY, H.M.B. (1969) "Psychiatric concomitants of fusion in plural societies." Paper presented at the conference on Social Change and Cultural Factors in Mental Health in Asia and the Pacific, Honolulu.

NAROLL, R. (1956) "A preliminary index of social development." American Anthropologist 58: 687-715.

NAROLL, R. (1959) "A tentative index of culture stress." International Journal of Social Psychiatry 5: 107-116.

NAROLL, R. (1970) "Cross-cultural sampling," pp. 889-926 in R. Naroll and R. Cohen (eds.) Handbook of Method in Cultural Anthropology. New York: Natural History Press.

NAROLL, R. and COHEN, R. (eds.) (1970) A Handbook of Method in Cultural Anthropology. New York: Natural History Press.

NAROLL, R., MICHIK, G., and NAROLL, F. (1974) "Hologeistic theory testing," pp. 121-148 in J. Jorgensen (ed.) Comparative Studies by H. Driver and Essays in his Honor. New Haven: H.R.A.F.

NIMKOFF, M.F. and R. MIDDLETON (1960) "Types of family and types of economy." American Journal of Sociology 66: 215-225.

OKONJI, M.O. (1969) "Differential effects of rural and urban upbringing on the development of cognitive styles." International Journal of Psychology 4: 293-305.

OLTMAN, P. (1968) "A portable Rod and Frame apparatus." Perceptual and Motor Skills 26: 503-506.

ORD, I.G. (1972) "Testing for educational and occupational selection in developing countries." Occupational Psychology Monograph 46, no. 3: 123-182.

PARK, J-Y., JOHNSON, R.C., DeFRIES, J.C., VANDENBERG, S.G., McCLEARN, G.E., WILSON, J.R., ASHTON, G.C., RASHAD, M.N. and MI, M-P. (forthcoming) "A Korean pedigree study of cognitive abilities."

PARK, R.E. (1928) "Human migration and the marginal man." American Journal of Sociology 33: 881-893.

PASCUAL-LEONE, J. (1969) "Cognitive development and cognitive style: A general psychological integration." Ph.D. dissertation, Universite de Geneve.

PELTO, P. (1968) "The difference between tight and loose societies." Transaction (April): 37-40.

POORTINGA, Y. (1975) "Some implications of three different approaches to intercultural comparison," pp. 327-332. in J.W. Berry, and W.J. Lonner (eds.) Applied Cross-Cultural Psychology. Amsterdam: Swets & Zeitlinger.

PORTEUS, S.D. (1937) Intelligence and Environment. New York: Macmillan.

PRESTON, R.J. (1970) "The development of self-control in the Eastern Cree life cycle." Paper presented to Northeastern Anthropological Association, Ottawa.

PRICE-WILLIAMS, D. (1975) "The cultural relativism of intelligence," pp. 51-64 in D. Price-Williams (ed.) Explorations in Cross-Cultural Psychology. San Francisco: Chandler & Sharp.

PROSHANSKY, H.M., ITTELSON, W.H., and RIVLIN, L.G. (eds.) (1970) Environmental Psychology: Man and His Physical Setting. New York: Holt, Rinehart & Winston.

RAPOPORT, A. (1963) "Mathematical models of social interaction," pp. 493-579 in
R.D. Luce, R.R. Bush, and E. Galanter (eds.) Handbook of Mathematical Psychology,
Vol. 2. New York: John Wiley.

RAVEN, J.C. (1963) Guide to Using the Coloured Progressive Matrices. London: Lewis.

RIVERS, W.H.R. (1901) "Introduction and vision," in A.C. Haddon (ed.) Report of the
Cambridge Anthropological Expedition to the Torres Straits, Volume II. Cambridge:
Cambridge University Press.

ROBBINS, R.H. (1973) "Alcohol and the identity struggle: Some effects of economic
change on interpersonal relations." American Anthropologist 75: 99-122.

ROGERS, E.S. (1969) "Natural environment—social organization—witchcraft: Cree versus Ojibway—A test case," pp. 24-39 in D. Damas (ed.) Contributions to Anthropology: Ecological Essays. Ottawa: National Museum of Canada.

ROSENBERG, S. (1969) "Mathematical models of social behavior," pp. 179-244 in G.
Lindzey and E. Arronson (eds.) Handbook of Social Psychology, Vol. 1. Reading,
Mass.: Addison-Wesley.

RUBLE, D.N. and NAKAMURA, C.Y. (1972) "Task orientation versus social orientation
in young children, and their attention to relevant social cues." Child Development
43: 471-480.

SACK, S.A. and RICE, C.E. (1974) "Selectivity resistance to distraction and shifting as
three attentional factors." Psychological Reports 34: 1003-1012.

SAHLINS, M.D. and SERVICE, E. (eds.) (1960) Evolution and Culture. Ann Arbor:
University of Michigan Press.

SAPIR, E. (1915) "The social organization of the west coast tribes." Proceedings and
Transactions of the Royal Society of Canada 9: 355-374.

SCHIMEK, J.G. (1968) "Cognitive style and defenses: A longtitudinal study of Intellectualization and field independence." Journal of Abnormal Psychology 73: 575-580.

SCOTT, W.A. (1963) "Conceptualizing and measuring structural properties of cognition," pp. 266-288 in O.J. Harvey (ed.) Motivation and Social Interaction. New
York: John Wiley.

SEGALL, M.H., CAMPBELL, D.T., and HERSKOVITS, M.J. (1963) "Cultural differences in the perception of geometric illusions." Science 139: 769-771.

SEGALL, M.H., CAMPBELL, D.T., and HERSKOVITS, M.J. (1966) The Influence of
Culture on Visual Perception. Indianapolis: Bobbs-Merill.

SELIGMANN, C. (1910) The Melanesians of British New Guinea. Cambridge: Cambridge
University Press.

SELYE, A. (1956) The Stress of Life. New York: McGraw-Hill.

SINHA, D. (1973) "Psychology and the problems of developing countries: A general
overview." International Review of Applied Psychology 22: 5-28.

SKINNER, A. (1911) "Notes on the Eastern Cree." American Museum of Natural
History, Anthropological Papers.

SOLAR, D., DAVENPORT, G. and BRUEHL, D. (1969) "Social compliance as a
function of field dependence." Perceptual and Motor Skills 29: 299-306.

SOMMERLAD, E.A. and BERRY, J.W. (1970) "The role of ethnic identification in
distinguishing between attitudes towards assimilation and integration of a minority
racial group." Human Relations 23: 23-29.

SPENCER, B. and GILLEN, F.J. (1899) The Native Tribes of Central Australia. London:
Macmillan.

SPENCER, B. and GILLEN, F.J. (1927) The Arunta: A Study of a Stone Age People.
London: Macmillan.

SPENCER, H. (1864) First Principles New York: Appleton.

SPRADLEY, J.P. and PHILLIPS, M. (1972) "Culture and stress: A quantitative ana-

lysis." American Anthropologist 74: 518-529.
SPROUT, H. and SPROUT, M. (1965) The Ecological Perspective in Human Affairs. Princeton: Princeton University Press.
STEWARD, J.H. (1963) Theory of Culture Change: The Methodology of Multilinear Evolution. Urbana: University of Illinois Press.
STEWART, M. (1973) "Tests of the carpentered world hypothesis by race and environment in America and Zambia." International Journal of Psychology 8: 83-94.
STONEQUIST, E.V. (1937) The Marginal Man. New York: Charles Scribner's.
STRODTBECK, F. (1964) "Considerations of meta-method in cross-cultural psychology." American Anthropologist 66: 223-229.
Superior Court of Quebec (1973) Testimony during injunction hearings of the James Bay Hydroelectric project.
SUZMAN, R.M. (1974) "Psychological modernity." International Journal of Comparative Sociology 14: 273-287.

TATJE, T.A. and NAROLL, R. (1970) "Two measures of societal complexity: An empirical cross-cultural comparison," pp. 766-833 in R. Naroll and R. Cohen (eds.) A Handbook of Method in Cultural Antrhopology. New York: Natural History Press.
THOMAS, F. (1925) The Environmental Basis of Society. London: Century.
TRIANDIS, H.C. (1964) "Cultural influences upon cognitive processes," in L. Berkowitz (ed.) Advances in Experimental Social Psychology, Vol.1. New York: Academic Press.
TRIANDIS, H.C. (1971) Attitudes and Attitude Change. New York: John Wiley.
TRIANDIS, H.C. (1973) "A review of the psychological dimensions of modernization." International Journal of Psychology 8: 170-181.
TRIANDIS, H.C., MALPASS, R.S., and DAVIDSON, A. (1971) "Cross-cultural psychology." Biennial Review of Anthropology.
TRIANDIS, H.C., MALPASS, R.S., and DAVIDSON, A. (1973) "Cross-cultural psychology." Annual Review of Psychology.

VALLEE, F. (1968) "Stresses of change and mental health among the Canadian Eskimo." Archives of Environmental Healty 17: 565-570.
VAYDA, A.P. (ed.) (1969) Environment and Cultural Behaviour. New York: Natural History Press.
VAYDA, A.P. and RAPPAPORT, R.A. (1968) "Ecology, cultural and noncultural," pp. 477-497 in J. Clifton (ed.) Introduction to Cultural Anthropology. Boston: Houghton-Mifflin.
VERNON, P.E. (1965) "Ability factors and environmental influences." American Psychologist 20: 723-733.
VERNON, P.E. (1969) Intelligence and Cultural Environment. London: Methuen.
VERNON, P.E. (1972) "The distinctiveness of field independence." Journal of Personality 40: 366-391.

WEITZ, J. (1971) "Cultural change and field dependences in two native Canadian linguistic families." Ph.D. dissertation, University of Ottawa.
WERNER, H. (1948) Comparative Psychology of Mental Development. Chicago: Follett.
WEYL, N. and POSSONY, S.T. (1963) The Geography of Intellect. Chicago: Regnery.
WHORF, B.L. (1956) "The relation of habitual thought and behaviour to language," in J.B. Caroll (ed.) Language, Thought and Reality. New York: John Wiley.
WHITING, J.W.M. (1968) "Methods and problems in cross-cultural research," pp. 693-728 in G. Lindzey and E. Aronson (eds.) Handbook of Social Psychology, Vol.2. Reading, Mass.: Addison-Wesley.

WHITING, J.W.M. (1973) "A model for psycho-cultural research." American Anthropological Association Annual Report: 1-14.

WHITING, J.W.M. and CHILD, I. (1953) Child Training and Personality. New Haven: Yale University Press.

WILLEMS, E.T. and RAUSCH, W.L. (eds.) (1969) Naturalistic Viewpoints in Psychological Research. New York: Holt, Rinehart & Winston.

WILSON, J.R., DeFRIES, J.C., McCLEARN, G.E., VANDENBERG, S.G., and JOHNSON, R.C. (1975) "Cognitive abilities: Use of family data as a control to asses sex and age differences in two ethnic groups." International Journal of Aging and Human Development 6: 215-230.

WISSLER, C. (1926) The Relation of Nature to Man in Aboriginal North America. London: Oxford University Press.

WITKIN, H.A. (1950) "Individual differences in ease of perception of embedded figures." Journal of Personality 19: 1-15.

WITKIN, H.A. (1967) "A Cognitive style approach to cross-cultural research." International Journal of Psychology 2: 233-250.

WITKIN, H.A. (1969) "Social influences in the development of cognitive style," pp. 687-706 in D.A. Goslin (ed.) Handbook of Socialization Theories and Research. Chicago: Rand McNally.

WITKIN, H.A. (1972) "The role of cognitive style in academic performance and in teacher-student relations." Paper presented to Conference on Higher Education, Montreal.

WITKIN, H.A. and BERRY, J.W. (1975) "Psychological differentiation in cross-cultural perspective." Journal of Cross-Cultural Psychology 6: 4-87.

WITKIN, H.A., DYK, R.B., FATERSON, H.F., GOODENOUGH, D.R., and KARP, S.A. (1962) Psychological Differentiation. New York: John Wiley. (Republished, Potomac, Md.: Lawrence Erlbaum Associates, 1974)

WITKIN, H.A., GOODENOUGH, D.R., and KARP, S.A. (1967) "Stability of cognitive style from childhood to young adulthood." Journal of Personality and Social Psychology 7: 291-300.

WITKIN, H.A., LEWIS, H.B., HERTZMAN, M., MACHOVER, K., MEISSNER, P.B., and WAPNER, S. (1954) Personality Through Perception. New York: Harper. (Republished, Westport, Conn.: Greenwood, 1972)

WITKIN, H.A., LEWIS, H.B., and WEIL, E. (1968) "Affective reactions and patient-therapist interactions among more differentiated and less differentiated patients early in therapy." Journal of Nervous and Mental Disease 146: 193-208.

WITKIN, H.A., MOORE, C.A., GOODENOUGH, D.R., and COX, P.W. (in press) "Field-dependent and field-independent cognitive styles and their educational implications." Review of Educational Research.

WITKIN, H.A., OLTMAN, P.K., RASKIN, E., and KARP, S.A. (1971) Manual for the Embedded Figures Test. Palo Alto: Consulting Psychologists Press.

WITKIN, H.A., OLTMAN, P., COX, P., EHRLICHMAN, E., HAMM, R., and RINGLER, R. (1973) Field-Dependence-Independence and Psychological Differentiation: A Bibliography. Princeton: Educational Testing Service.

WITKIN, H.A., PRICE-WILLIAMS, D., BERTINI, M., CHRISTIANSEN, B., OLTMAN, P.K., RAMIREZ, M., and VAN MEEL, J. (1974) "Social conformity and psychological differentiation." International Journal of Psychology 9: 11-29.

WOBER, M. (1966) "Sensotypes." Journal of Social Psychology 70: 181-189.

WOBER, M. (1967) "Adapting Witkin's field independence theory to accommodate new information from Africa." British Journal of Psychology 58: 29-38.

WOBER, M. (1969) "The meaning and stability of Ravens Matrices test among

Africans." International Journal of Psychology 4: 229-235.

WOBER, M. (1974) "Towards an understanding of the Kiganda concept of intelligence," pp. 261-280 in J.W. Berry and P.R. Dasen (eds.) Culture and Cognition. London: Methuen.

WOHLWILL, J.F. and CARSON, D.H. (eds.) (1972) Environment and the Social Sciences: Perspectives and Applications. Washington: American Psychological Association.

Il suffit d'aller à la banque pour trouver de l'argent ?

Comment vit-on dans un pays pauvre ?

Comment est-ce qu'on devient riche ?

Pourquoi le monsieur dort-il dans la rue ?

Si papa perd son travail, on n'aura plus de maison ?

Est-ce qu'on se sent différent quand on est pauvre ?

Comment peut-on aider les pauvres ?

Être riche ou pauvre, c'est juste une histoire d'argent ?

Suivi éditorial : Astrid Dumontet
Réécriture et correction : Karine Forest
Mise en pages : Pascale Darrigrand
Conception graphique : Emma Rigaudeau

www.editionsmilan.com

ISBN : 978-2-7459-5696-5 – Dépôt légal : 2e trimestre 2015 – Imprimé en Chine

les riches
et les pauvres

Textes de **Pascale Hédelin**
Illustrations d'**Élodie Balandras**

MiLAN

Ça veut dire quoi,
être riche ?

Les gens riches ont bien plus d'argent que les autres.
Ils peuvent donc s'acheter plus facilement ce qu'ils désirent
et posséder beaucoup de choses. Leur vie est confortable.

Quelqu'un de riche a une ou plusieurs belles maisons.
Il peut s'offrir des œuvres d'art, des voitures de luxe, des bijoux
très chers, de grands voyages, ou encore des chevaux
de course... Et il a **beaucoup** d'argent à la banque.

Quand on est riche, on est plus **libre** de faire ce qu'on veut. On profite de la vie sans souci d'argent : on n'est pas obligé de travailler, on peut dépenser ses sous sans compter... ou en donner à ceux qui en ont besoin.

À travers le monde, il existe des gens assez riches, très riches... ou extrêmement riches : les milliardaires ont d'énormes fortunes. Tu vois, finalement, on est toujours **plus riche** ou **plus pauvre** que quelqu'un d'autre !

Ça veut dire quoi, être pauvre ?

Les gens pauvres manquent d'argent. Ils ne peuvent pas s'acheter tout ce dont ils ont besoin, ni vivre dans de bonnes conditions. C'est tout le contraire des gens riches !

L'argent est **indispensable** pour vivre, car il faut payer la maison, la nourriture, le chauffage, la lumière... En France, les personnes pauvres habitent des logements en mauvais état, bruyants, mal chauffés, qui ne coûtent pas cher.

Ceux qui sont pauvres ne peuvent pas se payer
de repas équilibrés, bons pour la santé, et se soignent mal.
Ils doivent **se priver** de ce qui paraît normal à la plupart des gens.
Dans notre pays, 1 personne sur 8 est dans cette situation.

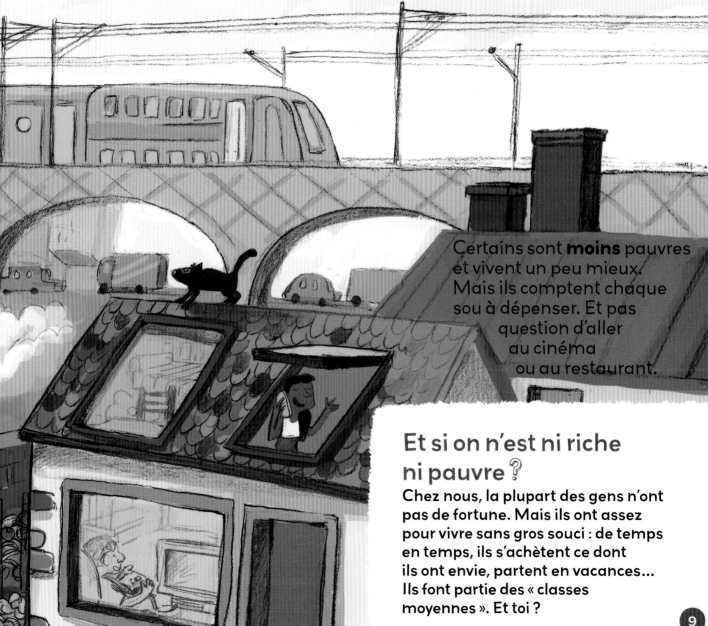

Certains sont **moins** pauvres
et vivent un peu mieux.
Mais ils comptent chaque
sou à dépenser. Et pas
question d'aller
au cinéma
ou au restaurant.

Et si on n'est ni riche ni pauvre ?

Chez nous, la plupart des gens n'ont
pas de fortune. Mais ils ont assez
pour vivre sans gros souci : de temps
en temps, ils s'achètent ce dont
ils ont envie, partent en vacances...
Ils font partie des « classes
moyennes ». Et toi ?

Y a-t-il toujours eu des riches et des pauvres ?

Depuis des milliers d'années, il existe des différences de richesse entre les hommes. Tout a commencé quand ils se sont mis à posséder des terres à eux...

Vers la fin de la préhistoire, les hommes se mettent à élever des animaux et à faire pousser des céréales. Ceux qui arrivent à avoir de précieuses **réserves** de nourriture sont les plus riches !

Au Moyen Âge, les seigneurs possèdent de vastes **terres** : c'est leur richesse. Les paysans, très nombreux, les cultivent pour eux... mais n'ont pas de salaire en échange. Ils sont très pauvres.

En 1789, en France, la plupart des gens sont misérables, alors que les nobles ont toutes les richesses et habitent de belles demeures. Le peuple se révolte contre cette **injustice** : c'est la période de la Révolution.

Il y a environ 50 ans, en France et dans de nombreux pays, tous les gens ont du travail et gagnent mieux leur vie. Ils forment la **classe moyenne**. Ils s'achètent les premiers appareils ménagers, comme le réfrigérateur ou le lave-linge.

Il suffit d'aller à la banque pour trouver de l'argent ?

La banque ne distribue pas de l'argent en cadeau, sinon tout le monde serait riche ! Chaque personne qui travaille possède une somme d'argent à la banque, et l'utilise.

Chaque mois, l'argent que tes parents reçoivent en échange de leur travail est envoyé à leur banque, sur un **compte**. Au fil des jours, ils s'en servent pour acheter ce qui leur est nécessaire. S'ils ne dépensent pas tout, ils font des économies.

40€

18€

25€

12

Quand tes parents ont besoin de billets pour faire des achats, ils les prennent dans un distributeur avec leur carte bancaire. Cette somme est retirée de leur compte. Ils **paient** aussi avec leur carte, ou un chèque. Là, l'argent ne se voit pas !

Toi, tu n'as pas de carte pour retirer de l'argent car tu n'as pas encore de compte.
Tu pourras en avoir un à partir de 12 ans. En attendant, tes parents te donnent peut-être de **l'argent de poche** ?

Qui a inventé les pièces et les billets ?

Les hommes ont toujours fait des échanges, une chèvre contre un beau tissu par exemple. Les premiers à échanger des pièces sont des marchands turcs il y a 2 500 ans. Les billets sont apparus chez des commerçants chinois il y a environ 1 000 ans.

13

Comment vit-on dans un pays pauvre

À travers le monde, il y a d'énormes différences de richesse d'un pays à l'autre. Dans les pays pauvres, la majorité des gens sont dans la misère : ils manquent de tout.

Presque tous les pays riches sont situés au **nord** de notre planète. Parmi eux, il y a la France et les États-Unis. Les pays pauvres sont surtout au **sud**, en particulier en Afrique, mais certains, comme la Chine, sont en train de s'enrichir !

Dans les pays pauvres, les gens luttent chaque jour pour **survivre**. Tout y est difficile : manger, boire, avoir un abri, se soigner... Beaucoup d'enfants travaillent pour aider leurs parents. Mais il y a aussi quelques riches sans souci d'argent !

Ces pays sont souvent **ravagés** par des guerres, ou des sécheresses, des inondations... Comme les gens ne mangent pas tous à leur faim, ils sont affaiblis, surtout les enfants, et des maladies se répandent.

Comment est-ce qu'on devient riche ?

Il est très rare d'être riche grâce à un coup de chance !
Pour le devenir, il y a différentes façons possibles,
honnêtes... ou malhonnêtes.

Si on est très doué pour un métier, par exemple commerçant, et si on a beaucoup de volonté, on peut s'enrichir grâce à son **travail** et ses **qualités**.

Parfois, des personnes sont riches **sans effort.** Certaines gagnent une fortune au Loto. D'autres naissent dans une famille riche... et le deviennent automatiquement.

Grâce à leur talent,
leur charme...
des chanteurs, acteurs
ou sportifs ont du **succès**.
Ils deviennent célèbres
et gagnent beaucoup
d'argent. Mais ça ne dure
pas forcément.

Les malfaiteurs
s'enrichissent
en **volant** les autres.
Ils attaquent
des banques
ou cambriolent
des maisons.
Des hommes
d'affaires malhonnêtes
gardent pour eux
de l'argent qui
ne leur appartient pas.

Et si on donnait de l'argent des riches aux pauvres ?

Les gens riches n'ont pas forcément envie d'être généreux envers ceux qui ont moins qu'eux ! Mais dans certains pays, comme la France, on estime qu'ils doivent partager un peu. Et des règles les y obligent...

Une personne qui travaille dur et gagne sa vie honnêtement **mérite** son argent. Et elle a bien le droit d'en profiter ! On ne peut pas le lui prendre de force, des lois protègent ce qui appartient à chacun.

Dans notre pays cependant, les riches donnent une petite partie de leur richesse en payant des **impôts**. Cet argent peut être utilisé pour aider les plus pauvres. Certains riches offrent aussi de l'argent pour soutenir ceux qui en manquent.

Des gens ont trouvé une autre solution pour partager sans utiliser d'argent : ils **échangent** des marchandises et se rendent des services les uns aux autres. Par exemple, un cours de guitare contre des légumes. Une bonne façon de s'entraider !

Est-ce que je serai riche si je travaille beaucoup ?

Travailler beaucoup ne rend pas forcément riche. Cela dépend des métiers. Et on travaille pour gagner sa vie... mais aussi si possible pour faire ce qu'on aime !

En échange de leur travail, les gens sont payés : ils reçoivent un **salaire** qui varie selon le type de métier qu'ils exercent et le nombre d'années passées à travailler.

Jacques est chirurgien. Il a fait de longues études, et a de grandes **responsabilités** : il sauve des gens. Il pratique son métier depuis de nombreuses années, passe beaucoup d'heures à opérer ses patients et gagne très bien sa vie !

Vincent a
un emploi physique,
dur et fatigant :
il est maçon.
Il est sérieux
et travailleur,
mais il est **débutant**
et n'a pas de diplômes.
Il a un petit salaire.

Au début, au restaurant,
Hélène épluchait les légumes
et gagnait peu. Aujourd'hui,
elle est chef cuisinière : elle crée
des plats et **dirige** son équipe.
Et elle a un bon salaire !

21

Pourquoi le monsieur dort-il dans la rue ?

Il y a des gens si pauvres qu'ils n'ont rien. Ils vivent dans la rue, et demandent aux passants un peu d'argent pour pouvoir se nourrir : ils mendient. C'est triste de les voir...

Les SDF, les gens « **sans domicile fixe** », n'ont pas de maison. Ils s'installent un petit coin dans une rue et se déplacent souvent. Des personnes ont pitié d'eux, d'autres sont gênées ou ne veulent pas s'en soucier.

des sous pour manger SVP

Ces sans-abri t'effraient un peu ou te font de la peine, car ils portent de vieux vêtements pas toujours propres et semblent si **malheureux** d'être tout seuls.

Georges avait une vie normale, avant d'être SDF. Mais il a eu de gros **problèmes** : il est tombé très malade et a perdu son travail. Il ne pouvait plus rien payer. Il n'avait ni famille ni amis pour l'aider. Et il a perdu tout courage.

Pourquoi maman donne des sous à ce monsieur et pas à l'autre ?

Elle est émue en voyant cet homme qui a eu bien des malheurs.
C'est si injuste ! Mais elle ne peut pas donner des sous à tous les SDF...
Par contre, un sourire ou un mot gentil peut leur faire chaud au cœur !

23

Si papa perd son travail, on n'aura plus de maison ?

Malheureusement, on peut perdre un jour son emploi et être « au chômage ». Par exemple quand l'entreprise pour laquelle on travaille n'a plus assez d'argent pour nous payer. Mais pas de panique !

Si ton papa se retrouvait sans emploi, il continuerait de toucher une partie de son salaire pendant un certain temps. Des pays comme la France **aident** les personnes en difficulté, pour empêcher qu'elles se retrouvent soudain sans maison.

Et puis, ton papa chercherait un nouveau travail. En attendant, ta famille devrait faire des efforts pour **dépenser moins** : par exemple, aller moins souvent au restaurant, offrir de plus petits cadeaux aux anniversaires...

De plus, même avec un papa au chômage, tu pourrais continuer d'aller à l'école et de te faire soigner à l'hôpital si tu en avais besoin. Car en France, ces services sont **gratuits** pour tous.

Pourquoi y a-t-il quand même des SDF ?

Les gens au chômage ne reçoivent de l'argent que s'ils ont travaillé. Et ceux qui n'ont pas de travail depuis longtemps ne perçoivent plus rien. Voilà pourquoi ils n'ont pas de maison. Mais ils peuvent trouver des abris d'urgence pour passer la nuit.

25

Est-ce que ça enlève tous les soucis d'avoir de l'argent ?

Être riche, cela ne suffit pas toujours à rendre heureux, car il y a des choses très importantes que personne ne peut acheter...

Les parents de Mathilde travaillent beaucoup et gagnent bien leur vie. Pour se faire pardonner d'être toujours occupés et de la faire souvent garder, ils offrent plein de cadeaux à leur fille. Pourtant ça ne la rend **pas heureuse**, c'est d'eux dont elle a besoin.

Grégoire a beaucoup de jeux chers. Il en prête aux enfants de son âge, en espérant se faire ainsi des amis. Mais ça ne marche pas. On ne peut pas s'acheter de **vrais amis**, ni payer une personne pour qu'elle vous aime !

Le chien de Jules et Léa est gravement malade. Même en payant une fortune, aucun vétérinaire ne peut le guérir. Tout l'argent du monde ne peut rien faire contre une **maladie** mortelle...

Où habitent les riches et les pauvres en ville ?

Dans les grandes villes du monde, les gens n'habitent pas les mêmes quartiers selon l'argent qu'ils possèdent. Bien souvent les gens riches et les plus pauvres ne se mélangent pas !

À Rio, au Brésil, les quartiers pauvres et riches sont nettement séparés. Les plus pauvres s'entassent dans des **bidonvilles** : des ensembles de cabanes misérables. Les plus fortunés ont de vastes maisons de luxe protégées par des grilles.

En France, au **centre-ville**, on a tout à sa disposition : les magasins, les écoles… Mais cela coûte cher d'habiter ces beaux quartiers. Les gens qui ont moins d'argent doivent vivre dans des immeubles autour du centre, ou encore plus loin dans la banlieue.

Aujourd'hui, les gens chargés d'imaginer les villes essaient de **mélanger** les habitants riches et moins riches. Ils construisent par exemple des appartements pas chers en centre-ville pour que tout le monde ait la chance d'y vivre.

29

Doit-on tout dépenser quand on est riche ?

Chacun fait ce qu'il veut de son argent : le dépenser ou le garder. Alors méfie-toi des apparences ! Quelqu'un peut te sembler riche et ne pas l'être et, à l'inverse, des gens qui paraissent pauvres peuvent en fait avoir des sous.

Pedro adore les grosses motos puissantes. Mais elles sont très chères et il a un petit salaire. Pour s'offrir celle de ses rêves, il a **économisé** pendant des années et s'est privé de vacances. C'est son choix !

Anna est riche, elle a du plaisir à s'acheter plein de choses chères. Et elle aime **montrer** sa richesse, pour se sentir importante.

Roger a aussi beaucoup d'argent... mais lui, il déteste le dépenser : il est **avare**. À le voir, il ne semble pas fortuné !

Quant à Sophie et Marc, ils n'ont l'air ni riches ni pauvres. Ils vivent **simplement**, ne gaspillent rien, mangent les légumes de leur potager. Mais ils ont une jolie somme d'argent de côté, à la banque, en cas de besoin !

Que ferais-tu si tu découvrais un trésor ?

À toi de choisir ! Le garderais-tu pour toi, pour t'offrir ce dont tu rêves – un voyage dans l'espace, par exemple ? Ferais-tu des cadeaux aux gens que tu aimes ? Ou bien partagerais-tu ton trésor avec les gens pauvres ?

31

Est-ce qu'on se sent différent quand on est pauvre ?

Quand on a peu d'argent, il y a beaucoup de choses qu'on ne peut pas faire comme la plupart des gens... Cette différence est difficile à vivre et on peut même en avoir honte.

Sylvie est séparée de son mari. Elle ne travaille que la moitié du temps et gagne peu d'argent. Comme beaucoup de mamans seules, cela ne lui suffit pas pour faire vivre sa famille **correctement**... et gâter ses enfants.

Cette situation la rend **triste**, alors elle a moins envie de se faire belle, de sortir... Et elle n'invite pas d'amis car elle ne veut pas qu'on voit son tout petit appartement.

Quand il va chez des copains, son fils Loïc se sent parfois **différent** d'eux. Lui, il n'a pas de console de jeux et ne part jamais faire du ski aux vacances d'hiver. Mais quand il joue au ballon, il oublie tous ses soucis !

Comment peut-on aider les pauvres ?

En France et dans le monde, on agit pour aider les plus pauvres.
Il y a des progrès, mais malheureusement, la pauvreté
ne disparaîtra jamais entièrement...

Chez nous, des personnes se regroupent en **associations**
pour distribuer aux plus pauvres de la nourriture et des vêtements,
et les abriter pour la nuit. Des gens célèbres s'engagent pour les défendre :
l'humoriste Coluche a créé les Restos du cœur.

Quand des pays pauvres sont touchés par des catastrophes, comme la famine ou une grave sécheresse, les pays riches leur envoient vite du secours : de la nourriture, de l'eau, des tentes, des médecins... C'est l'**aide humanitaire** d'urgence.

Pour aider ces pays en difficulté, des spécialistes des pays riches apprennent aux fermiers à mieux cultiver la terre pour se nourrir. D'autres construisent des **écoles** pour que les enfants puissent avoir un métier et une vie meilleure !

Être riche ou pauvre, c'est juste une histoire d'argent ?

Quand on dit que quelqu'un est « pauvre », ça ne signifie pas toujours qu'il manque d'argent. Et on peut aussi être « riche » sans posséder de fortune !

« Pauvre Emma, elle a encore eu un zéro en calcul ! » Emma n'est pas pauvre, mais on a **de la peine** pour elle parce qu'elle a des difficultés en mathématiques et que cela la rend triste.

Li-Mei n'a pas une famille fortunée, mais elle a pourtant de grandes richesses : elle est très douée pour le dessin, elle parle deux langues et invente des poèmes. Ses nombreux **talents** sont aussi précieux qu'un trésor !

Marc aimerait expliquer à ses élèves de CE2 que de porter des vêtements chers, de marque, ne rend pas supérieur aux autres. Et qu'on ne juge pas la **valeur** des gens à ce qu'ils possèdent, mais à ce qu'ils sont...

C'est quoi, la richesse intérieure ?

Cette richesse-là ne se voit pas au premier coup d'œil. Il faut connaître la personne pour découvrir toutes ses qualités : la gentillesse, la générosité, par exemple. Cela en fait quelqu'un de très intéressant !

Découvre les autres titres de la collection

 les gros mots

 les châteaux forts

 la nuit

les cheveux et les poils

les saisons

 la famille

 le bien et le mal

le Moyen Âge

la ferme

 la danse

 boire et manger

 les émotions

l'eau

 les Égyptiens

la montagne

 les dents

 le football

les oiseaux

 les loups

 bobos et maladies

 les poneys